Questions of consciousr

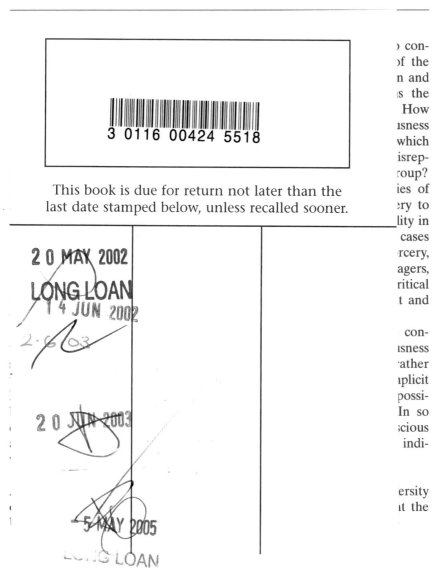

) con-
of the
n and
s the
How
isness
which
isrep-
roup?
ies of
ery to
lity in
cases
rcery,
agers,
ritical
t and

con-
isness
ather
iplicit
possi-
In so
scious
indi-

ersity
it the

ASA Monographs 33

Questions of consciousness

Edited by Anthony P. Cohen
and Nigel Rapport

London and New York

First published 1995
by Routledge
11 New Fetter Lane, London EC4P 4EE

Simultaneously published in the USA and Canada
by Routledge
29 West 35th Street, New York, NY 10001

Phototypeset in Times by Intype, London
Printed and bound in Great Britain by
TJ Press (Padstow) Ltd, Padstow, Cornwall

British Library Cataloguing in Publication Data
A catalogue record for this book is available from the British Library

Library of Congress Cataloguing in Publication Data
A catalogue record for this book has been requested

ISBN 0–415–12395–X (hbk)
ISBN 0–415–12396–8 (pbk)

Contents

Contributors

Anthony P. Cohen, Professor of Social Anthropology, University of Edinburgh.

James W. Fernandez, Professor of Anthropology, University of Chicago.

Kirsten Hastrup, Professor of Social Anthropology, University of Copenhagen.

Allison James, Lecturer in Social Anthropology, University of Hull.

Bruce Kapferer, Professor of Anthropology, University College, London.

Tamara Kohn, Lecturer in Anthropology, University of Durham.

Roland Littlewood, Professor of Anthropology as Applied to Psychiatry, University College, London.

David Parkin, Professor of African Anthropology, School of Oriental and African Studies, London.

Nigel Rapport, Lecturer in Social Anthropology, University of St Andrews.

David Riches, Senior Lecturer in Social Anthropology, University of St Andrews.

Cris Shore, Lecturer in Anthropology, Goldsmiths' College, London.

Andrew Strathern, Andrew W. Mellon Professor of Anthropology, University of Pittsburgh.

C. W. Watson, Senior Lecturer in Social Anthropology, University of Kent.

Preface and acknowledgements

This book is the outcome of the 1994 Annual Conference of the Association of Social Anthropologists of the Commonwealth, held at Hamilton Hall, the University of St Andrews, 21–24 March. In convening the conference, we broke with recent ASA tradition by strictly limiting the number of papers in order to allow much more time for discussion, and to provide the opportunity for a discourse to grow around the papers. With the same objective, we asked our speakers to relate their papers to those of the other contributors, and invited our Chair-discussants to be forthright in their observations, and directive in organizing the discussions. All willingly collaborated in this effort, with the consequence that the conference was judged to have been both pleasurable and academically successful.

It is to take nothing away from the individual papers to say that the progress made at the conference grew out of the discussions, and their fruitfulness will be evident from the chapters we publish here as the revised conference papers. Our first thanks go to the conference members, who responded so constructively and interestingly to *every* paper. Secondly, we owe a special debt of gratitude to the Chair-discussants, for taking on a more than usually onerous obligation, and for discharging it with such success: John Davis, Roy Dilley, Ladislav Holy, Signe Howell, Wendy James, Sandra Wallman and Roy Willis.

All but two of the papers presented at the conference have been revised for this book. The two which are missing, and which will be published elsewhere, were by Henrietta Moore and Georgina Born, and we thank them again for their contributions. Our authors have made our editorial task relatively simple, by completing their revised papers more or less on time and, in most cases, not more than 30 per cent over the maximum permitted length. They were a little less assiduous in preparing their texts according to the publisher's instructions, and for overcoming their lapses in this regard, we are indebted to Helen Sang of the Department of Biochemistry, University of Edinburgh, for her ingenuity, skill and labour on her wordprocessor.

The University of St Andrews, in the person of David Riches, was a most genial, generous and considerate host, and our thanks to him again, on behalf of all those present, for his endless help. He could not have done more to provide the conditions for a successful conference.

We are grateful to the British Academy for helping to fund the foreign travel of some of our speakers, and to the School of Philosophical and Anthropological Studies, University of St Andrews, and its head, Stephen Read, for help with the costs of preparing the manuscript for publication.

Finally, our thanks to Heather Gibson of Routledge, with whom it is a pleasure to do business.

APC and NJR
Edinburgh and St Andrews, January 1995

Introduction

Consciousness in anthropology

Anthony P. Cohen and Nigel Rapport

> This is the ground of anthropology: there is no . . . valid way to elimin-
> ate consciousness from our activity or those of others. . . . We can
> pretend that we are neutral scientists collecting ambiguous data and
> that the people we are studying are living amid various unconscious
> systems of determining forces of which they have no clue and to which
> only we have the key. But it is only pretence.
>
> (Paul Rabinow 1977)

QUESTIONS

Western social thought is built upon the Cartesian notion of self consciousness (as expressed in the *cogito*) as the distinguishing characteristic
of humanity; it is impossible to imagine what our intellectual traditions
might have been like if they had not proceeded from this premise. This
makes all the more remarkable the fact that social anthropology, the most
questioning of social science disciplines, has taken consciousness largely
for granted, neglecting – even, perhaps, denying – its significance and
relevance. Anthropologists have apparently been content to assume that
it is there, somewhere, and to regard its explanation as somehow beyond
our reach. If we have tied ourselves up in knots of philosophical *angst*
about the difficulties of understanding other cultures, we have largely
dismissed as 'not our business' the more fundamental problem of understanding other minds. The great modernistic paradigms provided anthropologists with justifications for this disinterest, and supplied their own
broad brush explanations which located consciousness in the structures
of historical materialism, or of the mind and human cognition, or of
culture, or of society. British social anthropology, of course, developed
predominantly under the influence of the last of these positions, and so
its practitioners became used to identifying the consciousness of any
individual with the structural logic of that individual's social circumstances. If I am a Nuer, then I must think like a Nuer. Anthropologists

thereby provided themelves with a simple means of defining away the *problematic* of consciousness. Their task was to provide a plausible inter-pretation of what the Nuer does. If social structure could not provide the answer, 'culture' could always be called in aid. In other than pathological or deviant cases, we simply assumed that people had similar kinds of consciousness if they could be depicted as 'sharing' culture or as being located within common social structures. Consciousness was simply not a problem, and the relationship of consciousness to either culture or social structure barely figured on the theoretical agenda.

This is such an obviously unsatisfactory position that it seems odd that it has remained unquestioned for so long. We do not suggest that the problems posed for anthropology by the difficulties of exploring con-sciousness are trivial: to the contrary (see, for example, Fernandez in this volume, pp. 25–6). But the consequences of failing to formulate and address them are that we have perpetuated the failings of anthropological practice: the generalization of thought and belief to whole societies; the subordination of individuals to these collective thought regimes; and, thereby, the construction of essential difference between 'us', individual-istic (sometimes preciously so) and creative, and 'them', apparently collec-tivist and passive. We do not accept the view that the problematic relationship of individual to society is a peculiarly Western preoccupation, but, rather, regard the denial of this concern to other cultures as, at best, a lapse of observation or a mistake of translation.

In this book, we have set ourselves the task of asking some basic questions. Can anthropologists approach consciousness more satisfactorily than they have done hitherto? What are the difficulties? Are there ethnographic devices which may be used to moderate or circumvent these difficulties? How do we know what people are conscious of? Is there such a phenomenon as 'collective consciousness', and how may the individual's consciousness be related to it? Is 'consciousness' the appropriate term for the work we entrust to this concept? How is consciousness related to culture and to social structure? How do consciousnesses impact on each other? What is the nature of the encounter between anthropologists' consciousnesses and those of the people among whom they study? How is consciousness manifest? Do the socio-anthropological idioms of 'agency' and 'embodiment' take the concept of consciousness any further? Do they finally overcome the philo-sophical and anthropological legacy of mind–body dualism?

If these questions have not often been put explicitly, we have routinely assumed unexamined answers to them in our ethnographic analyses. When the questions have been asked explicitly, anthropologists have tended to reject them as being either too difficult, or too trivial, or as the province properly of other disciplines. These responses do not do justice to the seriousness of the questions. Ethnographic reports have always been littered with imputations of belief, thought, knowledge and emotion to the societies and social groups with which they were concerned. But what kinds of evidence have we adduced for the authenticity or generality of the consciousness which we claim to have discovered? Are these claims for which evidence may even be possible; and, if so, what forms might such evidence take? If the evidence can only be inferential, or circumstantial, would this matter?

THE NEED TO QUESTION

When, prior to the postmodern turn, Geertz talked of the destabilization of disciplinary genres, he had especially in mind the recourse to the humanities made by social scientists in search of explanatory analogies (Geertz 1983: 19, 23). Since then, as Parkin makes clear in his chapter in this book, disciplines across the humanities and social sciences have looked to anthropology for similar inspiration. In opening our enquiry into an anthropological perspective on consciousness, it seemed prudent to keep disciplinary boundaries as open as might seem fruitful. This was not just a matter of pragmatism or expediency, but since our exploration of the relationship of consciousness to culture would inevitably lead us to problematize the latter, it seemed obvious that we must aim for an optimally inclusive approach. Not suprisingly, the psychoanalytic and the psychiatric loomed quite large in our discussions. However, as will be apparent from the essays which follow, we have taken seriously the commitment to an open-ended approach to the conscious self. Far from assuming the integrity of the conventional dichotomies of psychic and social, mind and society, we are trying to test them. As Strathern argues here, an anthropological concept of consciousness should encompass both.

The same must be true of our approach to another hoary old dichotomy which for so long has been used to pre-empt questions of consciousness: the distinction between the 'inner' and 'outer' person. Anthropologists used this dichotomy as an avoidance strategy, arguing that anthropology could deal only with what was empirically manifest (the outer), and must be content to treat anything else (such as the 'inner') as either a matter for imagination (fiction, philosophy), or for specialized scientific investigation (psychology) with a discovery objective different from anthropology's. As genres blur and/or change, so that it has become proper (if not obligatory) for anthropologists to write reflexively, deconstructively and politically, then, correspondingly, it now seems inadequate to write as if the outer life of symbolic forms, institutions and norms is all there is, or as if an outer life of overt behaviours somehow speaks for itself or is intrinsically meaningful, a social fact somehow independent of the creative consciousness of the individual.

Those whom we used to see and describe as role-players – realizing scripts written by a social *deus ex machina* – are now recognized as intentional, interpreting, imaginative, conscious agents. If this change of approach brings the self more squarely into the frame than previously, it is not because anthropology's object has shifted from society to the individual, but because we can no longer rest content with nineteenth century assumptions that social behaviour originates in social and historical forces beyond and 'outside' the individual. By the same token, we can no longer simply derive consciousness-driven behaviour from the social categories to which we analytically consign its individual perpetrators. If we were to continue past anthropological practice and treat the individual's consciousness as if it was simply identical to or derivable from that of the collectivity to which he or she supposedly belongs, we would thereby continue to deny or, at best, to misrepresent individuality and selfhood by gross simplification. If we continue merely to predicate the individual's consciousness on culture, we risk the conceptual sloppiness of sliding from one invention to another. If we continue to resign ourselves to the inaccessibility of consciousness, then we resign ourselves to a view which by now we know to be false: that what you see is what you get; that behaviour can be taken at face value.[1] Further, we would have to rest content with defending our imputations of consciousness as being somewhere between invention and best guess.

The consequence of acknowledging the self is that anthropology has also to acknowledge the problematic complement of culture: the mind. In so doing, it has to broaden its own problematic. Anthropologists must now recognize that they cannot know other cultures without understanding other minds. Whatever else we may have learned from our recent tortured debates about reflexivity, autobiography and anthropological writing, we do now know that knowledge of our own minds and cultures is implicated in our knowledge of other peoples'.

THEORETICAL APPROACHES

Competing explanatory paradigms of consciousness might conveniently be plotted on a scale one pole of which would be a 'closed' view which sees nothing in nature that is not ultimately explainable by 'natural science': by a notion of an objective world and a physical theory of mind; and at the opposite extreme, an open view which, emphasizing the unconfined scope of the imagination and the potential infinity of linguistic expression, sees a subjective quality in conscious experience which cannot be accounted for in purely objective terms (Cornwell 1994: Section 10, 4–6). Traversing the scale, a sample of the diversity of studies might include the following:

1 Francis Crick, *The Astonishing Hypothesis. The Scientific Search for the Soul* (1994): conscious awareness, sentience, feeling and intellectualiz-

ation derive from the assembly of nerve cells in the brain, their networks and oscillation. Neurons fire and consciousness results; humans are no more than the sum of their molecules.

2 Hans Moravec, *Mind Children* (1988), and Colin Blakemore, *The Mind Machine* (1988): the brain resembles a programmed digital computer; the brain is an evolved biological computer which gives merely the impression of free will.

3 Roger Penrose, *The Emperor's New Mind* (1990): mechanical computation could not possibly propagate consciousness. But the latter could be an outcome of microcosmic physics: the effect of quantum gravity in the brain.

4 Daniel Dennett, *Consciousness Explained* (1991): the self is an illusion, no more than a series of 'multiple drafts' or 'narratives', with no central focus or continuity.

5 Colin McGinn, *The Problem of Consciousness* (1992): consciousness is an intractable problem which Dennet is explaining away rather than explaining. Accounting for the presence of consciousness in a world of physical objects and processes, understanding the self, free will, meaning and knowledge, simply transcends our natural powers; it is too great a problem for human intellect ever to surmount. And Patricia Churchland, 'Can neurobiology teach us anything about consciousness?' (1994): even if we eschew the mind–body dualism, and despite the spectacular advances in neuroscience made this century, how human consciousness emerges from networks of neurons still escapes scientific understanding.

6 John Eccles, *How the Self Controls Its Brain* (1994): a purely materialist explanation for consciousness is by no means inevitable. Some form of dualism is inevitable.

7 John Searle, *The Rediscovery of the Mind* (1992): to insist on treating 'objectively observable phenomena' alone is to ignore the mind's essential features. While we might accept that both consciousness and intentionality are biological processes of the brain, and that they are essentially connected, we do not need to accept a materialist orthodoxy which would either eliminate consciousness (because it is observer relative, or because it is really something else, such as language or environment) or else would reduce it to something more basic, such as computation. Rather, we must insist that consciousness and intentionality are both intrinsic and eradicable. We all have subjective, qualitative states of consciousness; we all have beliefs, desires, intentions and perceptions, which are intrinsically mental.

8 Gerald Edelman, *Bright Air, Brilliant Fire* (1992): the way the brain develops and works (before as well as after birth) is more like an object undergoing natural selection in an ecological habitat than a computational system. Hence the ceaseless novelty, creativity and

change of our mental processes. To be human is to go beyond physics; science will not ultimately explain the human individual.

This diversity of view may seem a morass which anthropologists might do well to avoid. There may be some comfort to be taken from Jerry Fodor's suggestion that 'no scientist has the slightest idea how anything material could be conscious' (1992: 5); and from Roy Porter's insistence that experimental neuroscience still tells us far less than the philosophical observations of moral narrative about 'the stupendously complex dialectical interplay of subjectivity, self and society', about the aspects of the 'soul' (the self, personality, individual identity) that really matter, and about the details of the subjective nature of consciousness (1994: 7).

More significantly, Edelman may have thrown us a lifeline with his characterization of consciousness as 'a habitat ultimately beyond the physical' (1992: 170–5). Pursuing his vision of anthropology as 'moral explanation', Louch once enjoined the anthropologist to contextualize local action in an account of the moral ecology of a social milieu (1966: 160–1). Here we have Edelman talking metaphorically of the ecological habitat in which a human brain lives and develops, the context in which the brain continuously creates for itself new ways to be. His argument emphasizes the brain's capacity for selectivity which enables it to utilize experience and, thereby, to associate action with value. In this way, rather than passively 'receiving' the world, the brain constructs it, informing its construction with value. It is clearly a view which focuses on individuals as the conscious originators of their behaviour. It allows to individuals a unique history of successful adaptation to the world, and unique possible futures.

Edelman's humane approach to the creativity of individual consciousness echoes Bateson's characterization of our human being-in-the-world (1958: 96; 1972: 8, 126, 457–8). Bateson argued that we can be conceived of as 'energy sources' who create order and impose it on the universe by purposively relating ourselves to the world and its objects through our own powers of discrimination. The mind aggregates differences (and thereby establishes connections among them): between ego and alter, between objects in the world. The motivation to make these connections is internally generated, so that we may be seen as active participants in our own universe. Order in the world is determined by individuals' states of mind.

It should also be noted that these arguments go well beyond Giddens' account of the self in 'modern' society as a 'reflexive project' which has continually to adjust itself to changes in circumstances and to the individual's unfolding life course (1991). Giddens stops short of Bateson and Edelman in at least two important respects. First, he depicts the self as engaging with a world which is somehow independent of it – and therefore has to be seen as not of its making. Secondly, he limits the 'agency' of individuals to reflection, and does not extend it to motivation: he presents individuals as perpetrators rather than architects of action (Giddens 1984: 9). His account of consciousness offers little intentionality to the individual, whose agenda for action appears to be determined elsewhere (see Cohen 1994: 21–2).

NARRATIVE AND CONSCIOUSNESS

It would be perverse to pretend that the concept of consciousness, which has eluded (or repelled) anthropologists for so long, can be simply grasped and its problems overcome merely because we have now decided to pay some attention to it. Much of the discussion in this book looks at various strategies of capture. Inevitably, prominent among these is metaphor, especially given the presence of Fernandez among our contributors. Although it does not appear repeatedly elsewhere in the book (but has a significant place in Kohn's chapter), we wish briefly to explore here the metaphor of narrative and begin by noting its usefulness as a means of representing a view common to Bateson, Edelman and Giddens of individuals as having distinctive narratives of their embodiment and being-in-the-world (even though the authors would differ on the extensiveness of these narratives). 'Narrative' expresses, and suggests a focus on, the development, continuity and change of the individual's acts of orientation. Individuals own – and perhaps come to be owned by – unique narratives which unfold and mutate as these individuals situate themselves within moral, social, cultural and historical habitats (see Rapport 1993: 78ff.).

The anthropologist's task, and our present problem, is to find some convincing ethnographic access to these narratives. The problem has been described succinctly by Searle as the 'terrifying feature' of consciousness: the ontology of mental states is first person but the epistemology and methodology is third person (1992: 16). If the project is to study the consciousness of others, then to insist on studying only those phenomena which may be regarded as objectively observable would be to ignore the essential subjective features of the mind. Anthropologists should come clean and acknowledge that, quite rightly (and, in any case, inevitably) we make recourse to intuition and imagination. Let us elaborate briefly.

A narrative is 'the recounting of a series of temporal events so that a meaningful sequence is portrayed' (Kerby 1991: 39). It may be expressed verbally or in gesture and behaviour. It is the individual's routine *modus vivendi* on which he or she reflects self consciously. This regular reflection may be regarded as a condition of our conscious being-in-the-world. As Barbara Hardy says, 'We dream in narrative, day-dream in narrative, remember, anticipate, hope, despair, believe, doubt, plan, revise, criticize, construct, gossip, learn, hate and love by narrative' (1968: 5). Stephen Crites regards narrative as the form of consciousness, the form in which we continue to experience and to organize experience (1971: 297).

To further explore this thesis, consciousness can be seen to grasp its objects in an inherently temporal way. In Augustine's words (1907: Book XI, xxviii): consciousness *anticipates, attends and remembers*; what it anticipates passes through what it attends into what it remembers; and what it remembers then provides the substratum for what it anticipates. Here are three modalities of our conscious experience, an orientation to past, present and future, the three always existing in a relationship of tension but always forming a cognitive whole. Crites' concept of narrative is experience by another name, but emphasizes the temporality of experience, and incorporates an Augustinian (and rather later social psychological view) of the continuous reintegration of experience throughout life: 'our sense of ourselves is at every moment to some extent integrated into a single story' (Crites 1971: 302). Narrative, then, is a lasting if selective chronicle of the temporal course of experience, fixed in memory.

Memory would seem to be a key to consciousness. It makes experience coherent by ordering the images drawn from experience in the narrative form of succession. But remembering is not yet knowing, and a narrative is not the simple recital of the chronicle of memory. In a narrative we recollect particular images, abstracting them from memory's stream, stopping the flow at certain points. Hence, experience is illuminated by 'recollecting' from the memory. Knowledge is recollection, a reordering of past experience. As Hastrup suggests, we make iterative journeys through memory to make ourselves aware of what we 'know' at a less explicit level of our consciousness.

If memory has a narrative form, so too does anticipation. We actively plan and resolve and project and make guesses and predictions of what may happen; we write anticipated events into a sequential process. We then act by using this anticipated sequence as an itinerary (to use Hastrup's analogy) from which we may well digress, either because we so choose, or because the journey is not wholly within our control. The point is that whether or not deviations occur, we can be aware of them because we can predicate our awareness of the events on our anticipation of the process. Memory recalls the past to the present; anticipation calls the future back into the present. The present is the decisive moment in the narrative. Narration itself is time bound, which is its essential virtue to us as ethnographers. It is a specifically situated point of access for us to the narrator's past and anticipated future: access, in short, to her or his consciousness. Through an appreciation of the narratives by which individuals locate themselves in their natural, social and cultural milieux, as continuously expressed in their words and behaviour, the anthropologist can gain access to the grounds (the 'moral ecology', in Louch's portentous term') for the actions.[2]

THE ETHNOGRAPHY OF CONSCIOUSNESS

The temporal specificity of narrative also alerts us to the fact that it is simultaneously incidental (any narrative is one among an uncountable number of behaviours and events in which the narrator is then engaged) and enduring (it is an ineradicable element in the narrator's aggregate narrative). A narrative should not be unduly privileged over the others which it complements, or from which it is abstracted, merely because of the more or less adventitious fact that it is in our notebooks.

The same caution should be applied to anthropologists' narratives. Fieldwork also is a narrative, usually recorded and written as such, and only artificially bounded from other narratives which constitute our consciousness. We have learned painfully (if belatedly) to situate ourselves *qua* anthropologists in the anthropology we write. Using what we have learned from this enforced reflection on our practices, we must now apply the lesson as a means of understanding better our 'informants'. To put the matter plainly, we are not doing the job if we do not apply insights about our own consciousness to the problem of interpreting others', a reciprocity which Fernandez demonstrates in his chapter by describing the influence on his own self awareness of people about whom he has written. Narrative as an isolate, an abstraction, makes no sense. That is why we have turned away so definitively from the timeless ethnography and the absent or disembodied ethnographer. As Virginia Woolf observed, 'life is not like that, so why should its writing be?' (1938: 148–9).

The anthropologist seeks intimate knowledge: knowledge behind the scenes, behind the masks and roles, behind the generalities and abstractions. The quest is not for the sensational, but for the knowledge which animates the public exchange, the forms of which, far from revealing this knowledge, may well mask it beneath the vagaries of symbol or the constraints of conventional idiom. It is the anthropologist's ability to display such knowledge which persuades the reader of the authenticity of an anthropological account. The display of this knowledge makes claims about the consciousness of those to whom it is imputed. The integrity of such claims has conventionally been assessed in the context of prevailing anthropological orthodoxies.

For so long, too long, British social anthropology has lived complacently with the comforting Durkheimian notion of collective representations. Yet, as we know all too well, there are profound problems with the notion of representativeness. Who or what is represented? Are these representations coercive, or unmediated? Is it enough for us to assume that they represent modes of thought, and to refrain from testing such assumptions? If all we can focus on is what people appear to do, rather than on what they may (less obviously) think, are we not professing a somewhat arthritic anthropology? And has the time not come to confess that, as ethnographers and writers, we do *not* hobble ourselves in this way: that we do indeed use all kinds of devices, not least our *own* consciousness, to imagine and then portray the consciousnesses of others?

If this last suggestion is valid – and we freely confess and defend our own practice in this regard – then there is a sense in which the consciousness of others should be more accessible to us now than it has previously been because of the collapse or redundancy of the old orthodoxy which stipulated the strict difference between the anthropologist and the anthropologized. Now, we do not assume our similarity to those whom we study: apart from being ethnocentric, we would thereby make our subject redundant. But neither should we *assume* our difference, or our difference in important respects, for that would be no less ethnocentric. Modern anthropology is conducted as a dialogue in which, so far as possible, the differentials of power are removed, minimized or neutralized. Our subject has refined itself to the point at which we cannot reasonably plead our exclusive concern with what is public or revealed, for we know that this is, or may be, mere gloss on what is concealed or is not obviously apparent. We have to engage with what Hastrup cogently calls 'the contact zone' to reach whatever lies beneath the merely apparent. For that is where the proof of our claims to authenticity now lies.

'Anthropology at home' has been a much misused notion (now succeeded in misuse and abuse by 'autoanthropology'). Unless contemplating their own navels, the very nature of their enquiry means that anthropologists are never 'at home', for their enquiry consists in asking questions, or in making questionable what those whom they study do not question, either because they properly see no need to, or because it does not occur to them to do so. The term was applied to anthropological research conducted within one's own nation-state (very rarely has it been done within one's own *society*, although the distinction seems often to have escaped anthropologists) and/or within one's own language (as if there was *an* English, or *a* French, or *a* Xhosa so totalitarian and so lifeless that any two of its speakers would necessarily attach the same meanings to the words they share).

But perhaps the greatest lesson to have emerged for the subject generally from this misnamed anthropology was the fundamental impropriety and inadequacy of taking consciousness for granted, and treating it as merely derivable from public manifestations of culture and behaviour: that is, of neglecting the contact zone, on the mistaken grounds that there is only one realm. It may be because both of us have undertaken our main research among people who speak versions of our mother tongue (English) that these distinctions between the ostensible and the concealed, the public form and the private meaning, seem so clear (and, yes, so dear) to us. The apparent semantic similarity (perhaps familiarity) of what we heard revealed to us even more strikingly the reality of its distinctiveness. As fieldworkers, we were immediately made aware of the difference between being able to make a competent and an appropriate sense of what we heard, the essential distinction which becomes apparent to all skilled ethnographers over time as they acquire fluency and experience in the cultures they study. Our research – in the very different contexts of Newfoundland, Shetland, Cumbria and Israel – suggested to us the inescapable distinction between public language and private thought, between communication (a social act) and interpretation (an individuated act), distinctions which we have subsequently pursued in relation to a variety of topics. For us, therefore, consciousness has been an explicit, if elusive objective, the *sine qua non* of our entire ethnographic enterprise.

But, far from claiming this as the exclusive objective of 'anthropology at home', it seems to us the defining and characteristic aspiration of *all* anthropology. The range of societies and topics addressed in this book justify that contention. To understand a conversation among young English children or silence in a Rio *favela*, a healing ritual in Sri Lanka or Temiar, a poet in Asturias, a demonstration in Zanzibar, a Euro-bureaucrat in Brussels, a Nepalese dreamer, is precisely to try to make sense of the consciousness of others. This is not a matter of a new departure in anthropology, but of rediscovering that we have *always* claimed, or have been enjoined, to be concerned with consciousness (our own as well as others') since Malinowski first wrote in his field dairy in 1917:

Principle: along with external events, record feelings and instinctual manifestations; moreover, have a clear idea of the metaphysical nature of existence.

(Malinowski 1989: 130)

We do not aim at consciousness because of academic machismo, but because its elucidation is such a vital concern of those whom we study and claim to explain. As Rabinow insists, there are no 'unconscious primitives' (1977: 151–2); and, as Shweder (1991: 14) says, if we use the word 'civilized' to describe those people who can explain their practices far better and with more imagination than the anthropologist, then the 'primitive' who leads an unexamined life does not exist. An anthropology of consciousness should contribute to the 'decolonization' of the human subject: to a liberation from what we have for so long presented as overdetermining cultural conditions and social institutions. It should temper and moderate the language which social scientists have used to alienate conscious, intentional behaviour from individuals, and to reify and typify it in impersonal abstractions: collective representations, praxis, habitus, and so forth. To pay attention to the consciousness of the individual and to the narratives in which it is expressed is *not* to privilege the individual over society; but, rather, is a necessary condition for the sensitive understanding of social relations and of society as composed of, and constituted by, subjective individuals in interaction.

ANSWERS

So far, we have identified some of the questions about consciousness which we feel need to be posed, have touched on some of the reasons why the attempt to address these questions has now become imperative, and have indicated in very general terms our own theoretical perspective on the matter. When we convened the conference from which this volume of essays arises, we sought a plurality of views and positions; the only argument we refused to accept was that the problem of consciousness was such that no progress was possible. The conference was intensely argumentative, but achieved a remarkable degree of agreement over the most fruitful directions in which to proceed. No less remarkable was the agreement, even among those who were formerly the most sceptical, that progress could and should be made. Before we come, briefly, to the individual chapters, we will mention some of these collective conclusions.

Let us begin with the most important, the question of the evidential basis on which we think we know what people are conscious of. Geertz's famous answer to the question, 'What does the ethnographer do? He writes' (1973: 19), is a curiously thin description of what actually happens. Before they write, they do all of those things which we gloss in the cliché of 'participant observation'. Above all, they listen. The point was forcefully made in our discussions that we may not listen with sufficient care, or that we may listen somewhat selectively. Notwithstanding these failings, we try to listen, and to make sense of what we hear; and, until we have and can show good reason for doing otherwise, we take what we hear as the expression of the speaker's consciousness. The sense we make of it is also, of course, an expression of our own consciousness.

The process of sense-making is complex, but part of it has to do with our attempts to contextualize, knowing that this risks closing a metaphysical circle, rather than subjecting our analysis to a definitive empirical verification (see Hobart 1985). We pay attention to the imagery and figures of speech which people use, although, of course, we also supply their meanings. In what may or may not be sleight of hand, we may attempt to substantiate our interpretations by locating them in what we call 'culture'; but invariably we display our evidence as being other than random, arbitrary or exceptional. We may not claim 'certainty' for our knowledge, but we defend it as documentable, and do it routinely for behaviour. Although we may have been wary of going even this far in respect of 'consciousness', our acknowledgement that behaviour *is* conscious must surely now incline us to admit that we *do* make claims about other people's consciousness and our grasp of it. In her chapter, Hastrup draws our attention to the care we need to take in depicting the 'contact zone' between the 'inner person' (consciousness) and the 'outer reality' of manifest behaviour.

The range of evidence of consciousness adduced in this book is enormous: cursing, dreaming, writing, trancing, multiplying personalities, sloganizing, 'sorcerizing', growing and playing. We state them here as verbs rather than as nouns following the powerful suggestion[3] that the verb signifies the processual and personified nature of action: its agency or intentionality – both implying consciousness – as opposed to its alienation or abstraction or reification.

The second issue is the relationship between individual and collective consciousness. Inevitably, participants and contributors disagree over the importance to be attributed to the individual and with regard to the precise nature of individual agency. Nevertheless, there is general agreement that the individual is certainly creative within (and possibly outwith) the current and received terms of the collectivity to which she or he belongs; and that the individual's activity of *interpretation*, of sense-making, requires us to develop a more sophisticated and sensitive view of the complexity of individuals and to refrain from seeing them as merely generalizable within 'cultures'. Rather than talking glibly of collective consciousness, we would now advocate the more cautious, 'consciousnesses within collectivity'.

Third, some of the work presented here may appear at first sight to deal with 'abnormal', or altered states of consciousness. This does not reflect a gratuitous anthropological infatuation with the exotic or the alternative. Rather, it makes the crucial point that both within and across cultures, there are a variety of modalities in which people can be conscious. 'Alternative' consciousness may be one among many kinds of consciousness none of which should be axiomatically privileged in analysis, and any of which may help us to understand what is going on in any of the other forms.

THE BOOK

In the preceding section, we outlined three overarching concerns – with evidence; with the variety of forms of consciousness; and with the collectivity – and we have grouped the chapters which follow accordingly. However, this means of organizing the book should not be regarded as anything more than a matter of convenience: most of the chapters address issues beyond those of the rubric under which we place them, and overlap with other rubrics.

Part I, then, is concerned with questions of the evidence for or manifestations of consciousness. In the first essay, James Fernandez shows that the consciousness of the ethnographer is mutually and reciprocally implicated in both those of the significant others he or she studies and those who are his or her disciplinary peers and mentors. Consciousness is the driving concern of anthropological enquiry and underpins our specifically designated problematics. He refers to the ethnography in his own *œuvre* to show the influences on the composition of his own consciousness, his 'personal thought line'. Microcosmically, this reflects the problem of individual consciousness – its peripheralization and temporariness in the collective condition. He argues that our sensitivity to categorizations of ourselves in terms of collectivity and/or peripherality should sensitize us to the ways we impose it on our ethnographic subjects.

The next two chapters both further illustrate the interactive nature of consciousness, and its implications, to which Fernandez draws our attention. Chapter 2 is based on a dream 'out of place' and what may be learned from it. Tamara Kohn's subject is Kamala, her Nepalese 'sister-in-the-field', who visits her in England, and appears to communicate via her dreams with those she has left behind. Being 'out of place' affords Kamala heightened consciousness of her self and home which she expresses by recounting her vivid nightly dreams. In turn, these offer the anthropologist insights into the society and culture she had studied which were not apparent to her while she was in the field. Kamala's altered consciousness thus finds its complement in Kohn's with which it has engaged sympathetically, even, perhaps, intersubjectively.

In Chapter 3, Allison James imagines the conscious experience of being a child, with its unresolved dilemmas, contradictions and puzzles. She shows how the child's developing consciousness interrelates concepts of body, age and identity. She identifies problems in the categories of 'child' and 'adult' which are raised within the consciousnesses of her young informants and by their epistemological puzzles. She asks, what might it mean to a child to be a child? How might our perception and understanding of the child's experience of childhood be emancipated from the adult's construction of it? In acquiring sensitivity to conventional adult views of adult/child categories, children become both increasingly adept at social behaviour and self conscious: they learn to distinguish between their categorical social roles and their individuality and selfhood.

We have alluded above to the question of the mutuality of consciousness among, *inter alia*, the anthropologist and 'informants'. In Chapter 4, Bill Watson takes this question further, by extending it to the author of fiction. Making reference to the work of Zola, Forster, Gissing and Naipaul, he argues that the differences between fact/ethnography and fiction/novel may be more apparent than real. A comparison of the consciousness of the novelist with that of the anthropologist, as they work within their distinct (and apparently opposed) genres, reveals significant similarities.

Both of them construct their texts by interweaving 'social facts' with personal narratives; both imaginatively juxtapose individual actions to historical circumstances. The expertise with which both 'read' social life and (however ambiguously) inform their texts with these readings derives from their own experienced and personal consciousness of it.

In Part II, we look at states of consciousness. In a careful speculation on dreaming, David Riches makes waking consciousness and consciousness of dreaming contingent; and then, like Kohn, substantiates the view that by dreaming, we rehearse certain kinds of preoccupation or consciousness. Dreaming, he says, is the continuation of social action by other means. At the moment of waking, the dream provides a liminal bridge between the different realities experienced in wakefulness and in sleep, and between the meanings which may be attributed to them in each condition. For, while sleep may offer a view of the possibilities and consequences of social action which may not be available in wakefulness – reality experienced during sleep may rehearse, as it were, wakeful reality – only the dream makes conscious the connection. Dreaming is thus seen as purposive social process which can be interpreted from and informed by any cultural vantage point.

Chapter 6 is based on a cross-cultural comparison of four cases of trance and spirit possession. In offering this survey, Andrew Strathern insists on the imperative need to find an approach to consciousness which does not perpetuate the false dichotomy of the psychogenic and sociogenic. Since consciousness is both experienced and revealed through bodily processes in ways which are culturally, socially and historically relative, the dichotomy can be undermined, or bridged, by the concept of 'embodiment' as the medium of consciousness. Thus, he argues that consciousness itself is revealed as a concept indispensable for the task of situating events and understanding experience socially and historically.

Like Strathern, Bruce Kapferer is concerned to display the embodiment of consciousness; and, in so doing, to discredit the Cartesian dualism of mind and body. He uses Searle's concept of intentionality to reveal consciousness as dynamic: as moving and motivating the body, and moving beyond it to create and substantiate a 'field of consciousness'. For Kapferer, consciousness is interactional, and must therefore be regarded as process. He makes his argument by detailed reference to instances of sorcery among Sri Lankan Buddhists, showing that consciousness resides in embodied experience which is heightened by sometimes extreme emotion. To understand consciousness, anthropologists must look beyond culture, narrowly conceived, towards passion, in order to appreciate the compelling nature of reality constructed in and by consciousness.

In Chapter 8, Roland Littlewood's review of theories of multiple personality disorder (MPD) gives us a panoptic survey of contemporary views of consciousness and the self. At different times, MPD has been regarded as indicating past or present trauma, or has been regarded as a type of psychological defence or of creative fantasy. The historical variation in the frequency with which the syndrome is diagnosed suggests that, as a pathology, it may be exacerbated by certain contemporary conditions; or that it reflects an homology between the dissociation of society and that of the individual; or, more prosaically, that MPD is a fashion which appeals to American credulousness and popular tastes for psychological flimflam, or an obsession with 'self-awareness'. There is the intriguing speculation that MPD may reflect a problem of resituating consciousness in cyberspace at a moment in which there seems no limit to the possibilities of electronic technology. Littlewood argues that diagnosis of the syndrome may be a consequence of 'expert relationships', of 'medico-legal commerce', and invites us to consider the contrast between the abnormality of multiple personalities, and the normal expectation that multiple aspects of the self should be comfortably and harmoniously encompassed within the person.

Finally, in Part III, we look at the relationship between individual and collective consciousness, at the location of consciousness within a collectivity, and at the generalization of consciousness. In Chapter 9, Kirsten Hastrup introduces an important distinction between consciousness and awareness, giving to the latter the connotation of explicitness. There are different kinds of explicitness, which may include silence or other communicative forms, all of which are built upon the foundation of consciousness which is implicit. She echoes Fernandez's argument in insisting that it is anthropology's task to retrieve ('redeem') the implicit. This distinction between consciousness and awareness suggests a conceptual discrimination to be found in several of the chapters between the mental conditions for and foundations of action, and action itself; and provides the basis for a series of discriminations – consciousness : awareness :: map : itinerary :: memory : recollection (and, possibly, :: collectivity : individual) – which theorize the relationship of thought and action.

In the following chapter, Parkin builds on Hastrup's consciousness/awareness distinction by characterizing consciousness as a 'meta-conversation': as being aware of being aware. Arguing that consciousness is embodied and inscribed materially, he offers the ethnographic case of Zanzibari Muslims who use the comportment and concealment of the female body as a symbolic medium – a 'blank banner' – for the narration of a plethora of complex statements. These concern sexuality and gender; the relationship of Zanzibar to its federal partner, Tanganyika; and Zanzibar's relationship to the cosmopolitan world. Above all, they are statements about Islam itself, making a direct analogy between the requirement for women to cover their bodies totally and the total explanatory 'coverage' and capacity of fundamentalist Islam which has no null hypothesis. The blank banner of Zanzibari Islamic discourse and demonstration is an illustration of how consciousness works: predicating itself on awareness through specific, material and embodied objects.

In the final, and most explicitly sceptical, chapter in the book, Cris Shore gives us the intriguing case of a documentable attempt to contrive a new consciousness, that of 'the European', committed to the objectives of the Union even at the cost of more chauvinistic attachments to nation-state. His study is based on his doubts regarding the essentialism of self and the accessibility to anthropologists of individual consciousness. His focus is therefore on social action and on consciousness as a folk concept, an idea-in-use. His data are of Euro-bureaucrats who see themselves charged with the creation of a supranational European consciousness, through the manipulation of symbols, icons, emblems, and by attempting to harness the power of the media. He sees these activists operating with neofunctionalist ideas of social institutions and of consciousness itself, and argues in similar theoretical fashion that anthropologists cannot go beyond the 'social facts' of 'collective representations', such as those of Eurocrats' Europeanism.

NOTES

1 A proposition long ago discredited by MacIntyre (1962).
2 Indeed, to bring the argument full circle and return to the propositions we reviewed above concerning the development of the brain, it could be argued that consciousness is characterized by our capacity to adapt to circumstances which we interpret by predicating them on narrative (cf. Humphrey 1982: 474–7; also Bruner and Weisser 1991: 145–6).
3 Made early in our conference by Wendy James: a suggestion which then significantly influenced the ensuing discussions.

REFERENCES

Augustine of Hippo (1907) *The Confessions*, London: Dent.
Bateson, G. (1958) 'Language and psychotherapy', *Psychiatry*, 21: 96–100.
Bateson, G. (1972) *Steps to an Ecology of Mind*, London: Intertext.
Blakemore, C. (1988) *The Mind Machine*, London: BBC Publications.
Bruner, J. and Weisser, S. (1991) 'The invention of self: autobiography and its forms', pp. 129–48 in D. Olson and N. Torrance (eds) *Literacy and Orality*, Cambridge: Cambridge University Press.
Churchland, P. S. (1994) 'Can neurobiology teach us anything about consciousness?', *Proceedings and Addresses of the American Philosophical Association*, 67(4): 23–40.
Cohen, A. P. (1994) *Self Consciousness: An Alternative Anthropology of Identity*, London: Routledge.
Cornwell, J. (1994) 'Is mind really matter?', *The Sunday Times*, 15 May: Section 10, 4–6.
Crick, F. (1994) *The Astonishing Hypothesis. The Scientific Search for the Soul*, New York: Simon & Schuster.

Crites, S. (1971) 'The narrative quality of experience', *Journal of the American Academy of Religion*, XXXIX: 291–311.

Dennett, D. (1991) *Consciousness Explained*, Harmondsworth: Penguin.

Eccles, J. (1994) *How the Self Controls Its Brain*, London: Springer-Verlag.

Edelman, G. (1992) *Bright Air, Brilliant Fire. On the Matter of the Mind*, Harmondsworth: Penguin.

Fodor, J. (1992) 'Can there be a science of mind?', *TLS*, 3 July: 5–7.

Geertz, C. (1973) *The Interpretation of Cultures*, New York: Basic Books.

Geertz, C. (1983) *Local Knowledge*, New York: Basic Books.

Giddens, A. (1984) *The Constitution of Society: Outline of the Theory of Structuration*, Oxford: Polity Press.

Giddens, A. (1991) *Modernity and Self-identity: Self and Society in the Late Modern Age*, Oxford: Polity Press.

Hardy, B. (1968) 'Towards a poetics of fiction: 3. An approach through narrative', *Novel*, 2(1): 1–17.

Hobart, M. (1985) 'Texte est un con', pp. 33–53 in R. H. Barnes *et al.* (eds) *Contexts and Levels: Anthropological Essays on Hierarchy*, Oxford: JASO.

Humphrey, N. (1982) 'Consciousness: a just-so story', *New Scientist*, 95: 474–7.

Kerby, A. (1991) *Narrative and the Self*, Bloomington: Indiana University Press.

Louch, A. (1966) *Explanation and Human Action*, Oxford: Blackwell.

McGinn, C. (1992) *The Problem of Consciousness*, Oxford: Blackwell.

MacIntyre, A. C. (1962) 'A mistake about causality in social science', pp. 48–70 in P. Laslett and W. G. Runciman (eds) *Philosophy, Politics and Society*, 2nd series, Oxford: Blackwell.

Malinowski, B. (1989) *A Diary in the Strict Sense of the Term*, Stanford: Stanford University Press.

Moravec, H. (1988) *Mind Children*, Cambridge, Mass: Harvard University Press.

Penrose, R. (1990) *The Emperor's New Mind*, London: Vintage.

Porter, R. (1994) 'A mind and its meanings', *TLS*, 4772: 6–7.

Rabinow, P. (1977) *Reflections on Fieldwork in Morocco*, Berkeley: University of California Press.

Rapport, N. J. (1993) *Diverse World-Views in an English Village*, Edinburgh: Edinburgh University Press.

Searle, J. (1992) *The Rediscovery of the Mind*, Cambridge, Mass: MIT Press.

Shweder, R. (1991) *Thinking through Cultures*, Cambridge, Mass: Harvard University Press.

Woolf, V. (1938) 'Modern fiction', in *The Common Reader*, Harmondsworth: Penguin.

Part I

Chapter 1

Amazing grace

Meaning deficit, displacement and new consciousness in expressive interaction

James W. Fernandez

Amazing Grace! How sweet the sound
That saved a wretch like me.
I once was lost but now I'm found,
Was blind but now I see!

THE HUMAN CONDITION

Newton's famous hymn, so widely known and widely sung in the Anglo-American religious tradition as frequently to be listed as simply 'Traditional', may stand in apt epigraph to my anthropological experience of consciousness and particularly self consciousness: that is consciousness of the possibility of, the desire for and the achievement of radical transformation of wretched self into something other, something more 'grace full'. For I have been mainly a student of religious and political movements which, recognizing a situation of deficit in their members, have promised to them or achieved for them, on a temporary or a permanent basis, such significant transformations in their lives. They promise and achieve conversions – a notion that I shall discuss under the rubric of tropic displacement – which are in effect conscious changes in their selves. These changes are most usually revitalizing in their consequences. The self and those with whom it is grouped are given or restored to a new life, to a state of grace.

Hence I have been conscious of myself professionally as a student of revitalization movements and of my career project as the study of revitalization. In this chapter I wish to continue to explore this revitalization of consciousness with the simple additional thought that in some way anthropology itself, perhaps the social sciences entirely, have themselves been revitalizing for the kinds of wretched selves who find themselves singled out and moved by Newton's hymn. I mean that through the 'amazing' work of our methods of abstraction we regularly transform self consciousness into system consciousness. And that's a good thing too. But would 'saved' or 'salvation' be apt words for the rapture or epiphany obtained by these mainly intellectual operations? We have at least returned the self to the whole (Fernandez 1986: Ch. 8). Or in a rather more recondite vocabulary I find useful and shall return to below: the social sciences have been revitalizing by saving us from the complexities and contrariness of cultural consensus by putting forth collective representations purporting to account for how systems operate so as to assure our social consensus.[1]

Revitalization theory is a long-established theory in anthropology (Wallace 1958) and it rests like all theories upon metaphor: in this case the organic metaphor (Nisbet 1969). It is a metaphor which like all metaphors fleshes out, enlivens and animates the bare bones of the theory and gives it pertinence in the consciousness of those in social science who deploy it for explanatory purposes! There is, as has been said, a 'shock of recognition' in effective metaphor that drives in a vital way deep into our consciousness, linking, thereby, in a gratifying way corporeal and intellectual experience, the orectic and the theoretical poles (Turner 1967).

Both personally and theoretically I have become over the years quite self conscious about the presence of the tropes in argument (Fernandez 1991), including my own, and in this colloquium on (self) consciousness I shall be deploying that self consciousness to argue for the centrality of these figurations of life and thought in self consciousness itself. That is to say I will be arguing for the centrality of meaning deficit, of figurative displacement and, as a consequence, new consciousness – all phases in the metaphoric predication of new identities – in the human condition.

Despite anthropology's penchant for demonstrating difference I shall argue that, in at least a general way, all we 'wretched mortals' are alike, in respect of the impetus of meaning deficit and thus live within and live out the human condition in comparable ways. That living within and living out, of course, takes many different interesting forms – they are differences that make an important difference – according to the different transformative root metaphors of existence chosen by particular cultures, which is to say by particular influential individuals, to cope with these deficits (Pepper 1942; Fernandez 1986; 1974; Ortner 1973; Turner 1974). Also no deficit can be discussed without reference to the pressure exerted by political and economic circumstances on the worldview implicit in the root metaphors embedded in social discourse. Also, too, this humanistic recognition of the universality of deficit is no doubt conditioned by having lived within the Judaeo-Christian tradition with its sombre and repressive emphasis on human sinfulness and its Nietzschean 'tragic sense of imperfection' (Sahlins pers. comm.)

Still, I shall argue for meaning deficit as motivating in the human condition in general. And in the present context I would argue that this meaning deficit consists in the impermanence and transitoriness of our individuality *vis-à-vis* our imagination of the possibilities of its perpetuity, as well as in the imperfection of the realization of our projects in practice *vis-à-vis* the more perfect models we hold of them in thought, which we test and upon which we operate! Of such wretched unrequitement and of such needful search for grace is self consciousness, sooner or later, surely though not uniquely composed.

TWENTY–TWENTY HINDSIGHT: THE ARGUMENT SO FAR

When we are under invitation to participate and offer argument in the situation of a collegial colloquium – and this goes to the situatedness of all problem-provoked self consciousness – we undertake first (at least someone as long in the tooth as I) to review, to bring into consciousness, the personal thought lines (PTL) in one's own work – in relation to the Great Thought Lines (GTL) of one's art and science or one's skilful practice from which one has learned and to which one desires to contribute. These are the skills and understandings of the PTL and GTL that are relevant to and might be seen as contributing to if not leading up to the subject matter.

So, self-conscious of consciousness as our subject matter, I shall first take advantage of the licence for introspection of my own mind as such a mind lives in its academic 'vat' hooked up mainly to its own thought lines and the network of thought lines, great and small, that are in some way interconnected with it.[2] But this intellectual web-building must necessarily be accompanied by some feeling of awkward self consciousness at appearing to hawk one's wares or, to tend the trope, jangle one's thought lines. So though I at first incline towards my own thought line(s) here, the hope is that it (they) can turn out to be more than 'one liners' brought forth over the years by a wretch like me. I am also conscious that in that wretchedness lies a transformative dynamic that can hopefully save my consciousness from itself, enabling it to hop out of the vat, as it were, into a different if not a larger world! Presumably that is what anthropology is mainly about.

The PTL I would like to use this opportunity to bring into question has to do with social and cultural consensus in interaction (Fernandez 1965) and its relation to 'economies of thought' or essentialization (stereotyping) processes by which self and others are identified (categorized) in the process of that interaction. Somehow or other societies manage, despite the contingencies generated by both existential unpredictability and the great diversity of self consciousnesses of which they are composed, to find through categorization processes enough consensus to cohere and get their work done. And societies expect to get work done by such motivating collective representation. And an important part of self consciousness lies in the fact that the self is conscious not only of its own pressures to be itself but of the consensual pressures to conform to expectations bound up in categorical allegiances imposed or freely chosen.

Simply put, satisfaction, that is positive self consciousness, or distress, negative self consciousness, derives from conformity or lack of it to categorical obligations. Social consensus and coherence is managed by these processes which are, often enough rather wretchedly, essentializing in implication. At the same time the confidence in coherent belonging or the consciousness of coherence lost can be managed by imaginative displacement of category of various kinds which result in new consciousness. And it is this displacement towards new consciousness which trope theory, as both a PTL and a GTL, addresses.

SHIPS THAT PASS IN THE NIGHT? ACADEMIC ARGUMENT AND ETHNOGRAPHIC WORLDS

It is one thing to self consciously put forth a thought line. It is quite another thing for an ethnographer to presume that we can hand such a line over to those among whom we do our ethnographies in any way that will be relevant to their self consciousness. Until very recently the people I have worked among in Africa and rural Spain have read little or nothing either from the GTL or the PTL and it is doubtful that much in either line would be immediately relevant to any deficits in meaning or material well-being they themselves were conscious of needing to repair. As the rural and working people I am now working with like to say, 'Más enseña la necesidad que la Universidad' (Necessity teaches more than University).

At the same time I would maintain that this thought line, my PTL in particular, is quite relevant to my ethnographic experience. Indeed, the first article in the series speculating on the nature of social and cultural consensus (Fernandez 1965) arose out of experience of the diversity of interpretations of symbols in an otherwise fairly tight knit religious group in Africa. And a further series of articles exploring the organizing images or metaphors of that religion arose directly out of the local explanations directly given to me trying to account for their religious ritual or indirectly to be found in the densely imagistic homologizing and sermonizing characteristic of the religion. My PTL, in other words, was anchored in their PTLs as these arose under the pressures (perhaps contorting) of ethnographic enquiry and text collection.

At the same time their thought lines underwent significant conversion in me as I elaborated their implications in my own. And many conceptualizations relevant to the GTL of the Western tradition appear which are quite beyond any economies of thought my informants were interested in. My academic self was conscious of a tradition of discourse – the vat – to which I needed to relate, *a consensual obligation* as it were to former and present colleagues in the ongoing discourse of anthropology quite unknown to my local ethnographic collaborators.

Much has now been written about this discrepancy of discourses between fieldwork and subsequent interpretation in academic milieux.[3] I would simply like to observe, however, that in recent years I have been invited to lecture on the theory of tropes, my own PTL in part but especially the GTL, in various parts of Spain and Latin America including in the province of fieldwork, Asturias. Very often there are participants from rural milieux in these classes, seminars and public talks quite like the rural milieux of much of the ethnographic material I later conceptualized. In these talks and seminars I use these ethnographic materials and show their possible conceptualizations. Therefore, as the world turns, the separation of discourses is happily or unhappily compromised at least for those villagers, quite a few actually, who have gone on for an education. And, of course, by no means is mine the only case in a globalized anthropology in which boarding parties now move back and forth with facility between cultural vessels. But does this mean an approximation of self consciousnesses – that intimate intersubjective knowing which the philosophers desire and some promise?

A PENNY FOR YOUR THOUGHTS: ON KNOWING OTHER MINDS

The problem of knowing other minds in other cultures both in general and in particular, has long been a major preoccupation of anthropologists. We don't have to list the abundant literature devoted to this problem from 'The Mind of Primitive Man' to 'The Savage Mind' or trace the gradual evolution in thinking on this problem from finding the savage mind exclusively elsewhere to finding it inclusively in ourselves – from inspection or circumspection of the distinctly other to introspection in the self.

I have argued elsewhere (Fernandez 1992) the difficulty or impossibility of knowing other minds in any adequate sense of the term 'know' and surely in cross-cultural context. And I have suggested the intrusive not to say imperialist motives that may be present in the desire to do so. One might, indeed, be sceptical of knowing the minds of one's most intimate family members or even one's own mind! The tentative little phrase politely intrusive upon the meditative states of others, 'a penny for your thoughts', may, in fact, value the expected product, the true thoughts of others, at about its actual value.

For some time now social scientists have been invited to live in a Goffmanesque world where one has to recognize how much people warp their intimate interiority in order to accommodate to the expectations of others in their presentation of self. In respect to the consciousness of the other self, the question arises whether there is in fact any there which is anything more than an inchoate – even mystical – feeling of entity (Fernandez 1980) and which will always be swayed and shaped by the contingency of social circumstance in its public presentation. Indeed the pragmatic argument would have it that consciousness only arises from the need of communication with others. It is a product of praxis, of social adaptation, and has no investigatable antecedent existence.

For the anthropologist this has been an enduring problem. When pursuing enquiry into alien mental states among the colonized and other subordinated populations we are always at risk of being told what it is thought we expect to hear. Indeed our method has been designed to circumvent such tergiversation in ethnographic conversation and by 'indirections find directions out'. But whether in fact we ever truly move beyond analytic understanding to synthetic understanding (Kant) in this quest for the mind of the other is an open philosophic question. The argument is to be made that, even in the most intimate conversations characterized by a high degree of mutual confidence, what is learned is an emergent and secondary elaboration occurring between participants and is not truly the bringing forth of the truly original, that is 'pre-objective' (Tsordas 1994), which is to say the truly intimate property of the consciousness of either party (Schafer 1980).

So there is plenty of reason for scepticism in the knowing of other minds and their (self) consciousness beyond their pragmatic consciousness of needing to present an identifiable self to take its place among other identifiable selves in the practice of everyday social life. But this scepticism, this irony, we might call it, inclusive for us all in the human condition, need not inhibit our anthropological enquiry. Indeed it might rather animate it. And this for two reasons. First, we may not be able to truly know other minds but we can surely learn from them (Fernandez 1992). Second, we may not be able to know other minds but we can admire their myriad and creative ways of practising their being in the world (de Certeau 1988). And in this learning from other minds and admiring the practice of other minds – it must surely be what anthropological ethnography is mainly about – one might argue lies the basis of such possibilities of that human solidarity to which any transcendent-anthropological imagination must inevitably be dedicated (Rorty 1989). And if anthropologists and more particularly ethnographers can pretend to moments of grace in the practice of our profession and in our 'rapprochement' to other minds and other ways of working in the world it is, perhaps, not to deepest insight into 'otherness' but to a state of perpetual learning from and admiration for the work of other minds in the world that we might turn. So let me turn to other minds in other vats from which I have learned or am still learning.

SOME IMAGINATIONS WHICH HAVE CAPTURED MY OWN AND SOME THOUGHTS ABOUT THE STRUCTURES OF THEIR IDENTITY

Anthropology, it is said, is animated by meaning deficit in two ways. Our commitment to professional displacements to other climes and other mores is autobiographically animated by a sense of meaning deficit in our own lives and cultures. Here anthropology is understood as a metaphor, a disciplinary trope which effects a displacement, both a turning away and a turning to, and which seeks to respond to the deficits to be found in modern life. Secondly anthropologists are often animated by the sense that somehow our theoretical analyses and explanatory vocabularies miss what is profound in human experience. In the case of our colloquium we worry that the experience of consciousness, the conscious self and cultural and human individuality reposing in these states are escaping us.

In the presence of these meaning deficits, in any event, our thoughts are often displaced in search of enrichment to the novelist's domain and the greater freedom and power to be found there for getting at the experiential in the human condition. Early in American anthropology a panoply of the most distinguished anthropologists of the period, Boasians all, turned, in the collection *American Indian Life*, to the novelist's art to seek to capture what their ethnographies had so evidently missed (Parsons 1967). In the many decades subsequent, this search for local experience continued in the life history movement in American anthropology. And most recently, in the 1980s, there have been two related movements which have sought to bring our reach closer to our grasp: experiential anthropology (Bruner and Turner 1986) and narrative ethnography or 'ethnography of the particular' (Stewart 1989; Abu Lughod 1991; Behar 1993; Lavie *et al*. 1993).

But these movements in anthropology have not focused as directly on the issue of consciousness in society as we are focusing here. In my view greater directness of focus – that knowing of other minds – can come about by listening to or eliciting some of the key images that, if not actually present in these minds are, at least, put forth by them and/or put into practice by them. In the study of this 'argument of images' we may well come as close as we can come to capturing the other's imagination whether that 'other' be the collaborator from the local culture of enquiry or the reader of our ethnographic interpretations of that collaboration. But the issue, as we see, is not only that of capturing the other's imagination but, as much or more, in having our own captured.

In the light of that understanding I turn to some imaginations in other ethnographic vats whose images and projects have exercised some power over my own imagination – that is to say, who have saved me from it and who have seemed to me for a variety of reasons exceptionally conscious of who they are in relationship to their milieu; exceptionally conscious of meaning deficits in their (individual or group) identities – which is to say their category membership – and exceptionally determined to take imaginative action in response to these conditions. I shall try and give in briefest compass an account of that category consciousness which is a crucial component of their identity.

These five contrasting individuals were not the only 'powerful imaginations' (Fernandez 1991) encountered in my years of fieldwork in African and Iberian societies but space hardly allows for a larger cast of characters.[4] With the exception of the last entrepreneurial character, I have written elsewhere about all these individuals (see especially Fernandez 1984b). I want to emphasize what should be quite obvious in the distinction between *character* and *individual*: I cannot possibly in this space, or perhaps any space reasonably available to the anthropologist as published author, do justice to the complexity of consciousness of any of these individuals *qua* individuals. The age makes us aware that these brief narratives are not in any sense master narratives but only 'partial truths' of these personages arising in the particularities of my interaction with them and produced out of a focus relevant to our concerns here in category and meaning deficit. And, of course, these vignettes are shaped and highlighted by my sense of contrast in their respective characters. I can only try and characterize their contrasting consciousnesses in the terms I believe pertinent to our colloquium without caricaturing them.

Keeping in mind such reservations I shall speculate about the consciousness of my interlocutors insofar as in my interaction with them I became conscious of it. For what I know of other consciousnesses is what I learned from what they put into practice in the process of engaging with my enquiry or what I can infer from their practices that came to my attention in living with them. Since my enquiry was never focused on the problem of consciousness *per se*, my interpretations are second order in nature. By all the aforesaid it will be understood that I will be particularly attentive in these ethnographic vignettes to meaning deficits, category anxieties, tropic displacements and transformed or new consciousness.

Antoine the Night Fool: a 'Nduman' accedes to peculiar power

Antoine was a young Fang man in his early twenties whose actions I have described elsewhere (Fernandez 1982: 187–90). When young he had been 'prepared' according to Fang custom with a powerful tutelary spirit and had every right to expect success in this world. In fact he found himself quite impoverished and without employment at a time when he was thinking of marriage. His response to his desperate condition and the villagers' categorizations of him as a know-nothing and failure (*mimia*) was a chain of bizarre actions centred about the search for the wealth which he was sure had been sent to him from Europe and which someone, possibly the ethnographers among other suspects, were keeping from him. The most bizarre action, though not without precedent in Fang culture, was to place himself every night at a central point in the village and around midnight to begin his booming but disembodied, virtually spectral night talk. This 'talk' involved his frustrated claims to wealth and success but also involved critical, often sarcastic, social commentary on his fellow villagers.

The deficit here seems clear: his impoverishment and unemployment in the presence of his 'prepared' expectation of a successful young manhood. His painful consciousness of his situation produced a tropic displacement into the bizarre midnight personage of an amazingly articulate and insightful, though caustic, social critic and social arbiter – a know-everything. Figuratively, he displaced himself from the bottom of the social order of village life to the apex, from the peripheries to the centre. Such displacement, as long as it was tolerated, provided him with a gratifying new consciousness: the 'amazing grace', if only at midnight, of esteem, prestige and power – the exercise of a kind of shadow government in the affairs of his co-villagers. But his pronouncements were so satirical and caustic that eventually the villagers tired of them. True, there was a certain *schadenfreude* among those villagers not commented upon one night in hearing the foibles of their neighbours exposed. But the next night it was their turn and so in village moot it was decided to force Antoine back to his meagre itinerant tailor's job in the district seat of Oyem.

Antoine taught me something about the difficulties of transition to competent young manhood among Fang particularly and in the human condition generally. By mystical means Antoine converted his category from 'know-nothing' to 'know-everything' and fleetingly occupied the centre and high ground in village life. But the tolerance of his satire was shortlived. This causes one to think about the social role and limits of toleration of public irony of the satirical and caustic kind in village relations and its usefulness as an effective category converter and meaning provider.

The Parrot's Egg and the Bull Who Crashes in the Kraal: two styles in communicating cosmic consciousness

I have also written extensively about these two successful African prophets (Fernandez 1966; 1971; 1982; 1986), the secretive enigmatic style of the one and the energetic organizational style of the other. One says successful because both at the time I knew them were in their mid-forties and had become the heads of large congregations. These congregations were composed, on the one hand, of Fang Equatorial villagers living in the backwaters of the French colonial world and, on the other, of Zulu in a South African urban underclass temporarily in service but with fundamentally transitory lives. As I have been at pains elsewhere to describe, the prophets took these dwellers as members of marginal categories, and made them, if only temporarily, members of vital congregations which appeared to dwell at the centre of religious worlds.

The consciousnesses of these prophets were in large part preoccupied with the organizational struggle over several decades first to separate themselves from subordination in the congregations of other prophets to whom they first belonged, to found their own congregations virtually in their own name and finally to build and hold membership by techniques of ritual cosmos building and healing. So it was not only an organizational challenge to which they were responding but a deeper sense of the material and spiritual deficiencies of African life. 'The Parrot's Egg's' genius lay primarily in the former technique – that is to say in intricate inward-turning ritual elaborations of a spiritual world of which he was the *axis mundi* and through which he effected both a centripetal influence and a kind of generalized healing influence in the lives of his membership. 'The Bull's' genius lay primarily in the latter technique of healing and his church was relatively poorly elaborated in respect to ritual. But he was powerful in direct hands-on healing of which he was the main ministrant and by which he made each member the centre of focus of the action of the Holy Spirit.

Thus I would not want to simply identify their prophetic consciousness with competitive congregation gaining and maintaining or with merely strategic views of ritual elaboration and healing, however conscious these two prophets were of their challenges and responsibilities here. For both men were also religious virtuosi with a persistent consciousness of the immanence of supernatural forces within them and without them to which they had access and which they could employ to the benefit of themselves and their congregations. And their congregations, I believe, were conscious of this power and its ability to bring about significant changes within and without themselves.

The Parrot's Egg was particularly attuned to the presence of ancestral shades and had powers to invite their presence among the congregation. Indeed, he himself had 'died' many times, so in having dwelt among the dead he could enable them to dwell among their descendants, the needful living, from whom they had been cut off by the influences of the colonial world. The night-long rituals of the Parrot's chapel were aimed at the symbolic death and resurrection, among the revivified dead, both of the prophet leader and of the membership. The Parrot's spiritual serenity combined with his fertile ritual elaborations and cryptic pronouncements in sermons communicated consciousness of ancestral presence and confidence that the dead could be brought to live among the living such that death itself would lose its power over them. We might say in terms of the 'poetics of displacement'[5] that the Parrot had great metaphoric powers to bring into existence by demeanour, ritual action and word, another religious world in which his followers might live during the night-long seance.

The Bull was much more a man of this world who wrestled more directly with despair, sickness and death and overcame these not by joining them or by ritual displacement to another world but by concentrating in his person the healing power of the Holy Wind. He was particularly conscious of the circumambient presence of this vital force over the land and in the sea and was adept, like many of his successful fellow Zionist pastors, in concentrating its energies within himself first and then, by the laying on of hands, passing the power on to the afflicted individual sufferers of his congregation who came before him. In terms of the 'poetics of displacement' he felt himself as a part vitally connected with the whole, that is with circumambient power which he was able to bring to bear upon the afflicted, changing their condition by making them also a part of that whole. His was part-whole healing and thus his displacement was mainly metonymic. The Bull, to suggest the categorical dynamic mainly involved, was a 'metonymic operator' while the Parrot was a 'metaphoric operator'.

Thus if I were to speak of the consciousness of these two religious leaders I would say that it consisted in a charismatic combination of an awareness of organizational requirements, individual and social deficits and religious sensibilities. We can only suggest here a central component of their sensibility: a fertile figurative imagination. I have elsewhere explored (Fernandez 1966; 1986; 1982) the 'argument of images', which is to say the communicative capacity of these two leaders and their extraordinary ability through verbal-visual and kinesthetic directly visual imagery to convey forcefully to the consciousness of their members supportive and ultimately category-changing supernatural presences. By employing the metaphoric names by which they were popularly known to that membership, 'the Parrot's Egg' and 'the Bull Who Crashes in the Kraal', rather than their proper names I mean to evoke the centrality of an evocative figurative imagination in their own self consciousness and in the intersubjectivity they established with and among their membership.

The material deficits in the lives of that membership seem obvious enough: high disease and mortality (particularly infant mortality) rates, poverty and marked relative deprivation. The meaning deficits are more complicated to explain but mainly consisted in loss of the ability to imagine nurturant contact with the relevant supernatural forces, with the ancestors and their powers and with more abstract animistic powers that reposed, for example, in the Holy Wind. By various figurative means these two prophets displaced their membership from their current ills to focal relationships of empowerment with these forces. In effect they brought about new consciousness in their membership, if not permanently at least for the more or less extended periods of worship.

In being with these prophets I learned something from their practices about the place of the figurative imagination and various metaphoric movements made by it in the capacity of religious movements to effect category change in their members (Fernandez 1974; 1979).

Ceferino, the 'Habanero': a village versifier in his old age

Part of the only 'partial truth' that reposes in these narrative accounts of the consciousness of significant others encountered in fieldwork is that they do not take into account the age factor, the change over time in consciousness of the awareness of needs in oneself and others. Take the case of the 'Habanero', the 'Man from Havana', a village versifier whose life history I took down in the early mid-1970s in an agro-mining community in the mountains of northern Spain (Fernandez 1993a). Ceferino was in his very old age when I sought to relive his life with him, and his consciousness of himself was of one who had failed in his emigration to Cuba, of one who had failed in his relation to women and one who had failed in his expressive and artistic talents to interest or impress his fellow villagers. For his poetry and plastic art, he felt, had gone largely unappreciated in the village. But in earlier days his had been a much more buoyant and confident personality, a formidable opponent in village repartee and competitive rhyming and a bachelor always teasingly on the point of committing himself to marriage (Fernandez 1976–7). The 'Ceferino and his problems' he was conscious of then was much different from the rather depressed Ceferino he evoked in his late eighties in our lengthy late afternoon talks.

But I think it fair to say, despite the necessity of recognizing the anchoring of consciousness in the phases of the life cycle, that overall Ceferino had long been conscious of himself as a peripheral person in village life and a person of greater talent and insight than his fellow villagers – a talent and insight doomed in its more enduring expression by a limited education and bad luck in his Cuban emigration. Socially and intellectually peripheral as he might feel, he centred himself through his voluminous ironic and only gently mocking verse on village social life which amused and entertained his fellow villagers more than he realized. Indeed, unlike the other peripheral consciousness we have considered here, Antoine the Night Fool, whose midnight pronouncements were satirical, even scornful, of village life, Ceferino always practised an inclusive and not an exclusive irony. And it was this inclusiveness that inspired more than toleration but appreciation in his fellow villagers.[6]

Thus, however peripheral to the possibilities of matrimony he might feel, he centred himself with a variety of mild inoffensive and rather purple love poems to young women and old spinsters alike. And however superior to villagers he might feel at one moment by writing verse in the mode of inclusive irony, at another he managed to capture the village imagination and become a figure of some centrality to them. His was thus a poetic displacement in a self consciousness which struggled for many decades with feelings of superiority/inferiority and consubstantiality. This particular struggle and the resultant displacement towards the centre could not, however, be easily sustained in his old age when he could no longer practise the writing of poetry, the carving of stone and wood, or the playing on his old violin; in short when he could no longer either physically or poetically move around with any facility between the centres and peripheries of village life – when he could no longer, in other words, make up in a lively imagination for the lack of meaningful social relations with his fellow villagers.

From Ceferino I learned, of course, to appreciate more profoundly the meaning deficits of old age in village life, but from his earlier verse I learned something not only about everyday practice in the presence of the struggle in self consciousness amidst feelings of superiority/inferiority and consubstantiality but also about the practice of displacement from periphery to centre and, more than that, of the centredness of the poetic consciousness however peripheral the poet, in actual social fact.

José 'Felechosa': an entrepreneur in a time of crisis

Whereas the interpreted consciousnesses of the preceding individuals all seem appropriately discussed in relation to the notion of 'poetic displacement' from deficit categories, for there is poetic movement in all of them, this last subject of my field experience, a very practical young village entrepreneur, seems much less so. His consciousness seems much more political and practical than poetical. He does have a very strong sense of the meaning deficits of his time and place, particularly the political and economic peripherality and dependency of his province, Asturias, which has produced in recent years a pronounced sense of crisis in Asturians. This consciousness of peripherality to and dependency upon the centres of political economic decision-making in Europe is a widespread awareness in the Europe of the mid-1990s, and in the EU is found not only in Spain and Portugal but in Ireland, Scotland and Greece as well. And while there is hope for the prosperity that the EU may bring there is an awareness as well of a decline in the indicators of economic well-being, employment rates, gross provincial product, terms of trade. Despite the regionalism of recent decades and an emphasis on provincial autonomy, there is an increased recognition of the failure of autonomy and of economic dependence, since all these indicators seem to be fashioned by events and political economic decisions taken elsewhere. There is a widespread sense of crisis which arises from being members of the category, 'the periphery'.

With the triumph of the market economies after the Cold War the tactic recommended for such feelings is privatization and entrepreneurial activity. And José Felechosa, a young 'villager' in his early thirties, has styled himself very much as a privatizer and entrepreneur. He thinks of himself as trying to counter the inertia of trade unionism, since Asturias has long had a socialist majority supported by workers' unions in the state-run mining and metal working industries. In recent decades these have been deficit operations heavily subsidized by the state from Madrid and hence dependency operations. In his view, socialist politics feeds into that dependency mentality. As a counter to the politics of dependency he argues a politics of entrepreneurial individualism. He speaks of 'provincial mentality' and the need to change it.

José is proudly conscious first of his own entrepreneurial antecedents – his grandfather owned and operated the first bus in the village and one of the first food stores in the village; his father and mother installed a supermarket and built a small hotel. Their enterprise enabled him to obtain a university education, though he has returned to the village to live. His own entrepreneurship followed naturally. First he arranged to produce for the wider market the famous *chorizo* sausages of Asturias and of his valley. He then founded a record company to produce local music and folklore on cassette and CD. For his politics is not only entrepreneurial and privatizing but a politics of the promotion of local Asturian culture. And third he struggled to finance and build a bottling plant for the health-giving waters of a famous local spring. This last enterprise demanded considerable capital investment which he had to obtain from private investors in Madrid and Barcelona as well as locally. He writes a weekly column for the main provincial newspaper in which he seeks to interweave global and local issues, Bosnia and provincial employment, American science and the Asturian university system. He writes mostly in the national language of Castilian but sometimes, for reasons of cultural nationalism, in the Asturian language of his valley and village. He has travelled widely in Europe and he honeymooned in America. He is conscious, in short, of thinking globally but seeking to act locally.

So it is difficult if not inappropriate to think of him only as a villager: for though he continues to live in the village he travels daily back and forth to the capital city and beyond in attendance to his many enterprises. And this is so even though in ironic contrast to his cosmopolitanism he is widely known in the province not by his proper surnames but by the name of his village itself.

There is much more to be said of this complex *individual*, and I emphasize that the term for his politics is the politics of individual effort. It is unusual for anthropologists – so often in reaction to the excessive

individualism of their own societies and often with significant communitarian sympathies[7] – to include in their fieldwork members of emergent
economic elites. But since José has and maintains village roots and strong
loyalties to the Asturian culture which is the main object of our study he
is certainly fairly to be considered, along with cattle farmers and miners,
in the spectrum of contemporary village consciousness. And he may be
the more interesting in respect to our interests here in his struggle as an
individual to negotiate the global and the local, peripherality and centrality, entrepreneurship and community loyalty.

There is, of course, plenty of international awareness among villagers
involved in mining and union activities. And these men are negotiating
the loyalties of national union solidarity in relation to village loyalties
and family loyalties. But José seems the more conscious of the possible
interlocking of centres and peripheries and the global and the local than
his fellow villagers. He has taught me – I should say *is* teaching me –
forcefully what anthropology has tried to teach itself in the last several
decades as regards its preferences for purely local study: that no study
can be purely local and that all local experience is tied into the network
of larger political economic systems. José Felechosa certainly seems to be
a metonymic operator in that system, *par excellence*, energetically relating
part to whole and whole to part. He is little interested in metaphoric
operations that will bring a New World into existence but rather in
bringing into being a new consciousness that can avoid peripheral categorization by more effectively exploiting the network of part-whole, causal
relations in the market economy world as it is!

WHAT CAN IT MEAN TO SPEAK OF MEANING DEFICIT?
WHAT DOES IT MEAN TO SPEAK OF CONSCIOUSNESS?

In simplest terms we have been defining consciousness here as that state
of awareness of self in relation to others provoked by the sense of
peripheralization of category: in the cases here discussed, peripheralization in respect to the rights and duties of respected young manhood;
peripheralization in respect to the nurturant categories of colonial power
on the one hand and ancestral-circumambient (animistic-animatistic)
power on the other; peripheralization of category in respect to normal
relations with the other gender and with the male-bonded administrative
structure of village life; peripheralization of category in respect to the
economic and political structures of emerging Europe. I have tried in our
interpretation of a central theme in the consciousness of these individuals
from my field experience to see their dynamic of the categorical in terms
of complex centre-periphery negotiations.

This perspective assumes our 'social animality', which is to say the
overriding importance of our relationships to other social beings (Bateson

1972: 177–94, 364–78) as fundamental to human consciousness. It assumes the centrality to our consciousness of managing and manipulating or being managed and manipulated, of being paid due attention to or of being neglected, of being in propitious if not prosperous exchange relationships with others or of experiencing status withdrawal and impoverishment, of engaging with or being disengaged.

These brute facts, we might say, of the human condition carry us only so far, or perhaps too far, and I have thus been further interested, insofar as space would allow, in the poetical and political practices, the practical poetics perhaps, of displacement of category, the search for cultural consensus or the mutuality of cultural forms, in the presence of these minor and major crises of everyday life. This interest involves rhetorical operators of various kinds and a close analysis of the 'argument of images', the evocation of images about which there is or can be cultural consensus, that these operators put forth in search of social consensus, which is to say a gratifying sense of common category. There is a theory involved here, to return to the PTL, about how the self works in the social world, the kinds of imaginative negotiations it is obliged to undertake, whose details I have been working out over the years but which I cannot present in any detail here. What I have tried to do in these four vignettes is to indicate something of the category sufferings and the centre-periphery negotiations going on in these quite distinct consciousnesses as their, for the most part, lonely selves seek to be effectively conjoined, which is to say categorized with others.

No doubt there are ideas about the 'evolution of consciousness' that must be incorporated here. At the very least, Weberian notions about the 'unprecedented condition of inner loneliness of the *individual*', of which Marx also spoke, which was an increasing condition of modern life (Weber 1958), a product of bureaucratic rationalization and the resultant isolating compartmentalization of life. We all know the thesis – in which loneliness is implicit – on the elimination of magic from the world and the consequent 'disenchantments' and decommunalization of modern life. Indeed in all these vignettes the 'practical poetics' of our expressive individuals proceeds consciously or semi-consciously towards a re-enchantment in which lonely individuals can become part of a larger and more meaningful whole – whether village social life, religious community or emerging political economic order.

CONCLUSION – FROM CATEGORIES SAVED: ANTHROPOLOGY AS CONVERSION

I have argued elsewhere a 'categorical imperative' (Fernandez 1984b) in respect to the inevitable conceptualizations and categorizations of the materials produced by normal social science investigation: 'Do not categorize others in categories in which you yourself would not willingly be a member.' Admittedly this Marxist dictum (Groucho Marx: 'I would not be a member of a club which would have me as a member'), while intended to raise our level of self consciousness about the categorizing processes of our scientific practice, would have, to say the least, a rather inhibiting impact upon that practice. Nevertheless, I believe that an anthropology practised with good grace is an anthropology inevitably aware of the problem of constructedness and constriction of categories in the social order and thus sensitive to both their possible invidious misapplication as well as to the constant imaginative struggle over appropriate categories. Such anthropological awareness may arise fundamentally from the fact that in moving our enquiry from culture to culture we move from categorical system to categorical system. Conversion, at any rate, can be understood as a convincing shift not only from peripheral loneliness to a more centred sociality, as we have argued, but from one category system to another. And this is the conversion that anthropology perennially offers through *its* displacements.

In point of fact, the subject we have before us, (self and other) consciousness, is pronouncedly a subject having to do with social categorization. For the consciousness of the self in important part arises, as we have argued, from a comfortable or uncomfortable awareness of the difference between the category or categories to which one has been socially assigned and one's own individual and often lonely sense of self. And as we might be aware, a good deal more than discomfort may be involved – indeed, quality of life if not life chances. Here I think is where anthropology in general and this volume in particular can make a humanizing benefaction of 'amazing grace' – converting its audience to a renewed awareness of those ever-possible category conversions that occur in consciousness. It can conduce to a less procrustean application of categories, and particularly those categories applied to the self which in the end afflict its consciousness by violating the social possibilities of its individuality.

So we might end on a post-cautious note about our own explanatory categories. I would reiterate the precaution that my vignette-like interpretations of these five 'consciousnesses' are but 'partial truths', and rather arbitrary editings on my part of what appeared to me salient, thematic, in what my interlocutors put into practice. Mine cannot be master narratives or master editings that entirely encompass and categorize the complexity of the awareness of the subjects being examined. They can only be appreciations of these consciousnesses, attempts to escape the loneliness of certain categories in order to embrace more useful ones, pragmatically and socially speaking. In an interesting way these conscious editings of mine approximate in their way to a theory of consciousness understood as a perpetual editing process by which complex stimuli of experience are taken by the brain and fixed into a never-ending sequence of 'multiple drafts'.

Beyond that I would also like to note that I myself have sought for a minor kind of conversion here, displacing myself from my lonely preoccupation with my PTL not only into greater and more enduring GTLs but also into other consciousnesses living in and grappling with contexts significantly alien to my own. 'Amazing Grace, how sweet the anthropology, that saved a wretch like me, I once was lost in *self*, was blind, but through the *other* now I see.'

NOTES

1 The distinction between 'cultural consensus', the agreement about the meaning of our actions in the world, and 'social consensus', the agreement to interact in a world, is made in Fernandez (1965).

2 The reference is to the 'mind or brain in a vat' problem by which philosophers in their way contemplate the problem of consciousness in relation to the inputs which stimulate our conscious sense of being engaged with reality. By the nature of the illustrative case in point – the brain in vat wired up by clever experimenters – the problem of consciousness becomes mainly a problem of convincing and unconvincing hallucinations. Since some might argue that the academic or the academic's life is animated if not 'controlled' by convincing hallucinations, there is a certain poignancy in this image. Hence my ironic use of this trope at this wretched juncture of my argument. For one of the best known (hallucinatory) treatments of the 'mind (or brain) in a vat' problem, see Dennett (1978). In terms of my own field experience among political and religious enthusiasts who seem from any settled down-to-earth empirical perspective to be often hallucinating, this philosophic model is also poignant.

3 My own belated effort in this regard (Fernandez 1984a) was published in *Dialectical Anthropology*, a journal devoted to the dialectical interaction between the sophistications of the 'vat' and the 'primitive world(s)' beyond it. See Diamond (1974).

4 Readers may wish to consult the large cast of characters, both argumentative persons and dramatic persons presented as the framing interactive network of individuals whose activities and thoughts constitute the core of the ethnography in Fernandez (1982: esp. 13–15, 18–23).

5 A phrase employed by Clifford (1988) particularly in his discussion of the French polymath Victor Segalen's search in exotic societies for the 'necessarily other' part of the self. But as regards the present author, the dynamics of displacement is a basic theme in Fernandez (1974).

6 See Fernandez (1993b) for a discussion of the distinction between the use of inclusive and exclusive irony in anthropological ethnography. Also see Huber's (1988: 7–9) distinction between 'romantic irony', in which the ironist considers him- or herself superior and outside the object of his or her irony, and 'classic irony', in which the ironist considers him or herself consubstantial and a member of the subject(s) of his or her irony.

7 Which in point of fact I happen to share and which have served to direct most of my work towards revitalization movements with a communitarian impulse (see Fernandez 1977; 1978).

REFERENCES

Abu Lughod, L. (1991) 'Writing against culture', in R. G. Fox (ed.) *Recapturing Anthropology*, Albuquerque: SAR Press.

Bateson, G. (1972) *Steps Towards an Ecology of Mind*, New York: Ballantine.

Behar, R. (1993) *Translated Woman: Crossing the Border with Esperanza's Story*, Boston: Beacon Press.

Bruner, E and Turner V. (1986) *The Anthropology of Experience*, Urbana: University of Illinois Press.

Clifford, J. (1988) *The Predicament of Culture*, Cambridge, Mass.: Harvard University Press.

de Certeau, M. (1988) *The Practice of Everyday Life*, Berkeley: University of California Press.

Dennett, D. (1978) *Brainstorms*, New York: Bradford Park.

Dennett, D. (1991) *Consciousness Explained*, Boston: Little, Brown.

Diamond, S. (1974) *In Search of the Primitive: A Critique of Civilization*, New Brunswick: Transaction Books.

Fernandez, J. W. (1965) 'Symbolic consensus in a Fang reformative cult', *American Anthropologist*, 67(4): 902–27.

Fernandez, J. W. (1966) 'Revitalized words from the Parrot's Egg and the Bull who Crashes in the Krall', *Proceedings of the American Ethnological Society 1966*, pp. 53–64.

Fernandez, J. W. (1971) 'Zulu zionism', *Natural History*, 80(6): 44–51.

Fernandez, J. W. (1974) 'The mission of metaphor in expressive culture', *Current Anthropology*, 15(2): 119–45.

Fernandez, J. W. (1976–7) 'Poetry in motion: being moved by amusement, by mockery, and by mortality in the Asturian countryside', *New Literary History*, 8: 459–83.

Fernandez, J. W. (1977) 'Passage to community: encounter in evolutionary perspective', pp. 84–112 in K. Back (ed.) *Encounter Groups and Social Change*, Selected Symposia of the AAAS, Boulder: American Association for the Advancement of Science.

Fernandez, J. W. (1978) 'African religious movements', *Annual Review of Anthropology*, 7: 195–234.

Fernandez, J. W. (1979) 'On the notion of religious movement', *Social Research*, 46(1): 36–62.

Fernandez, J. W. (1980) 'The dark at the bottom of the stairs: the inchoate in symbolic inquiry and some strategies for coping with it', pp. 13–43 in *On Symbols in Anthropology: Essays in Honor of Harry Hoijer*, Malibu: Undena.

Fernandez, J. W. (1982) *Bwiti: An Ethnography of the Religious Imagination in Africa*, Princeton: Princeton University Press.

Fernandez, J. W. (1984a) 'Exploded worlds: text as a metaphor for ethnography (and vice versa)', *Dialectical Anthropology*, 10: 15–26.

Fernandez, J. W. (1984b) 'Moving up in the world: transcendence "in" symbolic anthropology', *Stanford Literature Review*, 1(2): 201–26.

Fernandez, J. W. (1986) 'Persuasions and performances: of the beast in every body and the metaphors of everyman', pp. 3–27 in *Persuasions and Performances: The Play of Tropes in Culture*, Bloomington: Indiana University Press. (Originally published in 1972.)

Fernandez, J. W. (1991) 'The ethnography of powerful imaginations', Munro Lecture, University of Edinburgh.

Fernandez, J. W. (1992) 'What I learned from "The Parrott's Egg" and "The Bull Who Crashes in the Kraal": the senses of time binding and turn taking in being with the other', pp. 209–16 in Christine Ward Gailey (ed.) *Dialectical Anthropology: Essays in Honor of Stanley Diamond. Vol II. The Politics of Culture and Creativity: A Critique of Civilization*, Gainesville: University of Florida Press .

Fernandez, J. W. (1993a) 'Ceferino Suarez: a village versifier', pp. 11–29 in S. Lavie, K. Narayan and R. Rosaldo (eds) *Creativity/Anthropology*, Ithaca: Cornell University Press.

Fernandez, J. W. (1993b) 'Emergencias etnográficas: tiempos heróicos, tiempos ironicos y la tarea etnográfica', pp. 33–67 in J. Bestard (ed.) *Después de Malinowski*, Tenerife: Federación de Antropología del Estado Español y Asociación Canaria de Antropología.

Huber, M. T. (1988) *The Bishop's Progress: A Historical Ethnography of Catholic Missionary Experience on the Sepik Frontier*, Washington DC: Smithsonian Press.

Lavie, S., Narayan, K. and Rosaldo. R. (eds) (1993) *Creativity/Anthropology*, Ithaca: Cornell University Press.

Nisbet, R.A. (1969) *Social Change and History: Aspects of the Western Theory of Development*, New York: Oxford University Press.

Ortner, S. (1973) 'On key symbols', *American Anthropologist*, 75(6): 1338–46.

Parsons, E. C. (1967) *American Indian Life*, Lincoln: University of Nebraska Press. (Originally published 1921.)

Pepper, S. (1942) *World Hypotheses: A Study of Evidence*, Berkeley: University of California Press.

Rorty, R. (1989) *Contingency, Irony and Solidarity*, New York: Cambridge University Press.

Schafer, R. (1980) 'Narration in psychoanalytic dialogue', pp. 25–49 in W. T. Mitchell (ed.) *On Narrative*, Chicago: University of Chicago Press.

Stewart, J. O. (1989) *Drinkers, Drummers and Decent Folk: Ethnographic Narratives of Village Trinidad*, Albany: SUNY Press.

Tsordas, T. (1994) *The Sacred Self: A Cultural Phenomenology of Charismatic Healing*, Berkeley: University of California Press.

Turner, V. W. (1967) *The Forest of Symbols: Aspects of Ndembu Ritual*, Ithaca: Cornell University Press.

Turner, V. W. (1974) *Dramas, Fields and Metaphors: Symbolic Action in Human Society*, Ithaca: Cornell University Press.

Wallace, A. F. C. (1958) 'Revitalization movements', *American Anthropologist*, 58(2): 264–81.

Weber, M. (1958) *The Protestant Ethic and the Spirit of Capitalism*, New York: Scribners. (Originally published in 1904.)

Chapter 2

She came out of the field and into my home

Reflections, dreams and a search for consciousness in anthropological method

Tamara Kohn

REFLECTIONS I

Introduction

'Oh my god, where is she', I hissed aloud as I dashed up and down the arrivals hall of Gatwick North Terminal. Of all times for the car to have broken down – when a Nepali-speaking woman would arrive in the chaos of Gatwick Airport with no contact other than a Durham phone number! 'We're nearly an hour late!' I picked out a man who could have been Nepalese – 'Excuse me! Do you know if the Nepal Airlines flight has come through yet?' 'Yes I think so . . .' 'Oh my god', and I dashed away again. Just as my husband Andrew ran up to join me I saw her there – half the size I'd remembered her – perched tensely on the edge of the seat, gripping a small rucksack. She leapt up when I said, 'Kamala, Kamala, *maaph garnuhos* [I'm so sorry!] – *Kasto Cha*? [How are you?]' – her face lit up, her hands shook as she reached out for contact, tears rolled down her cheek. I can only imagine the relief she must have felt.

In this chapter I wish to discuss problems of method in the anthropology of consciousness against a backdrop of what happened during Kamala's visit. Kamala was our 'sister' in the field, who came to stay with us in the UK for six weeks in July/August 1993. Andrew and I lived in Kamala's home in Tamaphok, a remote hill village in East Nepal, for nearly a year (in 1989). Even after we left her parents' house to live for a second year on our own nearby, we had her assistance daily for our research. When we left, we promised, as most anthropologists do, to return before too long. We also said (and this, I believe, is less often promised) that we would invite Kamala to visit us in England. Three years, two jobs and one baby later – the time was right for all of us, and we arranged for her to come during the summer break in her school-teaching year. The occasion raised what I consider to be important and compelling questions about consciousness and method in anthropology.

These questions include the following. What does travelling do to a person? In other words, how might one's reflexive, 'conscious', awareness of self, home, and other be altered by going away to somewhere very new? To what extent is it possible to tap into 'the field' (wherever that might be) through a familiar informant's travelling tales and dreams? How can such a possibility be used to reorient the existing literature about fieldwork, travel and informants abroad? And finally, how do our styles of enquiry (which change in different contexts and with different audiences) affect our resulting notions of consciousness and 'culture'?

Kamala's first experiences of the West, her awareness of difference, her consciousness of self, her memories of home – these were not always just spoken of directly nor acted out, but were felt by us in other ways, through her silences, laughter and tears and in discussions about dreams and their meanings. Unsolicited, her dreams were recounted almost daily over the breakfast table which took us back to the birds, houses, gods, woods and people of East Nepal. This was strange and wonderful for us, because we had only very occasionally heard about dreams when we were living in her home.[1] The meanings she attributed to some of these UK dreams told us something of her thoughts about the visit she was experiencing as well as of her home and family in the far-off hills. There were times when you could physically sense her lapping up the sounds, sights, tastes and textures of Britain. I felt I was seeing a different Kamala. Was it a Kamala changed by this confrontation of 'otherness'? Or was it a Kamala processing and reassessing her identity in the face of senses awakened by change?

How can consciousness (and here, as I later explain, I am using 'consciousness' in its broadest sense as something akin to 'awareness') be understood through things sensed and dreamed? How can experiences such as dreams, which are traditionally categorized in the West as part of the 'unconscious', be extended into 'consciousness'? In addition, of course, the consciousness of the anthropologist is as relevant as the informant's, for it is with the memories of our 'sister' in her own home context that we could understand better what she was experiencing in ours. If I had not felt close to Kamala on a daily basis in her home territory, my own senses would not have been as alert to what she was doing and feeling in ours. Elsewhere I have argued that through 'incomerness', intermarriage, travel and the meeting of others speaking other languages, the senses are especially active and noticeable (Kohn 1994). It is at such junctures that consciousness of culture and self may be particularly strong. Kamala's experiences in the UK not only appeared to me to confirm this pattern, but they seemed to offer a new indigenous view on 'the field' or 'the culture area' from without. Without attempting to elicit 'data' during her visit to my home, I learned a good deal about Kamala and 'her village', 'her people'. It follows that if one's consciousness is raised through an experience such as travel, then it is with the traveller, perhaps even within her dreams of home and away, that one can augment or enrich ethnographic accounts of her 'home' society.

'Out of the field'

Accounting for travellers' experiences is by no means a new thing. A vast literature exists on travellers in the UK, and historical works on diaries of travel in this country (e.g. Batts 1976; Clifford 1947; Moir 1964; Gard 1988; Johnson and Boswell 1924) are especially rich sources of descriptive detail. The historians who refer to these diaries are naturally interested in just that – detail on the life and landscape of the UK – the places visited – as witnessed by literate travellers. While diaries and letters written by American and European travellers may indeed describe their experiences with reference to their homes far away, there has been no interest, to the best of my knowledge, in teasing this out as a source of data about perceptions of life and landscape in their home countries. The focus is always on the place visited rather than the homes, people and lifestyles left behind.

Likewise, there have been anthropologists and other writers who have recorded Western life and landscape through non-Western eyes. These tend to be accounts which record *second hand* what these visitors *say* about the West and its people, places, conveniences, etc., rather than the reflective, descriptively rich essays we tend to find in a European diary. Nigel Barley, in a popular account, reports how the Indonesians he brought to the Museum of Mankind to build a rice barn viewed London and Londoners. They were shocked that all British were not white, and that they were not all rich. They marvelled at the Underground, central heating, and the notion of mortgages (1988: 182–98). But it is the contextualizing of these reactions, with knowledge of the places left behind, which gives them meaning. Barley could often explain some of the problems and ideas expressed by his visitors by juxtaposing them with what they had to say about their homes or what *he* knew or imagined to be their home experience. He reported how his visitors tried to make sense of the British monarchy with the comment: 'It is like the Minang people of Sumatera ... There it is the women who own everything and the poor men are sent abroad to work for them. You are just like them. We are sorry for you' (Barley 1988: 183).

One could look at many other such examples. Coburn has written about bringing an old Nepalese woman to America (in press), and Good describes how he brought a Yanomama girl from the Amazon to New Jersey as his wife (1991). Another genre of text is provided by literate non-Western travellers, e.g. K. M. George's *American Life Through Indian Eyes* (1967). We can generalize from all of these to suggest that people make sense of 'others' by making reference to themselves. This is the foundation of the reflexive movement in anthropology. It is not clear, however, to what extent anthropologists have looked beyond their navels to see how context might effect their *informants'* reflexivity. To what extent has reflection of informants 'out of the field' been seen as providing new ethnographic data about 'the field'?

Of course there is ample opportunity for anthropologists to pursue these questions. Few people in the world that anthropologists study are 'homebodies' (Clifford 1992: 97). Studies of nomads, migrants, refugees and people on pilgrimage abound (e.g. Delaney 1990), and yet one need not focus on such groups who are by definition 'travellers' in order to understand something about the experience of travel. Indeed, the Yakha are Tibeto-Burman people who are indigenous to the middle hills of East Nepal, and yet travel has long been important to them. Men from Yakha and other tribal groups in East Nepal have, since the early nineteenth century, been recruited as fierce and reliable soldiers for both the British Gurkha regiments and for the Indian and Nepalese armies. In recent years, young men have travelled seasonally to Sikkim, other north-east Indian hill states, and even as far as Saudi Arabia for paid labour. Some have tried to find work in Kathmandu – in sweet and carpet factories for instance. Others have migrated with their families to the Tarai – the southern flatlands of Nepal which border India – to exploit the richer farming land there (Russell 1992). Yakha women do not often travel outside the region, but they frequently marry men from other Kiranti groups, and this takes them away from their familiar homes to villages many hours' walk away (Kohn 1992).

Travel to a new country and movement from one village to another constitute very different scales of 'travel', and yet it is in the process of crossing over, in every context, that new possibilities of understanding may emerge.[2] We are all of us in transit between homes, careers, seasons and identities. We have not examined the reflexivity embedded in this process fully enough. It was only after the fact of Kamala's visit that I fully realized how significant crossing over can be to an understanding of others.

Enriching our fieldnotes on the village of Tamaphok and the ethnic group called the Yakha had not been our intention when we brought Kamala to the UK. Arranging the trip was a delicate and at her end quite nerve-racking experience. First she had to obtain a Nepalese passport in Kathmandu. Then we had to send her formal letters of invitation and support, money for a visa and bank statements to show we could look after her for six weeks. When nearly three months had passed and we heard nothing, we assumed the packet had been lost in the post. Then, suddenly we heard from a friend in Kathmandu – Kamala had arrived to purchase the ticket *in advance* of her visit to the embassy for the visa! Two days before the flight was to arrive in London, we still had no news about her visa and only knew that there was political violence and mayhem reported in Kathmandu.

After her arrival, Kamala was able to tell us what her experience in Kathmandu had been. She had arrived at the British Embassy on 22 June armed with her passport and photos and our packet. An official read our letter and said, 'You need a letter from your headmaster as proof that you are a teacher at the Tamaphok school . . . and you must give us proof of your friendship with these British sponsors'. She had to turn around and travel back – eighteen hours on a night bus and six hours' walk in each direction to fetch the headmaster's note and all the letters we had written to her over the years. Finally, she got her visa a day before her flight (the first plane she had boarded since her childhood trip with her Gurkha father back from Malaysia). Then to the arrivals hall at Gatwick where she expected us to be waiting, although we had never exchanged any direct correspondence about the arrival plans. And we were not there! Certainly all these events contributed to the traumatic nature of this woman's first-time travel to a Western country. If it is feasible to say that consciousness of self and other is strengthened through travel, then this sort of travel would be the most vivid example from which to draw (over, for example, the experiences of seasoned business travellers or even Nepalese soldiers in the Gurkha regiment of the British army who learn to expect a certain degree of inefficiency and miscommunication along the way, and who have each other's company).

When we finally rescued Kamala from her seat in the arrivals hall, we got into our car and drove to Andrew's mother's house in Sussex. On the road stories poured forth about the fiasco with the embassy and the extra trip east, new births, marriages and deaths in the village, what the plane trip was like, etc. Then she looked out the window at the thick woods on either side of the road and exclaimed – 'You have jungle here too – this is like the jungle in the Tarai! – I thought it would be so different!' Kamala's very first comment on her new surroundings were made with direct reference to what she had left behind in Nepal (my 'field'). She made sense of the new through the old. The world compacted – condensed – into places which grew similar jungles of trees. We shall see further examples of such linking processes shortly.

Of course, it is highly problematic for me to be referring so persistently and bluntly to 'the field' at all in the aftermath of a postmodernism which questions the validity of all anthropological units of study – 'village', 'native', 'culture', 'field'. Yet, even when one realizes that many contemporary anthropologists do not study in villages but in cities, businesses, hospitals, pubs, etc., still 'the notion of fieldwork as a special kind of localized *dwelling* remains' (Clifford 1992:98). 'The field', Clifford suggests, is 'both a methodological ideal and a concrete *place* of professional activity' (1992: 99). But it is more than this. It is also a place where the informant resides (whether this be in a village, a traveller's caravan, a street corner or an office block) – where the ethnographer is seen to be *more* of a stranger who has more to learn (about the 'other's' language, beliefs, fears, joys, memories). It is in this sense that I can raise questions about a place which is seen as being 'out of the field' for both the ethnographer and the informant.

There have been occasions when anthropologists have, out of necessity, done their interviewing of informants 'out of the field' (not to be confused with anthropology done in the field site but on the verandah!). For example, the work by the Kroebers on the Yahi Indians of northern California was elicited from Ishi – the sole survivor of the tribe – in the University of California Museum of Anthropology between 1911 and 1916. The book Theodora Kroeber wrote about Ishi attempts to give us a view of his cultural memory and life experience through his eyes and from the recorded recollections made after he stumbled into the white 'Saldu' world (Kroeber 1964). The ethnographers could not enrich these narratives with participant observation, but they could learn through Ishi's words, reaction, and dreams experienced near the end of his life, far from his tribal home. It was clear in the text that Ishi was returned to his lost home and friends through dreams. For example, one of these (day?) dreams was clearly triggered by his experience walking on a beach with 'Majapa' (Kroeber?).

> It is with Majapa I walk, through the sands of the Edge of the World. Outer ocean brings to me a shell like the shells of the Little One's necklace. Her baskets are in my room in the museum-watgurwa. Thus and thus our Dreams, the Little One's and mine, come close
>
> (Kroeber 1964: 180)

As 'last of his tribe', Ishi became representative of his extinct community from 'out of the field'. This sort of study became rather unusual in the post-Malinowskian field-centred academy. The way the 'other-from-the-field' has been viewed has changed dramatically over the decades. At the turn of the century we saw the 'other' as an entirely moveable novelty and researchers toured and exhibited 'primitive' human specimens at world fairs (See Stocking 1982: 217) Beginning in the 1930s and 1940s, there was a distinct preference to see the 'other' purely 'in context' – in a bounded, reified 'field' *out there*. A more recent focus on the globalization of culture has encouraged us to eliminate or at least contest these boundaries as well as our ideas about where and how our own knowledge about others is created. The argument I am putting forward is that if the 'other' leaves the field and is entirely out of the context of his/her everyday life, he or she (unlike the silent physical and cultural 'type' paraded at the fair) may have a *new* and interesting tale to tell about 'the field back there'. 'Out of the field' is where informants have much to reflect upon and dream about, and where we, in our place, have a good deal to learn about them and ourselves.

DREAMS

Dreams are given very different authority in different societies, and yet it is clear that the contents of dreams are always culturally informed. Tedlock, in her recent edited volume on dreaming, suggests that instead of focusing on 'the dream' as text, our gaze should be redirected at dream*ing* as a psychodynamic process – a communicative event (Tedlock 1992: 30). A question which one can raise is whether the narration of dreams which occurs in certain contexts far from home can be seen as a technique for keeping in touch with the social self – a psychic radio receiver of sorts which can be used to maintain relations with family and friends. This seems to have been the case for Ishi reflecting on his dreams in San Francisco, and it also seems to have been the case for Kamala reflecting on her dreams in the UK.

It was our second morning in our house in Durham, and we wanted to walk with Kamala around the town and cathedral. As we were getting our things together, she said:

> I had a dream last night. There were two trees full of small birds and large spiders' webs. I shook both of them and many many birds fell out dead upon the ground. I put them into a pile. My auntie's daughter, Man Maya, helped me to gather them together.

'Do you think this dream means anything?', I asked. 'No ... no,' she replied, 'there is no meaning.'

If I had been in Tamaphok I might have pursued this, but it didn't occur to me to do so as we got ready to go out for the day in Durham. A few mornings later, Kamala said:

> In my dream last night I saw ama [mother] – she was lying in bed and looked sad. She must be sick or hurting. I know now that I must go home before long to be with my mother and father.

She said this while holding tightly our son Ben who wriggled to reach his bricks. I felt she was about to cry, but before I could think of what to say or do she excused herself. While she was upstairs I realized that for several days running the mornings had been full of the recounting of her dreams, and that she had never done this in Nepal. The nights in the village had always ended with everyone saying to one another '*raamro sapanaa dekhnuhos!*' (see good dreams), but the days rarely began with a recalling of them. Why was this? Was it just that Andrew and I tended to emerge after most of the family was up and about, and that they had finished that bit of the morning chat by the time we joined the circle around the fire? Was it because in Durham I became Kamala's confidante and while we were close in Tamaphok, there were many others with whom she could share dreams? Or was there a need, far from her home and hearth, to 'touch base' through dreams – were dreams thus more active and memorable in my house than they were in hers?

When she came back down, I asked Kamala if she felt she was remembering her dreams more than usual since she arrived in England, and she thought for a bit and said yes. Did she think that there was a reason for this? She thought some more and said no. Of necessity, 'etic' conjectures must follow.

Having Kamala with us, speaking much of the day in Nepali, evoked a new vibrance in my memory of 'the field'. Not only did memories come alive for me, but new ideas, associations, meanings were communicated by her. This takes us a step beyond the familiar and connected notions that one needs distance from the field in order to write, and that field-acquired knowledge is transformed and/or processed when one gets away (see Ottenberg 1990: 144–48 on 'headnotes', and Cohen 1992 on 'provisional ethnography'). Dreams I had not been offered before, local meanings of dreams I had never had occasion to ask about, ideas about the cosmos which many hours of taped interviews had not uncovered in the field, were all volunteered three years later and thousands of miles away in my own home ground. I was expanding my knowledge of Tamaphok through Kamala's reflections in Durham. To state it more generally, when travelling, the informant is bombarded by great difference/foreignness interspersed with the apparently familiar, and this can lead to new reflections on self and 'culture'. The next example takes us out of the dream and into the cosmos.

One fine afternoon we took Kamala to see Brancepeth Castle – a rather splendid fortress in a small village outside Durham. Next to the big castle is a lovely old church full of crypts and surrounded by tall leaning gravestones. One particularly large gravestone is horizontally placed.

'Look!', Kamala exclaimed, 'that gravestone is like a Yakha gravestone – Yakha also have man-sized "tables" over the graves. Ours are engraved too!'

She directed us to take at least five pictures of her next to various gravestones. Then, as we walked through the empty musty church we talked in Nepali about Christianity and the use of churches.

'Not everyone goes to church to pray, Kamala', I said. 'Do you?', she asked. 'No . . .'

But before I could try to explain she smiled and said, 'If you have a clean heart, then there is no need to pray [*praarthanaa garnu pardainaa*]. It's only those who do not who must worship gods by praying. I don't pray either.'

I suddenly realized that while I knew a great deal about the Yakha pantheon of gods and the various *pujaas* (offerings) which are made to them for a great variety of reasons, I knew little about 'prayer'. Yakha ensure good health and good harvests and fortune by making periodic offerings to gods, and in the village we could ask about these actions because we witnessed them. The cleanliness of one's heart and 'prayer' did not enter into the equation. Clearly, however, Kamala's words point to a whole realm of consciousness of self *vis-à-vis* the cosmos which in Nepal we had had little occasion to witness or discuss.[3] Prayer only came naturally to the fore in the context of an introduction to a visible, palpable Christian church which Kamala could identify somehow in her own social memory – the same burial stones, the perceived familiarity of variable individual 'values'.

'Prayer, then, is something quite separate from making offerings?' I continued. 'Of course. Don't you make offerings to Jesus?' 'Well actually, I'm not Christian, and don't really believe . . .'.

Again she interrupted to connect:

It's just like what we Yakha do in Tamaphok. For travellers and visitors to our village we say we are Hindu or sometimes Buddhist, but we have our own gods really – *pang cyang, jangali cyang* [Yakha words for household gods and forest gods] – we are not really Hindu nor are we Buddhist – I suppose there is no way to make it simple with a name.

What I was getting at, and what she was telling me were *not* really the same thing, but here is that magic of worlds colliding – of different orders of cosmology becoming similar in the attempt to locate the self in the world of the other. I already knew from being with tribal people in East Nepal that visitors who asked about religion were given these relatively easy, if inaccurate, answers. And in Durham, when I brought Kamala to a feminist discussion group, I overheard her explain to one of the members, who happened to be a high-caste Nepalese woman studying in Newcastle, that she was Buddhist but did not believe in Buddha. Explaining the inexplicable – trying to cram one's own cosmology into another's vocabulary – is what happens when different people speaking different 'languages' make sense of themselves to others.

Perhaps the small reflections on her beliefs back in the Brancepeth graveyard were as new to her as they were to me. New contexts trigger the senses, activate the dreams, and affect one's reflexivity and relationships with others. In that shady, enclosed place so sensually different from the open hillsides where her dead relatives and friends rested in Nepal,

Kamala searched out the horizontal slab – 'just like ours'. Discussion was triggered by the similar in the context of general difference. For travellers generally, this might be the case. But for those travellers called 'anthropologists', so well trained to home in on the exotic 'other', the familiar is not always so easy to focus upon.

CONSCIOUSNESS

How does this all fit into an anthropology of consciousness? How can tales about travel, the individual dreamer finding 'sameness' in the foreign, and the reluctant anthropologist far from an imaginary 'field', help us to understand 'consciousness'? What *is* an anthropology of consciousness in the British anthropology of the 1990s? It certainly is not a clone of the American version of the same. I made a point of joining in on the sessions hosted by the Society for the Anthropology of Consciousness at the November 1993 American Anthropological Association meetings in Washington DC. I thought these would give me some tips, but instead I was transported into another universe, certainly into an as yet undeciphered anthropological patter.[4] Paper titles included: 'Zen and the Art of Restructuring Reality: Commonalities Between Shamanic Mastery and Schizophrenic Disaster', and 'Thoughts on the Relationship of Geometry and Analogy to the Aesthetic/Contemplative Experience: The Sri Yantra Configuration'. The pamphlet the Society produced spelled out:

'Current areas of interest' for an anthropology of consciousness:
States of consciousness: Trance possession, dissociation, dreams and the psychophysiology of states of consciousness.
Ethnography of shamanic, spiritual, and magical training . . . Indigenous healing practices . . . Linguistic, philosophical, and symbolic studies . . . Anomalous phenomena: Critical studies of precognition, remote viewing, out-of-body experience, near-death experiences, and other psychic and paranormal phenomena.

This particular genre in the study of consciousness clearly thirsts to unpack exotic, extra-normal, and *supra*-conscious experiences. However, I think that the study of consciousness can just as well be embedded in the normal as it is in the paranormal; in the everyday as it is in metaphysical experience; in association as well as in dissociation.

Consciousness in its broadest sense is often seen as what one knows – an awareness which can be spoken of and recorded. As students of society and culture, anthropologists have counted on gaining access to this sort of knowledge of the individual's sense of self, group and other. This has been done in anthropology for very different reasons throughout the history of the discipline under rubrics ranging from 'personality and culture' to 'cognition' to more recent discussions about 'experience', 'globalization', etc. Methods of participant observation have allowed us to see that an informant's consciousness of self and society is both spoken and lived. If narration, interview and discussion evoke the informant's consciousness of self, group and other, we say that action (see Reynolds 1980) or praxis is driven by this knowledge. And yet, social experience is larger than that which is reducible to words and deeds. To reach even closer to an individual consciousness (and thus to better describe the collectivity of 'culture'/'society' which informs it), our method should aim to take in more – the feelings, emotions, dreams and senses which eyes and ears can only partially capture. It is clearly impossible to separate mind, body and feeling from one another (see Erchak 1992: Lutz 1988). I know who I am because I know how I feel. The key to consciousness is in the knowing, not in the ability to speak fully of this knowing. As Dennett suggests:

> the conscious mind is not just the place where the witnessed colors and smells are, and not just the thinking thing. It is where the appreciating happens. It is the ultimate arbiter of why anything matters. Perhaps this even follows somehow from the fact that the conscious mind is also supposed to be the source of our intentional actions . . . If a sleepwalker 'unconsciously' does harm, he is not responsible because in an important sense *he* didn't do it . . . What more must be added is consciousness, the special ingredient that turns mere *happenings* into doings.
>
> (Dennett 1991: 31–2)

Awareness, appreciation and intention, then, are three parameters upon which anthropologists of consciousness may focus.[5] If these are revealed at a ritual seance, or during an out-of-body experience, that is surely very colourful. If they are felt and heard in a living room far from the 'exotic' hub of 'culture', that is just as valid.

Consciousness in the everyday and consciousness in the extraordinary are equally accessible to us. Our methodology remains a key to unlocking the experience and sensation of 'doing'.

DREAMS AND THE CONSCIOUS INDIVIDUAL

From this we could say that anthropologists are specialists in both etic analyses of all actions and emic analyses of intentional actions – 'Why are you waving that burning branch in the air?' 'Who is going to inherit this land?' 'What does that part of the ceremony mean?' 'Who can you marry?' One thing that stands out about these sorts of enquiries into intentions and meanings is that the answers tend to be used to explain something about cultural, local, shared beliefs and practices. Now what about the dream? Not the dream itself, but the awareness of the dream in one's waking life? In the West, the dream is stereotypically dismissed as a 'happening' which only accidentally reflects past social realities and which generally is not part of what we would normally consider 'intentional' and essential action. For people in many non-Western societies, however, the dream is understood as far more than a happening – it is a 'doing' – it is part of the conscious life and shapes people's presents and futures. Carrithers tells us that Sinhalese dreams can be portents and 'are subject to the same principle of interpretation as that which rules the interpretation of all human action' (1982: 27). We cannot, therefore, relegate dream contents and meanings to something popularly known in the West as the 'unconscious' which only reflects one's own inner state or past experience. Edgar, who has worked with dreamwork groups in the UK, suggests that 'once the imagery of the dream has referential meaning ascribed to it, it becomes a *conscious* metaphor' (1994). Conscious, yes, but of whom and of what period in time? Only of the self? (the ego? the id?) Only shadows of the past?

For Kamala, it is very clear that dreams may tell us in a 'doing' sort of way about people other than herself and about the future. Through her dreams, she was sure that several members of her extended family suffered illnesses during her time in the UK. Some dreams, she said, are warnings. Depending entirely on where one is, various options for action are possible to deal with these.

> If I am in my village and I dream about an ill relative or friend who is far away then I have several options. I can consult a *dhaami* [a shaman who conducts a ritual based on contagious magic using clothes of the ill person, left behind for that purpose], or I can do my own *pujaa* [offering], or I can write him a letter, or maybe I can do all three.

Kamala's dreams, which happened in the context of her relatively short visit abroad, only left her sad. Her options were limited here – there were no *dhaamis* to consult, no *pujaas* to offer, and letters would take far too long. 'I cannot do anything but return home,' she sighed.

During one morning chat about a dream in which Kamala saw fish, she said that this meant someone she is close to would be getting money. 'Is this true for anyone?' I asked. 'Oh no. For each person the meaning may be different. When my father dreams about milking a cow, then someone will have money.' This is interesting on one level because I have never known Kamala's father to have milked a cow in his day-to-day life. None of Kamala's immediate neighbours or friends in the Yakha community raised cows for dairy products. So the dream was an elaboration of a waking reality – perhaps it was noticeable and particularly meaningful because it was out of the ordinary. But the dreams of cows and fish are interesting on another level because one can see that Kamala's accounting of dreams is both intimately linked to the present and future of family and friends – is intensely social – but is at the same time distanced from the idea of 'one culture/one meaning'. Different people within the same society/ethnicity/family may associate dreams and their meanings entirely differently. However, she also indicated that

> some dreams are sure – fixed. If you dream of frogs, for example, then you will fall and hurt yourself, no matter who you are.

This is universal, as is the meaning of felled green trees (death).

> When a small stone falls in a dream, a baby will be dropped. I have known this to be true, and my father and mother have as well.

So universality of meaning is judged by people agreeing on dreams and the realities/outcomes which occur in their waking lives. The conversations in my living room were different from those which I remember through my fieldnotes. The former were not about the Yakha. They were about Kamala the individual dreamer, Kamala with her mother and father, Kamala with her best friend Man Maya, dreaming about birds, people and places in their shared worlds.

When we are in 'the field', trying to account for what is 'common-sensical' to our informants, we have to work quite hard to ask the right questions in order to elicit a sense of local meanings and feelings. One must listen carefully to the effect of context on one's style of narrative. When in the field we asked about 'the Yakha', we got 'the Yakha do this' sorts of answers. When we asked, 'Who can *you* marry?', we wrote about 'Yakha' not 'Kamala's and Bhim Bahadur's' marriage rules. However, when Kamala visited us in the UK, the focus was personal, emotive, intense, and answers often led us away from 'the Yakha' and towards a more honest, socially adaptive *self.*

From the 'local's perspective', a consciousness of self (in Erchak's sense of self as both unique individual and something which ties us to other people in our culture; 1992: 1,171) *vis-à-vis* the visiting 'stranger/anthropologist' is at a lower ebb at 'home' – it needs to be wheedled out, elicited, asked, verbalized. *Away* from home and the familiar, consciousness of self *vis-à-vis* other is heightened. It pours out of people when they are first thrust into the foreign: every observation of difference is rich with conscious recognition of some familiar thought or way of life 'back there'. Every emotional response is made sense of by the awareness of being in a new place, being confronted by a strange language, food, sight or smell.

The anthropologist knows this to be the case for herself when she looks at journals and notes which describe the first few weeks or months in a very new place. It is a time rich with sensations, observations and emotions which inform the descriptions and analyses which follow and form the crux of ethnography (Kohn 1994). It is because we can be conscious of our own experiences that we can locate others'. It is because I was first quite lost in Kamala's home and culture and only slowly became familiar with her language and way of doing things that I could imagine how she felt when she first arrived in England. Emotions are cognized through culturally specific lenses, but they may be imagined both within and between humans from different cultural backgrounds. This is perhaps why we can cry when we watch foreign films, or historical dramas – Kurosawa? Shakespeare?

Generally, anthropologists who have attempted to account for their informants' emotions, dreams, senses, etc., have tended to look to language as the key, and to linguistic fluency as a prerequisite to access. Hardman's study of the 'indigenous psychology' of the Lohorung Rai (another Kiranti hill tribe in East Nepal) suggests how ideas about self and an individual's relation to the 'social and metaphysical world' are based upon the state of three psychophysical bodily substances (*niwa*, *saya* and *lawa*) (1981: 161–2). The ethnographer's knowledge of these ideas was acquired through ability to spot the usage of these three terms in local sayings and everyday speech. Erchak would generalize that ethnographers' depictions of 'the self' in other societies tend to be 'presented as "ethnopsychologies", psychological concepts and categories "from the native's point of view" ' (1992: 12–13). The key to understanding individual experience in other cultures, therefore, is seen to be locked into 'native categories' – phonemes, words and sentences. Anthropologists continue to teach their students that one can only properly learn about what others do and feel when one is 'fluent' in their language, and that these things can only be impressionistic-ally sensed (and can therefore not be recognized as proper ethnographic data) when one is new/illiterate. This idea is not confined to the academy. Eva Hoffman, in an autobiography about her experience as a Polish immi-grant striving for fluency in America, writes:

> The thought that there are parts of the language I'm missing can induce a small panic in me, as if the totality of the world and mind were coeval with the totality of language. Or rather, as if language were an enormous, fine net in which reality is contained – and if there are holes in it, then a bit of reality can escape, cease to exist.
>
> (Hoffman 1989: 217)

But surely narration (both the informant's and the ethnographer's) comes out of an experience which is far larger than the narration itself can express? Erchak, paraphrasing Goldschmidt, has suggested that 'cognition makes possible the symbolic world of meaning which is the essence of language and culture. Emotion makes this world subjectively one's own' (1992: 177). Yet, one is aware of thought and emotion simultaneously. As Leach has eloquently put it,

> Feeling is a total experience; we become conscious because of messages that reach the brain through the eyes, ears, nose, mouth, fingers,

stomach, genitals. . . . But these messages are alternative simultaneous metaphors of one and the same world out there; we do not end up with separate constructions, a sight world, a sound world, a smell world and so on. All is transformation.

(Leach 1979: 104)

Likewise, perhaps, for messages which reach the brain in one's waking and sleeping lives. Dream theorist Hearne would confirm this. He has suggested that dreams are a continuation of our everyday thoughts, and that we use symbols and visual and verbal puns in dreams because our brains are turned down too low to receive a full set of images. And yet, none of these holistic models answer whether we are variably conscious of our feelings and our dreams. Do we, for instance, have different sorts of dreams and intensities of dreams when we move from home to the far away and foreign, and would such a variable consciousness mean anything – tell us anything new?

REFLECTIONS II

This all began as a simple recollection of dreams. I was startled by these dreams because I never thought of Kamala as a dreamer, and I never thought that dreams were something worth pursuing when I was in the field and few mentioned them to us. So many other things had to be asked back then which seemed so much more 'to the point' – social structures, marriage patterns, agricultural practices, etc. Now that her visit is over, I am left wondering many things. I still cannot be sure why Kamala offered her dreams to me every morning in Durham and not in Tamaphok. Was it a question of variable vividness? Of more or less available allies? Of a freedom in the one place which was lacking in the other? Of a need to reach back home which didn't exist in the home itself? Or a bit of all of these? What will Kamala's responses to this chapter be? What is hidden in the copious notes that Kamala took in her diary? To what extent was Kamala's recounting of dreams a way of referring to a common ground between us which was initially constructed in Nepal: was she talking to me through her dream talk? Answers are not forthcoming, nor are they entirely necessary. The questions the situation raised are what interest me – Kamala's dreams have certainly heightened *my* consciousness. They have helped me to dispel the notion of the fluent fieldworker well into 'the field' as being the sole centre for learning of individual consciousness and group 'culture'.

This is a methodological problem which is relevant to all anthropologists. In general we have been trained to talk to individuals and write about cultures. We all deal with people who move from place to place through time (even if that movement usually stops short of our living rooms), and people whose lived and dreamed experiences of 'world', 'place', 'self' and 'other' change significantly in consequence.

An anthropology of consciousness must account for the numerous and changing contexts in which individuals find themselves. To look at these is not to look at a number of static frames which can be isolated (the village, the town, the nearest cinema, the army, the neighbouring country, etc.), but to look at the processes which link them, the mechanisms (e.g. emotional adjustments) required for moving between different contexts. If our knowledge of others is 'dialogical', it means that 'it' is not reified into something really 'out there' in the field, but something which is produced through a process of interaction with others. Fabian calls this the 'intersubjective nature of ethnographic investigations' (1990: 765). In the global context of the 1990s, these investigations need not and will not occur in only locally relevant places – the solid, scarcely moving 'field' – but may move and thus be transformed in the process.

Anthropologists not only distance themselves from the field in order to write – to record what is known. They also distance themselves in order to experience – to expand what is known. However, it is not only fieldworkers and other intellectuals who are mentally equipped to travel. An unfortunate pre-modern, post-colonial assumption made but not necessarily admitted by many anthropologists is that it may not be 'appropriate' or 'fair' to bring informants to visit them in their own home countries.[6] What do people think is lacking? The attitude is even clearer outside the academy – while consultants are paid more than handsomely to join local counterparts in 'the field', these counterparts are rarely brought back to the UK to write reports. I believe that our understanding of others and other places, both in development and the anthropological academy, would only be enriched by more attention to the thinking and feeling which is activated away from familiar 'fields'. We should redirect our gaze to the many dreamers and travellers who are learning about who they are in newly reflexive ways. Consciousness awakened by change happens all around us, all the time – it is both lived and narrated in the normality of everyday encounters, in the active reforming of ourselves and our societies in our reflections and our dreams.

> We did relatively little talking in the airport while we waited to see Kamala off on her flight home. There were many tears and held hands. She gave Ben a picture of herself standing in a fine sari outside her home in Tamaphok – 'stick it above your bed to remember your auntie Kamala', she whispered. Then floods of tears and a bit of panic, as we tried to explain what she had to do between putting her carry-on bag through the scanner and finally boarding the plane, and then she was swallowed up by much taller crowds. Such similar emotions, and yet such contrasting circumstances when we left Tamaphok to return to

England – in the village we had had the relative formality of a small ritualized farewell, when *tikaas* [blessings placed in the form of a wet red paste mixed with uncooked rice] were placed by each family member on our foreheads. Yet the same tears which rolled down cheeks in the village were rolling down cheeks in Gatwick airport.

Months later, her visit had taken on that distant, partial, dream-like quality. A letter from Kamala suggested that this had been her experience too. 'Was it all a dream?' she wrote, followed closely by, 'in my opinion, dreams are usually good.'

NOTES

I am very grateful to the following for their helpful feedback on initial drafts: Luisa Belaunde, the late David Brooks, Leslie Carlin, Michael Carrithers, Iain Edgar, Robert Layton, Caroline and Filippo Osella, Nigel Rapport, Dan Rose, Andrew Russell, Bob Simpson and Charles Stewart. I would also like to thank all who commented on the original paper presented at the 1994 ASA in St Andrews.
1 In one, for example, the 'auntie' from next door told us that she had seen us in her dream, and our house was falling down. In another, which occurred during the nationally celebrated festivities of Dasain, Kamala's father ('Apa') was quite amused to tell us about a dream in which his sergeant-major during his time in the British Gurkhas (thirty years previously) was telling him to clean his rifle. The infrequency with which we were privy to dream narration in the field can be juxtaposed with the almost daily recounting of Kamala's dreams in the UK.
2 See Dan Rose (1990) on 'reversals'. It is from him that I have borrowed the useful expression 'crossing over'.
3 David Brooks read and took notes on a draft of this chapter shortly before his death, and in these he suggested that we may not have asked about 'prayer' (as an internal and thus non-observable state) because we were not ourselves religious. This is a helpful criticism which points to the way in which the relevance of questions and 'the field' itself is constructed by the ethnographer – it is in this sense, perhaps, that David noted that 'the field is a state of mind'. Perhaps an irreligious mind does not ask all the 'right' questions about belief (see Evans-Pritchard 1981), just as a person who has not experienced childbirth or intense bereavement may not properly engage with the 'other's' experience of these events. Hastrup and Hervik's collected volume (1994) deals most effectively with issues of experience and anthropological knowledge.
4 I have since been informed, perhaps ironically, that I should have attended the Society for Psychological Anthropology sessions to learn about current ideas in the field of consciousness.
5 One may be aware of feelings of pain, or one may appreciate the beauty of a rose, without thinking very clearly or articulating with speech. Kirsten Hastrup, in this volume, also describes this sensory breadth of consciousness, but has chosen to limit the definitional scope of 'awareness' in a very different way. The problem here, however, is less definitional than methodological.
6 Of course, racist immigration laws and travel restrictions only exacerbate and perpetuate power imbalances and prejudice. Discrepancies in money power are

often mind boggling. Kamala bought her cousin a sweater in an Indian shop in Southall for around £10, which is equivalent to two months' worth of average daily earnings in the village. Yet, while we cannot eradicate these imbalances, we can still strive to reciprocate hospitality.

REFERENCES

Barley, N. (1988) *Not a Hazardous Sport*, London: Viking.
Batts, J. S. (1976) 'British manuscript diaries of the nineteenth century: an annotated listing', Totowa, NJ.
Carrithers, M. (1982) 'Hell-fire and urinal stones: An essay on Buddhist purity and authority', in G. Krishna (ed.) *Contributions to South Asian Studies 2*, Delhi: Oxford University Press.
Clifford, J. L. (ed.) (1947) *Dr. Campbell's diary of a visit to England in 1775*, Cambridge: Cambridge University Press.
Clifford, J. (1992) 'Traveling cultures', in L. Grossberg, C. Nelson and P. A. Treichler (eds), *Cultural Studies*, New York and London: Routledge.
Coburn, B. (in press) *Nepali Ama in America*, Santa Barbara, Calif.: Ross-Erikson Publishers.
Cohen, A. P. (1992) 'Post-fieldwork fieldwork', *Journal of Anthropological Research*, 48: 339–54.
Delaney, C. (1990) 'The *hajj*: sacred and secular', *American Ethnologist*, 17(3): 513–30.
Dennett, D. (1991) *Consciousness Explained*, Boston: Little, Brown.
Edgar, I. (1994) 'Imaginary fields: the cultural construction of dream interpretation in three contemporary British dreamwork groups', unpublished PhD thesis, Keele University.
Erchak, G. M. (1992) *The Anthropology of Self and Behaviour*, New Brunswick, NJ: Rutgers University Press.
Evans-Pritchard, E. E. (1981) in Andre Singer (ed.) *A History of Anthropological Thought*, London: Faber and Faber.
Fabian, J. (1990) 'Presents and representation: the other in anthropological writing', *Critical Inquiry*, 16: 753–72.
Gard, R. (ed.) (1988) *The Observant Traveller: Diaries of Travel in England, Wales and Scotland in the County Record Offices of England and Wales*, London: HMSO.
George, K. M. (1967) *American Life Through Indian Eyes*, Madras: Janatha Printing and Publishing Co.
Good, K. (1991) *Into the Heart: An Amazonian Love Story*, London: Penguin.
Hardman, C. (1981) 'The psychology of conformity and self-expression among the Lohorung Rai of East Nepal', in P. Heelas and A. Lock (eds), *Indigenous Psychologies: The Anthropology of the Self*, London: Academic Press.
Hastrup, K. and Hervik, P. (1994) *Social Experience and Anthropological Knowledge*, London: Routledge.
Hoffman, E. (1989) *Lost in Translation: Life in a New Language*, London: Minerva.
Johnson, S. and Boswell, J. (1924) *A Journey to the Western Islands of Scotland and The Journal of a Tour to the Hebrides* (1775–1785), reprinted 1970, Oxford: Oxford University Press.
Kohn, T. (1992) 'Guns and garlands: cultural and linguistic migration through marriage', *Himalayan Research Bulletin*, 12.
Kohn, T. (1994) 'Incomers and fieldworkers: a comparative study of social experi-

ence', in K. Hastrup and P. Hervik (eds), *Social Experience and Anthropological Knowledge*, London: Routledge.

Kroeber, T. (1964) *Ishi: Last of his Tribe*, Toronto: Bantam.

Leach, E. (1979) 'Of ecstasy and rationality', in M. Csaky (ed.) *How Does it Feel?: Exploring the World of Your Senses*, London: Thames & Hudson.

Lutz, C. A. (1988) *Unnatural Emotions: Everyday Sentiments on a Micronesian Atoll and Their Challenge to Western Theory*, Chicago: University of Chicago Press.

Moir, E. (1964) *The Discovery of Britain: The English Tourists 1540–1840*, London: Routledge & Kegan Paul.

Ottenberg, S. (1990) 'Thirty years of fieldnotes: changing relationships to the text', in R. Sanjek (ed.) *Fieldnotes: The Makings of Anthropology*, Ithaca and London: Cornell University Press.

Reynolds, V. (1980) *The Biology of Human Action*, 2nd edn, Oxford: W. H. Freeman.

Rose, D. (1990) *Living the Ethnographic Life*, Qualitative Research Methods Series 23, London: Sage.

Russell, A. J. (1992) 'The Yakha: culture, environment and development in East Nepal', unpublished DPhil thesis, University of Oxford.

Stocking, G. W. (1982) *Race, Culture, and Evolution: Essays in the History of Anthropology*, Chicago: University of Chicago Press. (Originally published in 1968.)

Tedlock, B. (ed.) (1992) *Dreaming: Anthropological and Psychological Interpretations*, Santa Fe, NM: School of American Research Press.

Chapter 3

On being a child

The self, the group and the category

Allison James

QUESTIONS AND REPLIES

In considering the question of the consciousness of children my thoughts immediately return to 1978, to a conversation I had with a twelve-year-old-boy. Still vivid, it encapsulates the essence of my enquiry. I had got to know the boy whilst doing fieldwork in the north of England. That day, as ever, he was bragging before his friends of recent escapades, bemoaning, in passing, the restrictions which age placed upon his everyday activities: not being allowed to smoke or drink, being too young to do this, too old for that. Perplexed and seemingly exasperated, the boy suddenly demanded of me: when are you an adult? As an adult, I could give no sensible reply. Age alone would have been of little help: sure, he could vote at eighteen but with local unemployment figures high and on the increase would he, in the eyes of those who mattered, yet be a man? At sixteen he could buy cigarettes; that he already did. At eighteen he might drink in the village pubs and clubs, but in the years till he reached that age he would certainly be practising. He would leave school at sixteen and, inevitably, swop one training ground for another in the guise of the then much despised YTS (Youth Training Scheme). Chickening out I dodged the question. Some fifteen years later the epistemological frame of his enquiry remains central for me, if not for him. He has no doubt found out, by now, what it means to be an adult. I, on the other hand, am still asking what it might mean to be a child. Through the course of this chapter I shall be attempting, at last, some kind of reply.

The background to this questioning is the debate about the social construction of childhood which emerged in the late 1970s (Prout and James 1990). In his book, *What is a Child?*, written in 1977, Nicholas Tucker delineated the traditional perspective towards the study of childhood. Offered by developmental psychology, in brief, this centred on the body of the child, a body envisaged as lacking the competencies of the adult model and possessed of its own distinctive (peculiar?) physical attributes, modes of reasoning and thought (Hockey and James 1993).

Still very much in vogue (see Burman 1994), this view positions the child as less than adult, as developing its nature through particular nurturing processes and as being un-adult or at least different from. It is a conception of the child which conceptually separates children off from the adult world and protects them through the institution of childhood. Children are yet-to-be. But the question which arose in the 1970s and which remains pertinent today is the extent to which the distinctiveness of children's biology can be said to determine, rather than simply contextualize, children's social experiences.

For John Holt, the answer in 1975 was that biology has very little to do with the way in which childhood is experienced. Objecting strongly to the conceptual boundaries which distance the social worlds of children from those of adults through discriminating social practices he sees few reasons for giving prominence to the biological factors of childhood. What a child is, Holt maintains, is largely a function of what adults think it to be. And within late modernity, he argues, this expectation is of a cute incompetent. It is a model of the self from which children need emancipating. Thus the 'escape from childhood' which Holt advocates depicts a transition for children from their contemporary state of protected dependency to the assertion of independent human(e) rights. In this perspective, then, a clear analytic distinction is drawn between the biological state of childhood and childhood as a social institution, with the latter seen as being the more vital in shaping the pattern of children's lives. From this social constructionist perspective it is the different social elaboration of 'the child', glossed by the universalizing term 'childhood', which accounts for the variation in children's life experiences both between and within cultures.

That this knotty problem is of pertinence to children as well as to academic enquiry is evidenced by the fact that these perspectives can be – and indeed are – marshalled to underpin very different policies in relation to shifting conceptions of what a child might be. In 1993, for example, multiple and conflicting images of 'the child' have been paraded through the British press in relation to calls for policy changes: the child as murderer and the child as murder victim; the knowing child inciting sexual interest and the innocent child suffering sexual abuse; the competent child soldier and the vulnerable child maimed by war; the despair of the homeless child and the cruelty of leaving a child at home alone (James and Jenks forthcoming).

From such a catalogue of differences it might appear that what a child is depends, largely, on where one cares to look. Instanced in different cultural and temporal settings, or even within one locale, a plurality of models of 'the child' may be articulated for and on behalf of children, disparately touching children's lives through their permeation of the fabric of major social institutions: the school, the family, the church and the state. In their everyday experiences of schooling and family life, through exposure to religious beliefs or the constraints imposed by legal systems, children encounter various definitions of the self-as-a-child through implicit and explicit reference being made to what children are or ought to be. And in this manner a myriad of child-specific practices, proscriptive and prescriptive, give shape and texture to even their most mundane social experiences. Alternatively forbidding and encouraging children's participation in particular social domains, allowing and disallowing opinions, praising and disapproving action, it is adults who seem to define what a child is. But – and this is the point I wish to tease out here – it is children themselves who have to literally embody the idea of 'the child'. Thus, my questioning of this taking on (or not) of a 'child' identity by children is as follows: what do children make of and do with the different versions of who they are supposed to be?[1] That is to say, as children, how do they deal with the multiple child-selves on offer as they become consciously aware of themselves as a child and, at the same time, become increasingly self conscious.

CONTEXTUALIZING CONSCIOUSNESS

Deliberate slippage between notions of consciousness and awareness, between self conscious embarrassment and consciousness of the self as an individual and as a person stakes out my engagement with questions of consciousness. As much colloquial understandings as they are analytic categories, these terms are mutually reinforcing and their interplay illuminating, as Charles Taylor's (1985) discussion of the concept of the person demonstrates. In it he draws attention to the difference between notions of being/becoming conscious and/or aware (see Hastrup, this volume), to the reflective distance between being oneself, an individual, and being a person and, through remarking these distinctions, Taylor addresses the possibility of being/becoming self conscious, that is being/becoming literally conscious of one's self through a critical evaluation of how or what others are, might or will be. For Taylor, consciousness is the process by which we, as self-interpreting animals, reflect on the significance of things – events, emotions, desires, feelings – privileging some above others. Consciousness, therefore, is not simply the process of representing external reality to the self; rather it is an evaluative process through which 'our understandings reflect what seem to us to be the truth about what we feel' (1985: 262). In brief, becoming conscious and/or aware is the process of engaging privately and reflexively with a publicly constituted discourse.[2]

To illustrate his thesis Taylor focuses on the idea of shame:

I am ashamed when I am shown up as contemptible or unworthy

before others ... This means not only that I must be self-aware in order to be conscious of what is shameful about me. It is also that what is shameful can only be explained in terms of an awareness of the person: for the shame of my situation is partly constituted by my appearing unworthy in public space.

(Taylor 1985: 264).

That is to say, 'the self-awareness involved with shame is not just a matter of some independent significance which is now in our ken; it is rather a significance bound up with our being self-aware beings, that is persons' (1985: 264).

That Taylor should have chosen the concept of shame to illustrate his ideas about the significant connections between awareness, consciousness, the self and the person, is interesting, for the research upon which I draw here, in my quest to understand children's understandings of childhood, also addressed ideas of shame and embarrassment and public definitions of social correctness, albeit indirectly. Initially conceived as an exploration into young children's understanding of difference and disability in the context of friendship-making, the research project, nominally, had an applied aspect. Its findings would allow me to discover which differences – physical and/or social in origin – children found significant about other children and the extent to which these impacted, adversely or otherwise, on their social relationships. But, as is the nature of the anthropological endeavour, the project gradually took on a slightly different tack. Increasingly, I was drawn away from thinking about which differences were significant and why as, through my daily contact with the children, they pressed upon me the multiple ways in which differences can be powerfully signified and enacted. In effect, I was exploring what Taylor describes as the evaluation of significances by individuals, of themselves and of others, a process which he sees as fundamental to a developing consciousness and awareness. Gradually, I understood that it was the idea of difference, rather than the particularity of its discrete manifestations, which mattered most.

Here, therefore, I interpret the children's recognition and use of the idea of difference as a feature of their developing self awareness, arising out of the distinctions children make between the self and others in the course of their everyday interactions – you're fat, I'm not, you're thick, I'm clever. That this leads to a consciousness of the self, of one's individuality, and sometimes to a shameful self consciousness, occurs through reflexive interpretation by the child of the gap between the self of the child (I) and the self as an object (me) upon which other people – children, teachers, health professionals and anthropologists – gaze, express opinions about or adopt attitudes towards.

The following ethnographic account provides evidence therefore of the possibility of talking *sociologically*, rather than simply psychologically, about identity, about the self and about consciousness (Cohen 1986). In doing so it enlarges upon G. H. Mead's (1934) observations of the child's engagement with the social world through demonstrating the subtleties involved in 'taking on' other people's attitudes towards oneself. It shows that this is not simply the process of uncritical adoption of others' opinions of the self. More complexly, it involves a conceptual reorganization of who I am through reflecting on what others say or think about me and – a point not fully developed by Mead – what I think or say about them. In this view, the self becomes an object for reflexive thought through the creative synthesis of a multiplicity of public and more private or idiosyncratic discourses about identity and as children move between different social domains they gain both confirmatory and conflicting perspectives on who they are or might become (James and Prout forthcoming).[3]

Two questions focus my discussion. First, how do children, as individual members of particular fragmented social groups – children at school, children from particular localities, of particular social classes or age categories – come to understand and live with their simultaneous membership of the more universalizing category 'child'? Second, in a Western society such as Britain, where autonomy, individuality and independence are taken as a mark of a *conforming* social personhood, how do children negotiate the paradox which this represents?

Depicted diagrammatically below, the glimpses of child life which I shall provide begin to tease out these implications through a series of ethnographic examples focused exclusively upon the body. These derive from fieldwork carried out in a Midlands primary school with children aged between four and nine years old and from interviews with parents, teachers and members of the medical professions. In both contexts I was actively seeking out the differences which make a difference to children (Bateson 1973) and, in doing so, was able to explore the different pathways of children's developing consciousness of the self. The examples discussed below illuminate, therefore, the intrinsic relationship which exists between the child's growing consciousness of the self as a child and children's own growing self consciousness, a developing awareness which, I suggest, is largely mediated through the recognition and evaluation of significant differences.

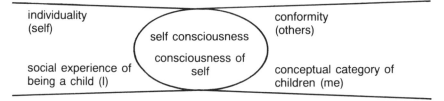

individuality (self)   self consciousness   conformity (others)

social experience of being a child (I)   consciousness of self   conceptual category of children (me)

That the body provides just one of many contexts through which children's consciousness develops and that this single domain is both exceedingly intricate and subtle simply underlines the complexities involved in becoming conscious.

DIFFERENTIATING BODIES

If stereotypes work to categorize, to 'heighten the perception of similarities within categories' and 'to sharpen the perception of difference between categories', it is no surprise that stereotypes are integral to processes of discrimination (Taylor 1981: 84). Here I am concerned with those discriminations which, through stereotyping, fragment the monolithic nature of the category 'child' and, at the same time, with those which firm up the distinctions between the 'child' and other life course categories. It is, as I shall argue, through experiencing both these kinds of classificatory processes that a child becomes conscious of his/herself as a child and as an individual. And in this process of becoming conscious one of the most visible, and arguably most powerful, sources of discriminating difference lies in the child's body.

In the late twentieth century the body of the child, like the adult body, has become a marker of identity, a symbol of and for the self (Turner 1984). Its perceived conformity registers a progressively prescriptive source of self consciousness as the body, increasingly, comes to serve as a sign not only of physical well-being but also of moral failing. Those whose bodies deviate or those who fail to maintain their bodies appropriately may find their social identities and personal integrity brought into question (Featherstone 1982). Whilst within the adult world at large the prominence of the body as a marker of identity may have only emerged in the late twentieth century, for children, along with other marginalized social categories such as elderly and disabled people, the signifying power of the body has long been part of their experience (Oliver 1989; Hockey and James 1993). Indeed, the very differences between their bodies and others may be the symbolic marker of category status, in the way that skin colour may work as an immediately visible symbol of ethnicity. Thus, in the case of children the physical disparities between the bodies of adults and children, as noted above, constitute a traditional category marker of childhood in Western cultures. The distinctiveness of the child's body – its small size, sexual immaturity, different skills, for example – is taken as a sign of the necessity of the boundary between childhood and an adolescent–adulthood.

Such a perspective registers the influence of developmental psychology in the history of childhood and the dominance of biomedical discourses in attributing identity, which together have produced the concept of the normal child. But that this vision of the 'normal' child is neither constant

nor unchanging has been noted by Armstrong (1983). He describes how·
it was constituted through competing medical discourses during the twentieth century. Child health surveys and welfare and development programmes, which monitored the child population, firmed up culturally
particular boundaries of normality for the growing child. The development
of growth charts, combined with advances in medical science leading to
the elimination of diseases, the control of chronic conditions and, more
recently, the reconstructive procedures of modern surgery (Alderson
1993), continue to refine the category of 'child' through rigorously survey-
ing its body.

Thus, though welcome, advances in medical science, ironically, may
have restricted the variations which any child's body might be said to
'normally' exhibit. Although birth defects can be corrected and disabling
illnesses controlled with drugs so that, for instance, asthmatic children
are no longer set upon an inevitable path towards invalidity, for those
others whose bodies fail to respond to treatment, those whose bodies
cannot be surgically altered, those whose bodies simply fall outside the
limits set for normal child-like bodies – too fat, too thin – the risk and
stigma of pathology remains. Indeed, it may have intensified.

That children themselves are constantly reminded of the powerful signifying potential of their bodies can be seen in parenting and pedagogic
practices. As adults anxiously scan their children's bodies for indications
of ill health and well-being or signs of abnormality, so children learn of
its potential as an identifying resource (Booth 1978). Thus, for example,
it is through questions asked about the body's health status in the context
of comments passed about its appearance that children get to know what
it means to be ill. 'You don't look very well' becomes translated into·
somatic feelings, and thence into concepts of ill health (and, by contrast,
concepts of well-being), legitimated through the adoption/negotiation of
the Parsonian sick role within the social context of the family or the
school (Prout 1989).

Unsurprisingly, therefore, the body comes to play a significant media-
tory role in children's developing consciousness. Through noting and
remarking upon differences between one body and another and through
having their own bodies singled out, children learn to distinguish between
anybody's body and their own and between normal and different bodies.
It is a process of classifying and assigning bodies which is done both in
relation to what the body does as well as what the body looks like, with
the former having more symbolic value than the latter for, as I have
described elsewhere, it is what any body does differently, rather than
the body's different appearance, which has the most significance as a
discriminating factor (James 1993). And in this process of classifying,
cultural stereotypes play an important role. The differences given significance by children are never randomly attributed. Instead, being stereo-

typical, they are infinitely generalizable, constituting a sense of otherness, through which individual children may come to see themselves as others see them.

However, these differences only gain significance through the comparably powerful idea of conformity, a conformity arising, I suggest, from children's shared experience of being members of the category 'child'.[4] It is, therefore, the emerging dialectic between sameness and difference which helps constitute children's consciousness of themselves as both individuals and as children. And, in turn, it is through recognizing and reconciling this dual aspect of the self that they may, in effect, become self conscious.

CONSCIOUSNESS OF BEING A CHILD

A first way in which the body quite literally embodies children's consciousness derives from its use in British society to distinguish between categories in the life course and to evaluate them. Being physically 'grown-up' is what visibly identifies and legitimates the conceptually 'grown up' (adults). As an example of what Lakoff and Johnson (1980) term the metaphors we live by, which provide a spatial framework for our conceptual thinking, height comes to take on moral qualities for the child. The growing body provides a ready symbolic vehicle for the increased social and personal responsibilities which age will surely bring as the child progresses towards adulthood. 'Haven't you grown!' 'Isn't he tall for his age!' 'What a big boy!' 'Isn't she grown up!' Thus, the adult world exclaims as it gazes fondly upon the growing child. Though culturally specific, such a constant reiteration of the positive evaluation of increased height offers the child a seemingly dispassionate (clinical?) commentary on his/her normality. Condensed in a single image, the body's increasing size provides a measure of any individual child's potential conformity to the category of child.

Thus, to be a 'normal' child necessitates having a body which does not retain its form. The child's body should, ideally, grow in size and change its appearance. Fundamentally a body in transition, the child's body must grow to conform to that of an adult. And that children are themselves conscious of the body's power as a cultural signifier is exemplified in the ways in which they talk about their changing bodies. Although rarely asking children directly about height, for example, it nonetheless cropped up regularly in the conversations children had with me and with one another at school for, on entering the world of the school, children's consciousness of being children intensifies. It is the school which, in Western societies at least, has been demarcated as the primary public space for children and is one important context where children's consciousness is nurtured through the socializing processes they encounter.

It is here too that stereotypes abound: stereotypes of identity are used by teachers to instil behavioural conformity into the children – good girls, real boys, bullies, little misses, and loners – and stereotypes of body size are promulgated between children to draw attention to the important category discriminations to be made between being a 'baby' and a 'child', and a 'child' and a 'grown-up'.

If entry into school signals the end of domesticated infancy and the start of childhood for children it is not surprising to find that the conceptual links tying physical size to age and identity which children have already met outside the school are in these ways forged into tighter bonds of conformity within its walls. Indeed, for children these links may take on a particular momentum as they discover for themselves the body's identifying power.

For example, during the last few weeks of the the summer term the staff at the nursery school were keen to prepare the children for their entry into the infant school the following September. They therefore spoke often of 'big school' as being the place where the children, as 'big children', would shortly be going, encouraging their four-year-old charges to begin to think of themselves as growing up. Primarily concerned with their changing status and the need to encourage children to become more self-reliant and responsible, the nursery school staff would gloss these expectations with a terminology centred on 'bigness'. Bad behaviour, tears or unwarranted interruptions were designated as stereotypical of 'little' children's behaviour, as versions of the self which the children would soon have to relinquish. As 'big' boys or girls such behaviour would not be permitted. Thus it was that on a pre-school visit to the infant school one four-year-old boy articulated his grasp of the social transition he was about to make in terms of his changing physical size: 'We're big now,' he told his friend. And yet he was not quite confident, nor yet fully self conscious. From me, an adult, he sought a more general assurance: 'I'm bigger, ain't I?', he asked. In his anxious enquiry can be seen, then, one instance of the search for conformity, a conformity which would place him safely in the category of 'normal' child. Although more characteristic of interactions between older children his question demonstrates that a consciousness of the desirability of conformity was already nascent at four years old.

Five-year-old Carol was more certain. Standing back to back with her friend she announced with a deal of satisfaction: 'I'm bigger.' I asked in idle interest if she would like to be tall, to which she gave the following curious reply: 'Yeah. . . . I want to be fifteen.'

This was no simple grammatical error. From Carol's point of view it was a logical reply, one which, I would argue, reflects her emergent consciousness of the body's identifying power. Through the conceptual blurring of physical size and social age – as discussed above, a conflation of genres common in adults' conversations with children – the body becomes a visible measure of the emerging social self. Carol can literally see herself as 'bigger' than her friend. She knows that bigger people are usually also older people and that adults are older than children and that it is towards adulthood that she must aspire. She is well pleased to be big; she wants to be tall; in fact, she wants to be as tall as she will be when she is fifteen. At this age, she confided, a girl can begin to enjoy adult activities. At fifteen, she would be tall enough, old enough and (adult enough) to smoke.

That it is a consciousness of the self as a child which emerges out of the conceptual slippage between age and body size was evident in many of the children's reminiscences about their own experiences of being younger and smaller. With seeming fond amusement they recalled the baby-selves they once were and, as mature six- and seven-year-old children, regarded with a patronizing affection the activities and behaviours of the 'little ones' at school, those who were younger and visibly smaller than themselves. In conversation with Paul during their second term at 'big' school, five-year-old Martin spoke of a time, seemingly long ago: 'Do you remember when I didn't like you . . . in the little [nursery] school?' Although this was just a few months earlier, both boys saw themselves as having entirely different identities, as being different persons. These were the memories of a bygone age, of the self literally in its infancy.

In the social context of 'big school', a public space where the independence of the body and mind is set as an explicit goal, the relinquishing of babyish dependency – of being little – is a high priority for pupils as well as staff. Thus, in their everyday encounters with one another, children would draw attention to those others who were not conforming to the category of child through their blatant exhibition of babyish behaviour. Those who noses needed wiping, who dribbled or were incontinent were easy targets for mockery. They had yet to demonstrate that they were convincing children. While in the privacy of the home bed wetting could be hidden, the euphemistic classroom 'accident' publicly declared a child's lack of self control through the highly visible loss of bodily control. The tears shed were those of social shame, reflecting the child's consciousness of the gulf which had opened up between him-/herself and those other more competent child-selves on display. And just such an emerging consciousness surely accounts for nine-year-old Camilla's outburst as she thought about life at home and those who would still baby her:

What [i.e. why] I like to be big and what I want to be older is because everyone treats me like I'm a little kid, like a baby. They say, 'Camilla, will you do that?' Like I'm a little baby. And my sister gave me this little toy to play with and, guess what, my mummy picked me up and put me in the chair and she goes, 'I'll feed you in a minute' and I said, 'No, I can feed myself.' And my sister she never gets dragged round like me. Like she always drags me around and shouts at me, like, 'Camilla, you silly little girl. Why have you been in my drawers? Why are you wearing my bra?'

The persuasive conceptual links drawn in these examples between size, age and category membership are promulgated daily by parents, by teachers and by other children. They deem small stature an unwelcome bodily attribute through its capacity to symbolize both social immaturity and physical dependency. Indeed, so great is the stigmatizing power of being little that the boy who is the object of Paul's teasing loses any social identity at all. 'He' has become 'it':

Paul: I scared a little first year. I was playing with it. I ran up behind it and went 'Aaagh!' and it jumped, didn't it?

Joseph: You know this little boy, with the brown coat on and the same hair as me? I just went like this [pretends to strangle him] and he went 'Aagh' and cried.

Achieving and fulfilling the status of a child is thus understood by children to be accomplished partly through abandoning the status of infant and one very eloquent statement of being a normal child lies in possessing a body which is child sized. Thus, children whose bodies are smaller than those of their contemporaries may gradually become self conscious of their difference through a dawning recognition of their own body's failure to conform.

For example, Lilly and her mother told me of many instances when Lilly's small stature had denied her what she regarded as her rightful identity. Twelve-year-old Lilly was often unable to find clothes to fit in fashionable teenage boutiques and the girls at school would teasingly hint that she bought her clothes from Mothercare, the well-known chain store selling baby clothes. Although not deficient in growth hormones Lilly had always been smaller than others in her class at school and in recent years had become clearly conscious of the stigmatizing potential which this difference can unleash: 'She's always been that much smaller ... and it becomes patently obvious sometimes and people tend to pat her on the head.' Lilly's self consciousness of her body only diminished when she went horse-riding for 'you don't look small on a horse'.

As children grow older and fast approach their next categorical identity of adolescent, small stature can become increasingly troublesome (Ablon 1990). Children with dwarfism, for example, are not able to outgrow the category of child; they remain child sized despite their increase in age and the development of cognitive skills. So self conscious do some children become of the conceptual demands for appropriate body growth and development that they willingly choose prolonged and incapacitating surgery to gain some extra inches (Alderson 1993: 36). However, as Alderson notes, other children may have their choices made for them by adults; being mere children it is assumed that their conscious consent about the normalizing of their bodies need not be obtained.

This latter observation raises a number of interesting issues about children's consciousness in revealing that the category of child is socially and culturally constructed by adults, in British society at least, as a category whose members, by definition, lack consciousness. For example, under the age of ten a child is not held to be responsible for its actions for it is said not to be fully conscious of their import; a child's evidence is still considered to be unreliable in court for, the question is raised, are children truly conscious of the difference between real and imaginary events; and a child does not have to give consent to surgery for 'when children's capacity to be "for myself" is denied, they are assumed to be "against myself", self destructive and in need of adult control'(Alderson 1993: 193). In the wake of recent 'home alone' cases in Britain, it would seem that adult denial of children's consciousness is set to continue. The NSPCC have recently recommended that children under thirteen years old should not be left alone at home for anything other than a short period of time. And those children who are the victims of adult abuse or neglect are construed as passive victims, unconscious actors on an adult stage (Kitzinger 1990). And yet, from the ethnographic examples given here, it is clear that children are conscious and, indeed, are self conscious at an early age; they know the demands made upon them both as individuals and as members of the category 'child'. They understand, through stereotypes of discriminating difference, what it means to be a child rather than a baby and have some knowledge of what being an adult might entail. The next section develops these themes, exploring how children become self conscious, not just as categorical members, but as individuals.

CONSCIOUSNESS OF BEING A DIFFERENT CHILD

Jerry's experience serves as an introduction to a more extended discussion of the self consciousness of children which, as suggested above, arises through the invocation of and reflection upon the idea of difference. Rather small in stature, bespectacled, academic and bookish in inclination, Jerry fitted uneasily into the tough, laddish culture of a working-class primary school (see James 1993). And yet he was neither teased nor excluded. At eight years old Jerry was not self conscious or embarrassed. Rather he was conscious of his self; he knew through what others said, not about him but about others like him, that his body did not conform to the implicit norms set for the appearance and behaviour of an eight-year-old male and had developed a compensating strategy. Sitting with him and some other boys one day, Jerry casually referred to himself as a 'titchy little boring person'. This good humoured admission of his own non conformity and his voluntary adoption of a stigmatized role took the other boys by surprise. Immediately they denied his self-ascription and in doing so offered him another version of himself, as perhaps different but nonetheless acceptable.

It is clear from this example that Jerry was particularly skilled at being a child. Other children may be less able and accomplished. This may mean that those who have bodies which deviate from the norms for normal child-bodies may become literally self conscious. Sandy, now a beautiful young woman, recalled for me a miserable childhood. Her skin, scarred by eczema, served to make her visibly different and other children commented openly on her different appearance:

> They used to call me Fungus and as I got off the school bus there was a group of girls ... who would throw apple cores at me ... it was awful ... [they'd] follow me round and knock into you, push you over.

As a young child Sandy was made to feel different and indeed felt different. In the summer sun she had to wear socks and shoes whilst the other children wore flip flops. She grew to dislike games lessons at school because wearing PE shorts exposed her red, sore legs for all to see and it was a difference which, with age, became compounded by the adolescent female gender role. Ashamed of her different skin, she covered it up, refusing the demands of fashion for V-necked shirts, scanty dresses and found experimenting with make-up difficult and, at times, painful. As an adult with a skin now blissfully free from eczema, she recalls her childhood as a time of developing consciousness:

> It was hard. I had my friends but the rest of the school knew. They knew you had something wrong with you. They don't make any bones about what they think and what they know. It was hard at school actually when you look back. The dinner ladies used to tell them off [the girls who teased] at dinner time and I used to think I'll just ignore it and think 'you haven't got a brain in your head'. It's not easy but it gets to a point you think you're coping with it and then you don't. Something happens and you don't want to go. It isn't very nice. Children are cruel. They really are.

These extracts, taken from a longer conversation with Sandy, chart the gradual patterning of a young child's consciousness of the self. As Sandy became aware of other people's opinions of her body – doctors', parents' as well as other children's – so a consciousness about her self developed into a strong self conciousness. The varied sources of this growing awareness she makes clear. As a young child periods of hospitalization, frequent contact with doctors, stringent medical regimes and restricted diets informed her of her own difference. She knew that other children did not have to follow such courses of treatment and that their skin was different from her own:

> I used to have coal tar bandages at home. They used to put them on and leave them on for a week soaked in tar. It was a joke. Mum said, when I was in hospital, 'I didn't have to ask where you were. I could smell you.' This coal tar drifting down the ward. But you had to joke about it. Mum'd say, '[you've] been in the lounge scratching, you can see the skin.' I'd say: 'It wasn't me, it wasn't me.' But I couldn't get away with it as no one else used to scratch.

In her denial – 'it wasn't me' – was Sandy refusing the me, the person that others saw, in an attempt to find a more favourable I?

What is certain in her account is that a consciousness that it was she who was the non-conformist, the different child, increased through considering, and at times taking to heart, other children's views about her self. Name calling and teasing singled her out from the crowd as having a body which was not just different, but one which, in her words, she was taught to see as 'wrong': 'they used to call me Fungus and ... would throw apple cores at me'. Having a different body, from the child's point of view, is what makes me different. Sandy makes this clear as, now distancing these events from her adult self, she told me that, 'they knew you had something wrong with you'.

Sandy recalled for me how, as a child, she tried to reconcile the negative vision of her self offered to her by other girls with a more private, and more positive self. Sandy described for me her developing consciousness of her own position and how sometimes she would try to attribute the other girls with similarly stigmatized versions of the self in an attempt to relocate the disgrace of difference, in the same moment as she was wrestling to come to terms with their version of who she was: she snapped, 'I used to think, you haven't got a brain in your head.' It was a struggle for identity which was sometimes successful and, for a while, Sandy would be able to retain a vision of her self as conforming. She managed to think of herself as one in the crowd, as a happy child with friends at school, rather than as the stigmatized other of another gang of girls. On other occasions, however, this version of her self was less easy to achieve. As if reliving the experience as she talked to me, Sandy reverted poignantly to the present tense in her account: 'something happens and you don't want to go [to school]. It's not very nice. Children are cruel. They really are.' Such a consciousness of difference is not, however, the sole dominion of those children who are chronically ill or disabled, for awareness can be triggered by even the most subtle of distinguishing marks: a long nose, a scar, heavy eyebrows. All children run the risk of being marked out as different, of becoming unhappily conscious of their own non-conformity. It is just that, for some, that risk is greater.

CONCLUSION

Elsewhere I have charted the temporal quality of children's developing consciousness, arguing that the identities which children may take on as children are a function of their gradual entry into the child's world of childhood (James 1993). Within the culture of childhood, that conceptual space which positions children *vis-à-vis* each other, individuality and independence vie with the pressure to conform and, as the examples have shown, it is clear that it is out of the gap between sameness and difference, the gap between conformity and individuality, that children's self consciousness emerges. That is to say, in the process of coming to terms with the paradox which these conflicting ideas represent children can become both conscious of the self – of my social status, my personhood – and self conscious, conscious of the me who is ashamed or embarrassed.

These ideas find support in Bluebond-Langner *et al.*'s work amongst children with cancer. In this she shows how in their day-to-day encounters with other children, children with cancer are made conscious of their difference through remarks made about their bodies. But it is not the specificity of the differences which counts most – the loss of hair or weight, the lack of energy or absence from school. It is the very idea of difference itself. The children describe how others fear that they might catch cancer or chide them for their inability to participate effectively in games. By contrast, at summer camps held for children with cancer, the idea of difference disappears. Although the children are conscious that their bodies are different from those of other children – that they are bald or sick from medication – they are no longer self conscious, for in the summer camp everyone is the same. Paradoxically, then, it is by being differently-the-same as others that, at last, these children feel able to be truly themselves: as one child put it, at camp 'it's okay if you can't do something or don't have hair' (Bluebond-Langner, *et al.* 1991: 74)[5]

In summary, then, I have shown how children's consciousness develops through focusing upon the interactions children have with other children and with adults, interactions centred upon what the body looks like. These have shown the ways in which a child's individuality can become highlighted, positively or negatively, through assessing and remarking the extent of his or her body's conformity. But the body is but a single vehicle for consciousness raising, just one arena where negotiations about identity take place. Replicated daily in other contexts and through other mediums, the complexities and paradoxes involved in becoming social are therefore perhaps the complexities and paradoxes of consciousness itself.

NOTES

1 It should be noted that some children have ambiguous identities as children because of a conceptual mismatch between their physical size/age and their activities. Examples would be those children who are described as 'gifted' (those whose intellectual abilities match those of adults) or children who act as carers for disabled parents. In the former instance concern is expressed over whether gifted children can have a 'proper' childhood, their minds being taken up with 'adult' activities. The latter group, those who bodies (and minds) are performing 'adult' tasks as carers, are frequently ignored, their work often going unrecognized by the state because, being children, they are unable to receive caring allowances. For further discussion of these ideas see Hockey and James (1993).
2 Taylor uses the term 'public' to refer to that which is shared, be it public space or shared values and standards.
3 This idea is explored in more detail in James and Prout (forthcoming) where it is suggested that, through adapting Mary Douglas' work on cultural theory and her use of grid and group, it might be possible to explore the ways in which children exhibit and develop their cultural competencies as they move between different social environments which are marked by different constraints. For example, children move between home, school and the neighbourhood and, within these environments, will encounter a variety of different social rules and boundaries, encounters which contribute to their knowledge of how to participate in the social world.
4 These ideas are discussed in greater depth in James (1993).
5 It may be, of course, that in the context of the 'cancer camp' other differentials come into play, such as social class or ethnicity.

REFERENCES

Ablon, J. (1990) 'Ambiguity and difference: families with dwarf children', *Social Science and Medicine*, 30 (8): 879–87

Alderson, P. (1993) *Children's Consent to Surgery*, Milton Keynes: Open University Press.

Armstrong, D. (1983) *Political Anatomy of the Body: Medical Knowledge in Britain in the Twentieth Century*, Cambridge: Cambridge University Press.

Bateson, G. (1973) *Steps to an Ecology of Mind*, London: Paladin.

Bluebond-Langner, M., Perkel, D. and Goertzel, T. (1991) 'Pediatric cancer patients' peer relationships: the impact of an oncology camp experience', *Journal of Psychosocial Oncology*, 9(2): 67–80

Booth, T. A. (1978) 'From normal baby to handicapped child: unravelling the idea of subnormality in families of mentally handicapped children,' *Sociology*, 12 (2): 203–21.

Burman, E. (1994) *Deconstructing Developmental Psychology*, London: Routledge.

Cohen, A. P. (ed) (1986) *Symbolising Boundaries*, Manchester: Manchester University Press.

Featherstone, M. (1982) 'The body in consumer culture' , *Theory, Culture and Society*, 1: 18–33.

Hockey, J. and James, A. (1993) *Growing Up and Growing Old: Ageing and Dependency in the Life Course*, London: Sage.

Holt, J. (1975) *Escape From Childhood*, Harmondsworth: Penguin.

James, A. (1993) *Childhood Identities: Self and Social Relationships in the Experience of the Child*, Edinburgh: Edinburgh University Press.

James, A. and Jenks, C. (forthcoming) 'Public perceptions of children and crime', *British Journal of Sociology*.

James, A. and Prout, A. (forthcoming) 'Hierarchy, boundary and agency in the experience of children: towards a theoretical perspective', *Sociological Studies of Childhood*.

Kitzinger, J. (1990) 'Who are you kidding? Children, power and the struggle against sexual abuse', in A. James, and A. Prout (eds) *Constructing and Reconstructing Childhood*, Basingstoke: Falmer Press.

Lakoff, G. and Johnson, M. (1980) *Metaphors We Live By*, Chicago: University of Chicago Press.

Mead, G. H. (1934) *Mind, Self and Society*, Chicago: University of Chicago Press.

Oliver, M. (1989) 'Disability and dependency: a creation of industrial societies', in L. Barton (ed.) *Disability and Dependency*, Lewes: Falmer Press.

Prout, A. (1989) 'Sickness as a dominant symbol in life course transitions: an illustrated theoretical framework', *Sociology of Health and Illness*, 4 (11): 336–59.

Prout, A. and James, A. (1990) 'A new paradigm for the sociology of childhood? Provenance, promise and problems', in A. James and A. Prout (eds) *Constructing and Reconstructing Childhood*, Basingstoke: Falmer Press.

Taylor, C. (1985) 'The person', in M. Carrithers, S. Collins and S. Lukes (eds) *The Category of the Person*, Cambridge: Cambridge University Press.

Taylor, S.E. (1981) 'A categorization approach to stereotyping', in D. Hamilton, (ed). *Cognitive Processes in Stereotyping and Intergroup Behaviour*, Hillsdale, NJ: Erlbaum.

Tucker, N. (1977) *What is a Child?*, London: Fontana.

Turner, B. S. (1984) *The Body and Society*, Oxford: Blackwell.

Chapter 4

The novelist's consciousness

C. W. Watson

If Euro-Americans have used the creative writing of Afro-Americans primarily as evidence of the blacks' mental or social 'perfectibility' or as a measure of the blacks' 'radical' psychology or sociology, then they have used African literature as evidence of African 'anthropology', of traditional and modern African customs and beliefs. Chinua Achebe, more often than not, is taught in anthropology classes in America; at Cambridge in 1973, Wole Soyinka was neatly shunted away from the Faculty of English and appointed instead to the Faculty of Social Anthropology! If we were forced to compile a list of the received critical 'fallacies' that we wish to avoid in the analysis of black literature, the 'anthropology' fallacy would most certainly stand near the top of our list, perhaps just beneath the 'perfectibility' fallacy and the 'sociology' fallacy (that is, that blacks create literature primarily to demonstrate their intellectual equality with whites, or else to repudiate racism). The anthropology fallacy, moreover, can be divided into its two components, the 'collective' and 'functional' fallacies. ('All African art is collective and functional', whatever this is supposed to mean.) Our list could be extended to include all sorts of concerns with the possible *functions* of black texts in 'non-literary' arenas rather than with their internal structures as acts of language or their formal status as works of art.

(Henry Louis Gates Jr 1984:5)

But our social novels profess to represent the people as they are, and the unreality of their representations is a grave evil. The greatest benefit we owe to the artist, whether painter, poet, or novelist, is the extension of our sympathies. Appeals founded on generalizations and statistics require sympathy ready-made, a moral sentiment already in activity; but a picture of human life such as a great artist can give, surprises even the trivial and the selfish into that attention to what is apart from themselves, which may be called the raw material of moral sentiment ... Art is the nearest thing to life; it is a mode of amplifying experience and extending our contact with fellow-men beyond the bounds of our personal lot.

(George Eliot 1856 [1963: 270])

The Golden Wing is a sociological study written in the form of a novel. Its theme is refreshingly simple in conception – but like the painting of a bamboo leaf, its austere form conceals a high degree of art.

(Raymond Firth 1947: xi)

Le roman dit des jolis mensonges qui contiennent des vérités profondes. C'est toute sa gloire trompeuse. Il n'a donc (selon votre point de vue) absolument aucune valeur, ou alors il est ce qu'il y a de plus important au monde.

(Julian Barnes 1994)

As the quotations above suggest, reading novels and making good sense of them is a difficult task, one which anthropologists are not always very good at. We know, or we should know, that we need to bring to the reading of novels a different set of assumptions from those we bring to reading ethnographies. Fundamental to this different set of assumptions is the understanding of the reader that what she or he is about to read is fiction, something made up, concerning invented characters and situations. And, consequently, since we consider fiction at least one remove from reality, very often we read it as entertainment, very superior aesthetic entertainment in some cases, but nonetheless entertainment and not to be confused with things as they are. When we read ethnography on the other hand, despite all the cautionary remarks made by anthropologists over the last few years indicating how an anthropological text is a highly contrived and composed account full of the ambiguity and irony we associate with fictional texts, we read the work, not as fiction, but as fact, that is, as close to reality as possible, not removed from it. This simple difference, then, between fact and fiction seems self-evidently the criterion by which we distinguish between ethnography and the novel, in just the same way as we might distinguish between history and the novel. Yet, what seems self-evident may be deceptive. And in fact I shall be arguing in some detail that the difference is often more apparent than real. Contrary to what we may have imagined, it is not the greater or lesser reliability of factual descriptions which differentiates the consciousness of the novelist from that of the anthropologist. More significant, I would maintain, is a further set of assumptions, one perhaps not so frequently articulated, which we make in our approach to the different genres.

Broadly speaking, in reading a novel we know we are being invited to extend our sympathies not to a general condition of things but to individual characters and circumstances (cf. the epigraph from George Eliot). This is true of almost any kind of novel, from the most absurd and fantastic to the most naturalistic and documentary. The craft of the novel lies entirely in the way our sympathies are engaged. In reading an anthropological text, however, the invitation is not to implicate ourselves in the narrative in this way, but to come to a more distanced and synoptic understanding of a general and representative set of circumstances. The anthropological text may frequently refer to individuals, case histories and specific circumstances, but the intention of the writing is always very explicitly to draw the reader on to the level of a totalization.

As readers, then, we distinguish between fiction and ethnography, and in doing so we are intuitively recognizing a difference between the consciousness of the novelist and the consciousness of the anthropologist. Both may be looking at and reflecting upon the same situation on the ground, but their understanding, interpretation and evaluation of what they see are different. Their consciousness, that is how they structure and organize their perceptions, is different and that difference is reflected in the kinds of texts they write.

There is, on the other hand, a very close correspondence between the intentions of anthropologists and novelists, which makes their writing complementary and mutually enlightening in a unique way. Other types of writing are, as we know, ancillary to ethnographic accounts. A geologist describing a landscape brings to it a specialist knowledge, a unique consciousness which informs his or her perceptions. The anthropologist sees the same landscape from a different perspective, one to which a geological knowledge, as well as other types of knowledge, may well have contributed. The novelist's perception as reflected in his or her text is different again, and intimately bound up in the context of the novel with the people and circumstances which are at the novel's centre. But an understanding of these people and their circumstances is also at the centre of the ethnography.

In sum, the novelist and the anthropologist can both be said to share the desire to explain the ways of man to man, but they differ both in the manner in which they interpret those ways, and, because of that very difference in interpretation, in the manner in which they compose, present and offer their accounts. There are, then, similarities in intention but differences in consciousness, that is in the attaching of significance, in the evaluation of social circumstances, in the weight ascribed to the representativeness of the individual life, and above all, in the way each moves from the level of the particular to the general and back again.

Within the limits of this chapter it is not possible to do justice to all these issues, important as they are to an understanding of how we should read both novels and ethnographies. What I have chosen to do, therefore, is to limit the discussion first to a description of how novelists, even though their understanding of the operations of society may be different, do indeed incorporate social facts into their novels, and how, consequently, the simple distinction between the 'fictional' and 'factual' stance adopted by the reader can, as I have already hinted, be misleading. Then, in the second part of the chapter, with reference to some examples, I go on to suggest that, in imaginatively juxtaposing individual actions (fiction) and general historical circumstances (fact), consistent with their perception of things, novelists contrive to qualify their judgements in a manner which should, at the very least, give anthropologists pause in relation to how they present their own conclusions.

ARGUMENTS ABOUT FACT IN FICTION

The debate about the reliability of the factual information contained in novels and the degree to which that information can be used by anthropologists and others anxious to understand social reality has in fact been frequently aired. On the whole, social scientists are much less circumspect than literary critics in their use of literary material as evidence of actual circumstances. Anthropologists, for example, will frequently cite a reference to a play or a novel or a short story with the intention of providing supplementary corroboration of conceptual or ethnographic points which they wish to make. Even at the stage of research it is considered good practice to read the fiction of a period and a place – where it exists – in order to acquire a 'feel' – an intuitive understanding – for a culture or, alternatively, to avail oneself of what is often viewed as an alternative or oppositional version to the reality of the presentation explicit in documentary accounts or in the lived practice of participant observation in fieldwork. Two related points arise here. The first is the way in which the fiction is appropriated to play a minor, ancillary role – very different from that accorded to archival and historical material – an optional extra in an ethnographic account; the second is the brute fashion in which very often the references are wrenched from the text without any consideration of context and therefore of meaning. Decontextualization such as this can, of course, lead to some strange and unacceptable misreadings when, for example, an ironic reference is read as straight.

In my own field of Malay studies the questionability of anthropological exploitation of literary sources was forcefully brought home by a damning review by Amin Sweeney of a book by the anthropologist David Banks entitled *From Class to Culture. Social Conscience in Malay Novels Since Independence.* Banks, who had carried out long periods of fieldwork in Malaysia, had read a great number of novels written in Malay by Malay writers and regarding this literature, in his words, as a unique source of information he had proceeded to build up from this reading an account of various characteristics of Malay society, in particular with relation to recent socio-economic development. Sweeney's sharp review condemned the whole enterprise as specious, his argument being both that it was naive to mistake fiction for documentation and that it was a cardinal error to confuse novelists with key informants in the field. Now, I have a certain sympathy with Banks – indeed I had better come clean and say that I have published articles in which I make exactly the same leap across categories as Banks (Watson 1989; 1993) – and my anthropological training and my experience convince me that novels are, as Banks states, a useful source: I recognize that there is a dialogic relationship between the fiction and ethnography. On the other hand, my literary critical sympathies and my reading experience prompt me to accept much of Sweeney's argument. In particular, despite the disrepute into which 'New Criticism' has fallen, I still find myself remembering my youthful enthusiasm for the iconoclasm of those critics who maintained that the 'play's the thing' and not 'how many children had Lady Macbeth?' In other words, I can understand the position which states that the extrapolation from text to life, at least at one level of sensibility, is categorically illegitimate, critically absurd and philosophically indefensible (cf. the whole argument of Olsen 1978): fiction should be left to the literary critic and real life to the anthropologist and philosopher(-king?). And yet, and yet . . . , repeats the voice of my anthropological consciousness.

What concerns us here, then, is the use of literature as a source. However, before we can consider the extent to which an anthropological use of literature might be considered legitimate, we need to consider the related question of what sort of discourse we take fiction to be. Questions of epistemology and contingency, ethics and make-believe are at issue here. In relation to one anthropological view, for example, there is a very telling aside in Max Gluckman's introduction to Elizabeth Bott's classic text, *Family and Social Networks* (1971: xiv), in which he describes how before the writing of her book she presented her material in several seminars at which she solicited the advice of anthropologists present about what she should do with her data. Their response was the suggestion that she work it up into a novel. The implication here – at least I think this is how we must take it – is that the information which she had gathered was so idiosyncratic and individual that it was impossible to generalize from, and that consequently it was to be more appropriately sited – after suitable fashioning – within that genre of writing which dealt with the highly particular and had little to contribute in the way of a representative or typical statement about the human condition, namely the novel, or at least one species of it, that which Greene circumspectly uses to define some of his own fictions – an entertainment. In this case, then, the anthropological audience was making a category distinction, not one, notably, which depended on either the origin of the source material or indeed upon the material's correspondence with some objective truth, but upon distinctions of form and style, and, more importantly, on *a priori* assumptions about what constituted anthropological knowledge – in their view, clearly, very much a generalizing science.

This perception, on the part of anthropologists, of a line of demarcation between fiction and ethnography, despite recent arguments that ethnography is itself a species of fiction, is clearly an enduring one, hence the frequently noted practice of making the strict division that many anthropologists have made between their fictional account of a society and their anthropological account (cf. Bruner's remarks on this [1993: 18]). Both texts usually deal with the same society and both attempt to convey to their readers an understanding of the society, but in the minds of the writers, at least, the two works operate at different levels or in different dimensions of understanding. A further point to be noted here, one which in any extended discussion would be quite critical but which there is not the time to attend to here, is the related demarcation dividing off the personal account of fieldwork, in the form of the autobiographical memoir or the published diary. (See some pertinent remarks by Brian Moeran [1990: 345–54] on this issue.)

In recent years this compartmentalization, not of experience itself, but of the inscribed transformations of that experience, have, as we all know, been radically challenged, and the challenges have been largely in terms of form, style and rhetoric with an emphasis on the need to recognize the constructed fictional nature of even the apparently neutral scientific discourse of the anthropological monograph. Nevertheless, the hesitancy about confusing the fictional and personal with the scientific and general remains strongly entrenched. However, rather than continuing to address the issue at the level of the style and rhetoric of anthropological accounts it may be advantageous to look more closely at literary texts not as examples of rhetoric but for the assumptions they contain about the uses of fiction or make-believe.

One of the frequently stated impulses which underlies the desire to write the memoir or the fiction is the urge to make the whole anthropological experience more accessible, to render that personal confrontation and growing together of the anthropologist and the people of the society in terms of vivid immediacy which better reflect the emotion of the experience than the monograph is able to do (K. Read 1965; Turner *et al.* 1992). Sometimes this impulse to write in a different mode seems to be coupled with a wish to reach a different audience; it is not simply the fellow-professional or student who is being addressed but, potentially, the wider public. Indeed there is an increasing tendency to popularise anthropology, perhaps fuelled by the expansion of general interest in travel and travel writing which, at its worst, leads some anthropologists to succumb to the professional temptation to exoticize the other, whether through self-indulgent caricature or through deliberate emphasis on the arcane and the repellent, but which, at its best, poses questions fundamental to the readers' understanding of themselves as well as others.

Whatever the motivation, the recent proliferation of different types of text (in 1991–2 alone texts by British anthropologists include those by Helen Watson [1992], Katy Gardner [1991] and Anna Grimshaw [1992]) has implications both for the redefinition of anthropology – if anthropology is what anthropologists do and if they are now doing different things from what they did in the past, then anthropology must now be different – and, consequently, for how anthropology is taught and, ultimately, practised. Novels, along with anthropological memoirs, documentary films, an introspective gaze at our own society and short experiences of foreign travel, do now constitute some of the substance of anthropological discussion, but only marginally so. What I imply throughout this chapter is that, as anthropologists increasingly recognize, the novelist's consciousness does not simply provide a supplementary or ancillary contribution to understanding, but is often capable of a far more nuanced description of cultures, which should be reflected in a greater incorporation of these texts into our anthropological practice. By more nuanced description what I have in mind are the numerous subtle ways in which great writers, sometimes almost unconsciously (cf. Lukács 1964), qualify and extend their accounts at those very points when the reader is about to lapse into the security of a generalization. At the same time, however, as advocating the importance of giving due weight to the novelist's perceptions, I would insist, like Sweeney, that we cannot simply extract at face value statements from the novel, and that we must evaluate those statements in context according to the proper protocols of reading. This means that we must be sufficiently aware of the structural conventions of the genre in which the work is written. How these conventions and traditions of reading operate we shall consider with reference to specific examples.

THE NOVEL AS AN ANTHROPOLOGICAL RESOURCE

Aristotle's dictum 'Fiction is more profound and truer than history' conveys a sentiment which, in the European cultural legacy, at least until very recently, has commanded universal assent: there is in great literature an understanding of the human condition which goes beyond what can be achieved in the scientific study of society. But, regrettably, although generally acknowledged, its import is frequently neglected or dismissed by the assumption that Aristotle is here perhaps referring to an almost metaphysical property of fiction, and that this mystical dimension of poetic understanding can be safely ignored when engaged in any serious discussion about culture and society. At best, fiction, indeed literature, and art in general, are regarded as cultural products, and it is within the context of cultural production, and not transcending it in the realm of some meta-discourse, that art should be discussed – or so runs the argument. It is therefore refreshing to see Aristotle recently reformulated in a way which stresses the continuing relevance of understanding the epistemological relationship between Dichtung and Wahrheit. In a recent article entitled 'Écriture romanesque et écriture de l'ethnologie', Gérard Toffin makes the point that: 'Quant à la littérature, quelle que soit l'école, réaliste, naturaliste, symboliste, etc., dont elle se réclame, elle est investie d'une fonction de connaissance. Même lorsqu'il réfute de la manière la plus catégorique toute finalité didactique, l'écrivain entend exprimer une vérité' (1989: 35).

The problem of course is to identify what sort of 'truth' is in question and to identify where, within the fictive product, the novel, the poem, the drama, it resides, or, if that is impossibly to reify the concept, to know how to recognize it. Toffin's lucid and well-argued article shows various ways we may go about this. Drawing in large part upon the example of Zola, he makes a strong case for the anthropological worth of the information contained in novels, laying particular emphasis on both the ethnographic pretensions which Zola had and referring to the meticulous fashion in which Zola actually conducted fieldwork. In addition to drawing our attention once more to the relatively well-known claims which Zola made for naturalism in *Le Roman expérimental*, in which he wrote 'Le naturalisme, c'est la méthode scientifique appliquée dans les lettres' (Toffin: 37), Toffin is able to refer to the recently published *Carnet d'enquêtes* (Zola 1986 – which appears in the same Terre Humaine series as *Tristes tropiques*) in which the lengths to which Zola went in order to document and authenticate the scenes and descriptions which would resurface in the novels are recorded in detail.

That Zola's novels can, then, be usefully mined by anthropologists and social historians wanting to understand everyday French social life of the late nineteenth century would seem to be irrefutable. Zola is as good a witness, if not much better, than any other contemporary ethnographer of the times. And yet this documentary accuracy, this faithful recording and representation of the minutiae of everyday experience, was surely not what Aristotle had in mind when he referred to fiction as being *spoudaioteron* (truer)? And even if it were, can we really accept Zola's claim at its face value? Have we not, since Zola, become rightly sceptical of the claims to transparency of even the most objective description, let alone those embedded within a context which is avowedly fictional and rests unashamedly upon (honest) deception? And of course in Zola's case there is still considerable argument (Toffin 1989: Lukács 1964) about whether the ethnography can be easily extracted from the context of the scientific and political theories of the writer.

In fact these questions are precisely those which Toffin (1989) addresses in his extended argument, but rather than pursue that here, I want to consider in more detail the views of Amin Sweeney, who made his remarks on the inadmissibility of confusing literature with reality in the context of understanding contemporary Malay society. The closing sentences of his review read:

> And whether or not the novel is presented as a slice of life [the metaphor of course derives from Zola (CWW)] or as pure fantasy matters little in our assessing what it *tells* us about society. The notion that the more realistic a novel is the closer it takes us to reality is entirely misguided.[1] The novel itself is reality; the realism it may employ is a convention, and of course, conventions are reality, too. An attempt to understand how literature works entails examining it as an institution of society in its own right. One must focus upon literature as form, literature as system, not literature as native informant.
>
> (Sweeney 1989: 121)

Sweeney has in mind here the various examples he has criticized in the course of the review of what he regards as Banks' naivety in taking the text of the novel to refer to social reality, what he terms 'reality on the ground'. Leaving aside for the moment the dubiousness of the positivism of this notion of reality, I want to take up just one of Sweeney's several arguments, the question of whether even the most meticulous recording of experience, once it is transposed – and thereby transformed in its generic character – into the context of a novel can reliably inform us about life.

One of Banks' justifications for using the novels as source material is one which Zola by implication would have endorsed:

> social scientists may find [in the Malay novels written by Malay writers] detailed descriptions of ceremonies and rituals drawn from the author's recollections. These descriptions may validate materials gathered through stricter social science observational techniques. In some cases, readers will find new information that awaits validation by social science observers.
>
> (Banks 1987: xi)

Sweeney objects that it is not a question of one validating another or of social science having stricter observational techniques: the two are independent of each other and employ different criteria of validity and strictness. More relevant to our immediate purposes, however, he argues that even if one did allow that social scientists and novelists were representing the same reality on the ground – rituals and ceremonies in this case – 'seeking fact in fiction is at best a risky undertaking' (1989: 103).

The very claim, however, that it is 'risky' also implies that it is possible, and Sweeney seems to endorse the possibility by going on to refer to

Joan Rockwell's argument (in Sweeney's paraphrase) that 'information in fiction produced as a background which makes specific events seem plausible may be accepted as factual', even though he questions that assumption in relation to '*traditional* [my emphasis] literature'.

Now in fact I think that Banks has a stronger case here than Sweeney admits. And certainly if one was to apply the general argument to Zola and ask about the authenticity of the incidental descriptions, then one would be hard put – once one has accepted of course the positivist premise in the first place – to sustain the argument that the embedding of the description in a novel renders it an unreliable representation of 'fact'. Indeed Zola was so adamant about the authenticity and verifiability of these incidental descriptions that he once commented, 'Si l'indication des sources, dans un roman, était chose usitée, je criblerais volontiers de renvois le bas des pages' (Toffin 1989: 48 fn.23), a comment which by implication seems to cause havoc with any neat stylistic distinction between social science fact and literary fiction.

That there is an important epistemological issue at stake here is something which has exercised a number of commentators who, like Rockwell, have noted that contained within literary fictions, particularly within the realist novel, there are descriptions which are intended to refer to a reality outside the self-contained universe of the literary work. Currie points to several examples of this. He notes, for example, how in *Guy Mannering* Scott 'turns aside' from the principal narrative in order to provide the reader with what is intended to be a factual account of gypsy life, which the reader, precisely because it is factual, not fictional, is required not to make-believe, but actually to believe (Currie 1984: 391). Webster dealing with the same issue borrows from Rabinowitz's distinctions between 'four audiences implied in any narrative literary text, correlative to as many different modes of the author'. It is these distinctions which are crucial because: 'The relationship between these several audience–author levels of narrative meaning are the basis for contextual discriminations between truth and fiction' (Webster 1982: 106). The example that he gives is of the difference between the relationship between the author and his assumed audience, called the 'authorial audience' and the relationship between the internal narrator and his intended audience, called the narrative audience. 'For *War and Peace*, the authorial audience accepts the reality of the War of 1812, while only the narrative audience accepts the reality of Natasha, Pierre and the other characters' (Webster 1982 106).

This, it seems to me, is a useful distinction to make because, although Webster goes on to stress that Rabinowitz is happy to *allow* for the 'simultaneity of the perception of both truth and fiction' (1982: 107), the point at issue is the different assumptions that author and audience are making of each other in reading the text, and the stress placed here on the 'device' of creating or merging the difference between authorial audience and narrative audience. (For this general discussion of author and implied author, a useful extended analysis – of which Sweeney seems to be aware – is Wayne Booth's *The Rhetoric of Fiction* [1991: 67–86].)

This is exactly the point made by Lamarque in his elucidation of how we distinguish truth from fiction in a narrative such as Llosa's *The Real Life of Alejandro Mayta*, but Lamarque, rather than talk about device and shared expectations, phrases his description in terms of a game in which author/narrator and intended/actual audience are aware of the rules. These are, he argues, 'institutionally-based relations'. In sum he writes:

> There is no reason why make-believe descriptions should not describe (truly) actual states of affairs. It is in virtue of other features, as we will see, that they are make believe . . . The defining feature of a make-believe fictive utterance, which includes fictional narrative, . . . lies in a network of institutionally-based relations at the centre of which is a set of attitudes I will label the 'fictive-stance'. The fictive stance is not a property of sentences or utterances but is an attitude taken towards them by participants in the 'game' of fiction. The fictive stance is made possible only within a complex conventional practice which determines storytellers' intentions and readers' responses.
>
> (Lamarque 1989: 147; cf. Fowler 1988: 67)

All this seems fairly straightforward and, despite the minor differences in terminology, there appears to be a consensus that fiction, particularly realist fiction, contains non-fictive material – again with a disturbing hint of positivism here which we need to bracket out for the moment – and by implication the anthropologists or social scientists who wish to avail themselves of this should feel free to do so.

In practice, however, there is a catch, something which is obscured by the too brief references to particular novels in the above examples, but one of which Sweeney is fully cognizant and which is brought out in his review article. The problem is that although we may agree that the conventions – the schemata in Sweeney's usage – imply a reading contract between author and reader which in principle makes possible the distinction between fact and fiction, and consequently allows the anthropologist to extract the facts in what Sweeney calls a 'raiding' operation, in numerous cases the task of distinguishing between authorial audience and narrative audience or of establishing what precisely the conditions of the contract lay down is highly problematic.

In *War and Peace* and *Guy Mannering* the reading rules are straightforward. The same is true of Zola. In *Au bonheur des dames*, for example, several pages are devoted to describing the content of department stores; in *Le Ventre de Paris* there are elaborate descriptions of the food stalls in

Les Halles. These are clearly intended to be authentic descriptions: the author has used various rhetorical and textual devices to win the reader's consent to take the description as accurate, that is to its having an exact correspondence to what is out there in the real world. The conventions having been established then, the description is to be evaluated by the reader on two levels: at the level of correspondence to reality, as ethnographic observation, does it faithfully represent what the readers themselves experience or can potentially experience? and, on the authentic level of fictional creation, does the description cohere in the context of the narrative and is it of itself emotionally or intellectually compelling? (cf. K. Burke quoted by Jameson [1983: 81] on the simultaneity of two similar sorts of appreciation). Here at this point we are only concerned with the reader's evaluation of the first level: correspondence with reality. In Zola's case the reader is assured if not of the absolute reliability of the description, at least of the value of testing it out through direct experience or indirectly through comparison with other descriptions. The description, therefore, can in this instance legitimately contribute to the reader's knowledge of the world, in exactly the same way as Banks claims in his use of Malay novels.

So far so good, but what happens when we move beyond Zola and Dickens and the European realist writers of the nineteenth century and consider contemporary writers who implicitly make large claims for authenticity such as Timothy Mo or Adam Thorpe; or Forster or Naipaul? Mo, for example, for the 'authenticity' of his novel *Sour Sweet* relied on his research into historical and anthropological literature. The 'facts' derived from the research have been incorporated into the novel, but where and how precisely, and what are the conventions which would allow one to distinguish between, for example, the accuracy of the representation of the Grandfather being brought over to live in England, and that of the patroness Mrs Law as being a typical character with Chinese immigrant communities? If we read Anthony Shang's account of the Chinese restaurant community in Britain we will in fact learn that bringing over grandparents to reside in Britain is an increasing demographic trend (Shang 1984: 20), so to that extent the fictional description is authenticated by social science observation, but there is no *a priori* way in which the reader without that knowledge can rely on textual or narrative cues to know this as a 'fact'. The most that one can say is that in this instance there is a creation of verisimilitude, the function of which is to imbue the narrative with the plausibility which in turn determines the artistic and literary success of the coherence of the plot, the idiosyncrasies of the characters and the humour of the satire.

At which point, however, it is well to point out that there are different types of novel, and that in some it will indeed be impossible to sift the ethnographic realism, but nonetheless this objection neither affects the usefulness of the analytical divisions of narrator and author nor denies the possibility that in many cases – Zola and the Scott example – it is possible very quickly to identify the indicators which allow one to make a distinction between imagination in fiction and truth in fiction. In trying to elaborate what these conventions are, in other words showing how in general terms the contract between narrator and implied reader is initially negotiated and subsequently interpreted in the reading, I want to look briefly at two more problematic instances where the success of the novel – and I mean success according to the large Aristotelian criteria – depends very much not just on the reader's ability simultaneously to perceive both truth and fiction, but on the creative tension which the reader understands to lie in the juxtaposition of the two.

FACT AND FICTION WITHIN THE NOVEL: TWO EXAMPLES

I have recently been teaching E.M. Forster's *A Passage to India* to students on a course entitled 'India in English Literature', the very title of which brings into immediate focus an implied correspondence between fiction and reality. The novel is generally recognized as treating several major literary themes, as the numerous critical works about it testify, but what concerns us here is whether in addition to exploring these several themes, it is also intended as a description of social conditions or a social milieu. Is it ethnographic as Zola's novels are ethnographic? What is the contract, in other words, which Forster is drawing up with his readers? For many of my students, at least on first reading, it was clear that the contract required them to read the novel in the context of the nationalist struggle in India, and it was consequently a novel about politics, which had to be evaluated according to its engagement with politico-historical referents of the period. For them, then, it was a good novel because it exposed the nature of the relations of power in colonial society in India. And such an interpretation can find plausible justification in the text. My own recent rereading[2] of the novel, on the other hand, convinces me that the novel is less about politics and more about the difficulties of interpersonal relationships and cross-cultural understanding, and to support this view I would argue from the text using recognized conventions of literary criticism. The procedures are well known, and I mention them here simply as a reminder that among literary critics there often exist differences in the evaluation and interpretation of a work, but the grounds on which the argument should proceed are well established. As Leavis pointed out in a famous passage, the response of the critic to an interpretation with which she or he disagrees is not to deny the premise but to say 'Yes but ...' and then proceed to frame the textual references within a different cast from that of her or his interlocutor (1969: 47). Because of its subtlety and complexity, *A Passage to India* lends itself to just such arguments about interpretation. To take up again the particular issue with which we are concerned here, one of these arguments is about the reliability of Forster's descriptions as applied to colonial India.

In a recent informative introduction to the book, P.N. Furbank makes the point that on its first appearance representatives of the three groups at the centre of the novel – Anglo-Indians, Muslims, Hindus – all praised the book for its general accuracy but each criticized the way in which their own group had been represented (Furbank 1991: xv). In the same introduction Furbank notes that Forster had gone to some pains to ensure the 'accuracy' of the details he provided and had been irritated to discover that he had made a mistake about legal procedures (Furbank 1991: xv). Now the significance of these remarks bears directly on those assertions by Currie, Webster and Lamarque mentioned above, concerning the assumptions which writers and readers make of how a text is to be read. It is clear that in this case Forster did expect of himself as a narrator that he would set the narrative in an historical context which was true outside the text – for him there was unambiguously an *hors-texte* – and he regretted the errors that he made. Secondly, it is clear that readers did expect 'factual accuracy', and when that was shown to be wanting in their eyes this detracted from the book's merits.

Other critics have, however, pointed out that the 'inaccuracies', however much in error if taken to refer to the historical reality, are nonetheless true within the text: the fact that a subordinate Indian judge, for example, would not have been allowed to try a rape case, does not detract from the literary and aesthetic coherence of the narrative. Where, then, does that leave us with the use that we can make of Forster as a witness? Can we exploit the material in the same way as we might Zola? Or, as Sweeney argues, in general is it better not to use the material of the novel but to have recourse, where it exists, to the raw documentary evidence – the substance of the *enquêtes* in Zola's case perhaps – and, consequently, should we be looking not so much to *A Passage to India* but to Forster's journalism and his memoir, *The Hill of Devi*?

My own feeling is that, difficult as it may be in the case of Forster to make productive those easy epistemological distinctions (author/narrator; audience/reader), not only is it possible, but indeed it is required of the reader: holding fact and fiction together in tension, as suggested above, is at the operational centre of the novel. At one level – the description of a physical landscape or the layout of a room, the description of dress – the convention tacitly agreed upon by the writer and reader is that there is a direct correspondence to something lying beyond the novel; whether the description is accurate or not may be open to dispute, but is not of relevance here – the issue is the agreement that there is correspondence. When, however, there is a shift away from physical to psychological description, a description of behaviour, then it seems that we are immediately engaging a different set of rules. The first of these is that when the description is of a generic kind – this is the way all Anglo-Indians behave, this is a characteristic of Indian Muslims – the implicit convention is that the author/narrator (here I don't think one can distinguish between the two) is making two statements simultaneously, the first that the general description again corresponds to reality, the second that in the context of the fictive population of the novel the statement is plausible and therefore true within the fiction. The reader is then free to challenge the description at either level. Thus we see one reader criticizing the scene in the club where the members all stand up when Heaslop comes into the room as being absurdly not true to life, and at another level the critic arguing that the narrative thrust of the novel and the fictionally created situation make this credible within the novel.

At a still more complex level, however, where the writer is representing not some generic circumstance but a highly particularised incident created out of imagined characters and situations, then what we have is not information which is directly open to exploitation as supplementary ethnographic data, but an analysis or interpretation of experience which is potentially more profound. In *A Passage to India* the incident of the collar stud is precisely of this kind. Fielding, Aziz and Ronnie are highly individual characters and yet their attraction for readers lies not simply in their fictional roles but in a likeness – deliberately implied by the realistic incidental detail in the text – to people that the reader knows or might know: there is thus a hint of the generic, the representative, about them. The fabricated, fictional scene of the loss of the collar stud enables the reader to keep both the generic and the particular then in a creative tension: the response of each of the three – Aziz's spontaneity in parting with his own stud, Fielding's acceptance of the offer and Ronnie's condemnation of Aziz, which arises from Ronnie's ignorance of the true situation – is both in tune with what the reader knows of them as fictional characters and at the same time reveals a wealth of information about the nature of personal relationships and cultural values within colonial society.[3]

It does not seem to me to be open to doubt that this is what Forster intended and this is what the reader expects from *A Passage to India*. It is, however, very difficult to sort out at any particular point whether it is with an authorial or narrative voice that the writing is being conveyed and at what points precisely the reader is being asked to move from a fictive stance to a factual one and back again. The game being played is a complicated one and the rules are being refined during the playing of the game. Currie and the others were right then to make the distinctions they did, but they were perhaps unaware of the subtlety of the reading shifts which take place.

One more example of the complexity of unravelling the relationship between fact and fiction within the text of the novel and then we will be in a position to review what anthropologists should understand as constituting the novelist's consciousness. V. S. Naipaul's *The Enigma of Arrival*, published in 1987, was received with widespread critical acclaim, and by universal consent is accepted as being one of the finest novels of the last thirty years. It tells the story of a middle-aged man of Trinidadian origins who takes a cottage in Wiltshire for a time, and recounts his experiences, observations and reflections during his stay there. There is not much in the way of plot or incident and the power of the novel comes from the long lyrical descriptions of the landscape, the warm idiosyncratic portraits of the people of the country and the unfolding disclosure of the memories of thirty years.

There is, however, one major difficulty for the reader in knowing how to read the book: the rules of the contract are not clear. The book proclaims itself on the cover as 'A Novel'. But this confuses the situation even more. Why does it have to announce itself as a novel? After all, most novels do not find this necessary. Perhaps it is because Naipaul has written books of travel and there is a desire not to mislead the intending purchaser, but this can hardly be the case because the conventions of the two are dissimilar. At least they usually are, since the travel works are written in the first person and are immediately sited within specific historical and geographical locations. But indeed this is where the problem lies in this instance, for *The Enigma of Arrival* is written in the first person and has a very exact historical and geographical anchoring, which readers with even the slightest knowledge of Naipaul, gleaned, say, from a dust jacket, will recognize as identical to his own. Perhaps, then, it is the confusing use of what seems to be the autobiographical 'I' which has led to the explicit enunciation of its being a novel, but nonetheless there should be other indications that allow us to distinguish the travel book from the novel, and if there are not, or if the overt fictional reference is minimal, then there are extreme difficulties to be found in negotiations of the reading contract. According to Webster's account of Rabinowitz, what distinguishes the two – the autobiographical (and ethnographic too according to Webster) from the fictional – is the collapsing of the author and the narrator into the one individual (Webster 1982: 106). When there is this exact congruence we can read the narrative as factual. But *The Enigma of Arrival* proceeds in precisely this manner: there is exactly this collapsing and it is deliberate. The voice of first person narrator in this instance is not simply a device for the creation of verisimilitude, assisting the reader to a willing suspension of disbelief; it is to be taken as the authorial voice itself, and for Naipaul to claim otherwise, and to argue that the reader who sees the narrative as autobiographical is naive, is surely disingenuous. The piquancy of the book derives from the reader understanding how close an autobiographical account it is, not that the reader is looking for any specious titillation in seeing personal details of the author revealed, but because she or he is engaged in a direct encounter with the novelist's observations and analysis, an encounter which is direct because it is not articulated in a fictional guise and does not require epistemological unravelling.

The nearest work which we have to *The Enigma of Arrival* in English literature is Gissing's *The Private Papers of Henry Ryecroft*, where a similar situation is created – a writer retires to the English countryside and recounts his observations and reflections – and there is there, too, a wonderful evocation of Englishness juxtaposed with the particularities of a man's life. The difference between the two, however, resides in the deliberateness with which Gissing creates the fiction, making it clear to the reader – paradoxically, through the manipulation of verisimilitude:[4] an elaborate explanation, true to literary conventions of the time (compare Dr Watson's elaborate fictions) is provided for the discovery of the personal papers – that Ryecroft is a fantasy, what Gissing might like to have been. For those who know something of Gissing's unfortunate life the fantasy is a very poignant one, but the assumptions the reader is bringing to the text do depend on a suspension of disbelief, while *The Enigma of Arrival* with the profound ambiguity which hovers over the status of the narrator at the very least questions whether a 'fictive stance' from the reader is appropriate.

In fact the convention which Naipaul is exploiting here – the ambiguity of the ontological status of the first person narrator – although relatively uncommon in English literature,[5] at least in its extreme form, constitutes the definitive criterion of a whole subgenre of the novel in Japanese literature, the *shishosetsu*, or 'I' novel. It would be inappropriate to describe the *shishosetsu* at any length here – Fowler's prize-winning book *The Rhetoric of Confession* should be read by anyone interested in the subject – but it is worth remarking that the writing and reading of these novels involves writer and reader in the most extraordinary contortions of negotiating between fact and fiction.[6] There is, for example, one famous instance of a writer's incestuous relationship with his niece being written into a novel, thus revealing the relationship to the writer's family for the first time through the published work and then the account of the revelation forming the substance of the sequel (Fowler 1988: 110). One consequence of this often tortuous introspection is a critical confusion relating to how one should deal with the text, with the response of one set of critics and writers being to condemn the *shishosetsu* as leading to a creative dead-end in Japanese literature. Such a criticism has its echoes today in the strong attacks on reflexive anthropology for its self-indulgence, its navel-gazing and its failure to go beyond an excessive preoccupation with the self of the ethnographer.

CONCLUSION

The Enigma of Arrival is, then, a *shishosetsu* novel with the conventions of which Japanese readers would at least feel comfortable, even though some of the nuances might escape them – as I am sure, given the density of the novel, they escape many English readers, including myself. If the manner of reading *A Passage to India* required that in the juxtaposition of truth-in-fact and truth-in-fiction the stress should be placed on making fact congruent with the fiction – the reader constantly asking whether and how it is appropriate to apply historical and psychological knowledge to evaluate the imagined situations – the reverse is true of *The Enigma of Arrival* where the reading constantly demands an alertness to the way in which stylistic technique, deliberate literariness and occasional fiction affect the quality of the documentary statement. Indeed it seems to me that we read the latter according to those norms of critical caution which Geertz and Clifford and others recommend to us when we read ethnography, a caution which reminds us both of the epistemic context out of which the writings are produced as well as the rhetorical conventions by which the reader is being persuaded to the truth of the ethnographic narrative, that is, a truth which in the absence of corroborating evidence we have to take on trust, in the same way as we trust, after suspending our disbelief, a fictional narrative. In both cases it is only the internal logical consistency of the account as sustained by the rhetoric of the writing which can direct us.

When, for example, Geertz reminds us of the fundamental irony underlying the anthropologist's relationships in the field – the ambivalence of honesty and deception at the heart of the informant's rapport with the anthropologist – and how that irony remains an absent present in the subsequent writing, and should consequently affect our reading and evaluation of the ethnography (Geertz 1968), the remarks apply equally to any documentary account, written or visual, journalistic or academic, personal or scientific. They apply also to a reading of the realist novel from Zola to Naipaul.

As of course will not have escaped Geertz, irony and ambiguity are the major tropes held up to critical scrutiny by the New Critics in their explorations of the weave of literary texts and their subtle disclosure of the variety of ways and levels at which literature can work upon the consciousness of the reader through plot and character, metaphor and theme, revealed through imagery, symbolism, parallelism, analogy, drama, dialogue, affect, satire and parody. The New Critics would, of course, stop short of any suggestion that they were offering guidance on linking the text to any ethnographic or historical reality – Jane Austen's novels are not intended to help us to understand historical change – but, nonetheless, the lessons that anthropologists can draw from their examples of textual reading convey to the ethnographic reader something of the task involved.

Raymond Williams writes in *The Long Revolution* (1965: 304) that as a category the novel should be regarded not as a genre comparable with drama and poetry but as an equivalent to literature in the range and diversity of its genres.[7] With the growth and expansion of experimental novels, magical realism and 'faction', the comment seems particularly telling. The assumptions within the reading and the nature of the pact agreed upon by writer and reader become progressively more complex. Nonetheless, the ways in which we are invited to read are susceptible to certain procedural rules.

The examples considered above by no means exhaust the range of the novel's possibilities, but they do at least indicate some of the complexities. In each case, Zola, Forster, Naipaul, the realist premise which the author lays down is that the novel is intended to make some statement about a reality beyond the text. The way in which the statement is framed may differ from those statements contained in writing which is not avowedly fictional, but the novelists in all cases consider themselves to be making the same kind of observation as the non-fictional writers. The 'fictive stance' which Lamarque and others see as definitive of fiction does not, then, exist – at least not in the neat form represented – as far as either novelist or reader is concerned.

Within the one text, however, as it has been the burden of this chapter to demonstrate, there are different orders of statement, from the reportage of Zola (or of Dos Passos, Dreiser and George Moore) where, observing the usual conventions of reading, the descriptions can be read as corresponding to what is recorded by – to use Dos Passos' famous phrase – the camera eye, to the subtleties of Naipaul where the blend of fact and fiction require an excessive alertness to the deceptions of the positivist fallacy. But to leave the argument here, concluding simply that the novelist does indeed have something to say about the nature of human society which anthropologists would do well to attend to, even though it has required extensive demonstration, is limited and unsatisfactory. The consciousness of the novelist is not fully explained by recognizing the relationship between text and empirical reality. The deeper question is to ask what sort of consciousness the novelist is laying claim to when the statements are not about the empirically observable world. What, for example, to return to Forster, is the status of Forster's statement on the limits of intersubjectivity contained within the incident of the collar stud? To answer that, it seems to me, we should be probing more profoundly philosophical questions about the explanatory power of novels, about whether novelists claim that power and whether, within the contingent idiosyncratic circumstances they describe, any claim to explanation is justifiable, given both the artifice with which those contingent circumstances are subject to the novel's systemic commitment to closure, and the questionability of any claim to meta-discourse in these postmodernist times.

NOTES

My thanks to my colleagues at Eliot College, Roger Clark, Malcolm Andrews and Andrew Butcher, for their suggestions and the references they provided, and thanks also to Nigel Rapport for useful editorial comments.

1 Cf. Barthes, 'aucune écriture n'est plus artificielle que celle qui a prétendu dépeindre au plus près la nature' (quoted in Toffin 1989: 39), and the views of Nabokov as presented by Rorty (1989: 144–68), who takes issue with him.
2 It is important to note that as much as interpretations can differ between one reader and another, although both may be fully alive to the contractual conditions of reading, they may also differ from one reading to another.
3 My argument here is similar to the general one which Strickland makes about the statements contained in realist novels requiring to be evaluated against social reality (1983: 156–60).
4 Lennard Davis (1983) makes a similar point about this manipulation of verisimilitude in an earlier period of the novel's history where again assessing the correspondence between fact and fiction lies at the core of the novel's appeal.
5 There is a classic instance of it in the Dutch novel *Max Havelaar*.
6 It was exactly this kind of negotiation which characterized the early English novel according to Davis. It was this ambivalent reaction – an uncertainty to the factual or fictional reality of the work – that I am maintaining was one of the major components in the phenomenology of reading during the early eighteenth century (1983: 24).
7 Bakhtin (1981) makes the same point at greater length in an essay entitled 'Discourse in the Novel', showing how the novel appropriates other genres. In this respect he takes some apposite examples from Dickens.

REFERENCES

Bakhtin, M. M. (1981) *The Dialogic Imagination*, trans. C. Emerson and M. Holquist, Austin: University of Texas Press.
Banks, D. J. (1987) *From Class to Culture. Social Conscience in Malay Novels Since Independence*, Monograph Series 29/Yale University Southeast Asian Studies, Yale Centre for International and Area Studies, New Haven, Conn.
Barnes, Julian (1994) *Times Literary Supplement* 11 March: 16.
Booth, W. C. (1991) *The Rhetoric of Fiction*, 2nd edn, Harmondsworth: Penguin.
Bruner, E. M. (1993) 'Introduction'. in Paul Benson (ed.) *Anthropology and Literature*, Urbana and Chicago: University of Illinois Press.
Currie, G. (1984) 'What is fiction?', *The Journal of Aesthetics and Art Criticism*, XLIII (2): 385–92.
Davis, L. J. (1983) *Factual Fictions. The Origins of the English Novel*, New York: Columbia University Press.
Eliot, G. (1856) 'The natural history of German life', *Westminster Review*, LXVI (July): 51–79; pp. 266–99 in T. Pinney (ed.) *Essays of George Eliot*, London: Routledge & Kegan Paul, 1963.
Firth, R. (1947) 'Introduction', in Lin Yueh-Hwa, *The Golden Wing. A Sociologi-

cal Study of Chinese Familism, London: Kegan Paul, Trench, Trubner. (Reprinted by Greenwood Press, 1974: xi-xv.)

Fowler, E. (1988) The Rhetoric of Confession. Shishosetsu in Early Twentieth Century Japanese Fiction, Berkeley and Los Angeles: University of California Press.

Furbank, P. N. (1991) 'Introduction' to E. M. Forster, A Passage to India, London: Everyman's Library.

Gardner, K. (1991) Songs at the River's Edge, Stories from a Bangladeshi Village, London: Virago.

Gates, H. L. Jr (1984) 'Criticism in the jungle', pp. 1–24 in H. L. Gates Jr (ed.) Black Literature and Literary Theory, London and New York: Methuen.

Geertz, C. (1968) 'Thinking as a moral act: ethical dimensions of anthropological field work in the new states', Antioch Review, 28 (2): 129–58.

Gluckman, M. (1971) 'Introduction' in Elizabeth Bott, Family and Social Network, London: Tavistock. (Originally published in 1957.)

Grimshaw, A. (1992) Servants of the Buddha. Winter in a Himalayan Convent, London: Open Letters. (Now published by Prickly Pear Press.)

Jameson, F. (1983) The Political Unconscious. Narrative as a Socially Symbolic Art, London: Methuen.

Lamarque, P. (1989) 'Narrative and invention', pp. 131–53 in Cristopher Nash (ed.) Narrative in Culture. The Uses of Storytelling in the Sciences, Philosophy and Literature, London and New York: Routledge.

Leavis, F. R. (1969) English Literature in Our Time and the University, London: Chatto & Windus.

Lukács, G. (1964) Studies in European Realism, New York: Grosset & Dunlop.

Moeran, B. (1990) 'Beating about the brush: an example of ethnographic writing from Japan', in R. Fardon (ed.) Localizing Strategies. Regional Traditions of Ethnographic Writing, Edinburgh and Washington DC: Scottish Academic Press and Smithsonian Institution Press.

Naipaul, V. S. (1987) The Enigma of Arrival, London: Penguin Books.

Olsen, S. H. (1978) The Structure of Literary Understanding, Cambridge: Cambridge University Press.

Read, K. E. (1965) The High Valley, New York: Charles Scribner's Sons.

Rorty, R. (1989) Contingency, Irony and Solidarity, Cambridge: Cambridge University Press.

Shang, A. (1984) The Chinese in Britain, London: Batsford.

Strickland, G. (1983) Structuralism or Criticism? Thoughts on How We Read, Cambridge: Cambridge University Press.

Sweeney, A. (1989) 'The Malay novelist: social analyst or informant? Or neither?', RIMA (Review of Indonesian and Malaysian Affairs), Double Issue: 96–124 (Sydney).

Toffin, G. (1989) 'Écriture romanesque et écriture de l'ethnologie', L'Homme, XXIX (111–12): 34–49.

Turner, E. with Blodgett, W. Kahona, S. and Benwa, F. (1992) Experiencing Ritual, Philadelphia: University of Pennsylvania Press.

Watson, C. W. (1989) 'The experience of rural poverty in Malay novels', Modern Asian Studies, 23 (I): 25–47.

Watson, C. W. (1993) 'Perception from within: malign magic in Indonesian literature', in C. W. Watson and R. Ellen (eds) Understanding Witchcraft and Sorcery in South-East Asia, Honolulu: University of Hawaii Press.

Watson, H. (1992) Women in the City of the Dead, London: Hurst & Company.

Webster, S. (1982) 'Dialogue and fiction in ethnography', *Dialectical Anthropology*, 7 (2): 91–114.

Williams, R. (1965) *The Long Revolution*, Harmondsworth: Penguin.

Zola, E. (1986) *Carnet d'enquêtes. Une ethnographie inédite de la France*, Textes établis et présentés par Henri Mitterand, Paris: Plon.

Part II

Chapter 5

Dreaming as social process, and its implication for consciousness

David Riches

Is it possible that without fantasies, visions, and dreams, an individual could emerge or exist – I mean a being who is someone without being Everything?

(Caillois 1965: 52)

INTRODUCTION

Dreaming is unconscious behaviour which includes striking imagery of social events. Or, dreaming is the continuation of social action by other means. Thus put, dreaming invites complementary investigation from the experimental *and* social sciences. Yet a meeting of minds as between the two sides has barely occurred. For the experimental sciences (from molecular science through to cognitive science, and taking in psychoanalytic approaches), dreaming amounts to a fundamental human behaviour. But in anthropology and sociology it has been largely regarded as something incidental – as something, moreover, which may be discussed as if scientific appreciations (apart from Freud and Jung) did not exist. The problem, of course, is that the sciences approach dreaming as if it were a universal phenonenon, and their explanations are couched in a distinctively Western discourse. Meanwhile, anthropologists (in the main) offer relativistic appreciations, emphasising the influence of culture on dreaming, ranging from how dreaming is construed through to the meanings people attribute to particular dream imagery (e.g. Tedlock 1987; Jedrej and Shaw 1992).[1] This perspective would want to add that even the category of dreaming is culturally relative.

In this chapter I explore dreaming in a way that a meeting of minds might occur. This means that a universalistic approach to dreaming will be retained: the quest is for a theory of dreaming which would hold good cross-culturally. At the same time, in the vein of interpretivist social science, due account will be given to people's (cultural) experience of dreaming. This agenda clearly requires a methodology where various analytical tools will be deployed, and a central aim in this chapter is to demonstrate the worth of certain distinctively *anthropological* tools. There is, of course, a tension here – which I believe occurs, one way or another, in all anthropological discussion. On the one hand I seek to deconstruct Western (including, by implication, Western scientific) notions of dreaming; on the other hand to do so I use concepts and procedure from a Western academic discipline. I think, at this point, the anthropologist puts the onus on the reader to say whether an intellectually compelling account has been provided. As regards my endeavours in this chapter, I should add that in other publications, in discussions on such topics as power (Riches 1985) and violence (Riches 1991), I have addressed similar methodological issues with similar anthropological tools. In what follows, among the tools employed will be notions of ideology and rites of passage and the distinction between operational and representational models. The rewards are a theory of dreaming as social process and speculations on the place of dreaming in the development of consciousness.

DREAMING: THE PHENOMENON

At the outset some ground assumptions must be provided as to what dreaming, as a phenomenon, is, and how it relates to 'neighbouring' phenomena. Care must be exercised here both because of the contaminations of Western discourse and because in all cultures, as I briefly discuss latter, notions to do with dreaming are particularly susceptible to ideological manipulation. But one has to break into the topic somehow.

First I presume that 'dreaming' is a respectable category. It corresponds to *something* worthy of anthropological elucidation, and it is the job of this chapter to establish what this 'something' is. This something will not correspond with Western ideas about dreaming as a phenomenon, nor can it correspond to notions, such as prevail in some non-Western cultures, where a differentiation is refused as between what might commonsensically be termed dreaming and other, quite different experiences – for example, Australian Aboriginal conceptions in which dreaming is classed as myth. Just as it is valid to deconstruct the Western ideas (by so doing, explaining them), so also must it be valid to deconstruct those of the Australian Aborigines.

Second, dreaming refers to a cross-reality experience. The context to this is that people's sense of reality is not seamless: as conscious life unfolds people slip from reality to reality. Some of this slipping may be deemed 'routine', such as when people pass from dreaming to a this-world reality, or when, during awakeness, people pass from a this-world reality to a reality of imagination. (By 'this-world reality' I mean the reality you are currently experiencing as you read these words.) Other slipping is induced, for example the passing into or out of the so-called altered states of consciousness stimulated by drugs or trance. One recognizes that all (I had better say, nearly all) such *classes* of reality are culturally framed, yet I am going to presume that from the standpoint of *individual* experience two discriminations implied here are universally valid. The first is between awake and asleep as objective states. This discrimination rests on the observation (which, I contend, everyone – everywhere – entertains) that people behave differently when awake from when asleep – this observation refers to the elementary difference between mobility versus long-term immobility. (Again, should this discrimination be refused I would suspect this is an ideological expression, and would seek to explain its social basis.) The second is a discrimination corresponding to the boundary between sleep and awake. I assert that people's subjectivity of the nocturnal/diurnal rhythm is not seamless – that upon waking there is, in this regard, a perception of qualitative change, and that, moreover, this perception incorporates in some essential way the feeling that such qualitative change lies outside one's control. The relation between the objective and subjective discriminations here is, I shall show, the basis for cultural elaborations on a notion of dreaming.

The question arises as to the relationship between the different realities which people subjectively experience. I would suggest that the fundamental issue here is not (for example) that individuals' experiences relating to one reality can influence the way they act in another, but that individuals 'in' one reality can know of the existence of, and recollect experiences in, another. I am interested in circumstances where an individual's awareness of another reality is (in the reality presently being experienced) given conceptual recognition. Dreaming, I contend, must be approached from this standpoint. To do the English word justice we may say that 'dreaming' is the stipulation, in this-world reality, of an(other) reality associated with sleep. Dreaming, in short, is a concept in the discourse of cross-reality experience.[2]

In my opinion not to address dreaming as a function of this-world reality is to render the concept, dreaming, pointless. For example, to examine the reality experienced during sleep in its own terms and from an 'internal' standpoint might be a perfectly respectable endeavour. But to call such an examination an investigation into dreaming, or dreams, would be to distort it from the outset, since 'dreaming' is a concept from a different reality. And this moves me to a crucially important point. This is that to equate the reality of sleep with dreaming is presumptuous: by dreaming all that is *necessarily* connoted is an experience which implicates sleep. To make an *equation* (even a partial equation) of 'dreaming' and sleep would be to beg the questions of what dreaming as an experience actually is and what sleep as an experience actually is. As we shall see, it is precisely the relation between these two that is at issue. Here I will only say that dreaming as social process relates to the way in which the individual, upon waking, senses a move into a new reality – the reality of 'this world'; and I use the word 'sense' to hint at the fundamental salience of dreaming, in terms of which this social function is important: the salience of consciousness.

Dreaming, then, is a form of knowledge. There are theoretical and substantive problems relating to knowledge and, with regard to dreaming, I have alluded to both already. It is necessary to review them now, regarding three points – the first theoretical and the second two substantive. The theoretical problem was hinted at when I spoke, above, of the individual, upon waking, *sensing* a move into a new reality. What sort of knowledge is implied by the notion of sensing? In other publications (Riches 1985; 1991) I have found Caws' distinction (1974) between operational and representational models useful for basing a distinction between two levels of knowledge, together with their respective functions. Representational 'knowledge' amounts to a considered reflection (concerning some phenomenon) on how things are; precisely because it is sustained through intellectual endeavour such knowledge is normally enshrined as what might be called overt culture. Operational 'knowledge', in contrast, amounts to an appreciation (of some phenomenon) at its moment of occurrence; such knowledge, also cultural, is tacitly held. The notion of 'sensing' clearly corresponds to the latter form of knowledge. I deploy these notions later. Here I shall simply reiterate my opinion, argued at length elsewhere (Riches 1991), that representational knowledge has an ideological function, and that operational knowledge may well refer to experiences which hold good *cross*-culturally.

The substantive matters relating to dreaming as a form of knowledge are of two kinds, firstly concerning the distinction between dreaming and dreams, secondly on the matter of distinguishing dreaming from sleep. 'Dreaming' expresses a type of experience, in this case the cross-reality experience associated with waking. 'Dreams', in contrast, refers to the particular imagery in which this (cross-reality) experience is manifest. Put crudely, we might say that dreams are the content of dreaming. That this distinction is subjectively valid comes from the fact that everyone knows, from everyday discussion, about the dreaming experience, but when observing a particular person dreaming (as they believe), they do not presume to know what his or her dream images exactly are.[3] The priority, and most especially, the relation between dreaming and dreams is something I discuss in the final section, when I speculate on the part played separately by both in the development of consciousness. I need say here only that this chapter is specifically concentrated on the topic of dreaming, which means that what it has to say may be taken in some measure as a complement to academic discussion, especially in psychoanalytic theory, which focuses on dream imagery.

A final word. In this chapter I shall be working to establish a connection between dreaming and sleep. I have already stated that to make an equation between the two, or to presume a particular relationship, would be precisely to beg the question. As the argument unfolds I shall be embracing some types of connection and rejecting others. It may be helpful if I clarify some conventions at the outset:

1 Dreaming is *associated with* sleep. This leaves the nature of the connection unspecified and, by implication, still to be revealed.
2 Dreaming occurs *during* sleep. This asserts a temporal overlap as between the two: 'dreaming' and 'sleeping' may be presumed to be essentially independent statuses, dreaming always occurring *while* the individual sleeps.
3 Dreaming is *intrinsic* to sleep. This asserts that dreaming is constituted in sleep: dreaming is an inherent part of the nature of sleep.

THE WESTERN DISCOURSE ON DREAMING

The way *dreaming* is described from society to society would seem, at first glance, to indicate that this does not correspond with a universal experience. To cite the classic contrast, in some cultures it is construed as a harmless, and essentially passive, fantasy, in others it reflects a deadly serious out-of-body experience. The task in this section is to deal with the Western cultural notions about the nature of dreaming, some of which stem from academic science, which may contaminate the exposition, in this chapter, of dreaming as social process. By dealing with these cultural assumptions I shall reiterate the way in which dreaming is a universal experience.

The key observation about Western ideas is that they are expressed in terms of idioms in which dreaming is intrinsic to sleep (in its duration). Dreaming *is* some sort of an experience during sleep, Western notions say. Western scientific theories play on this in that they generally posit sleep as time when, through dreams, the human mind/body is, on behalf of the awake existence, in some manner refreshed. For example, neurological theories hold that in dreams overload in the brain, built up from the awake existence, is processed and eliminated (e.g. Crick and Mitcheson 1983); cognitive science considers that dreaming enhances the individual's unconscious capacity to be a conscious meaning-maker (e.g. Foulkes 1985: 201–2); Freudian theory famously considers that in dream imagery disguise and resolution are given to the individual's often contradictory (daytime) desires.

All this is in contradiction with the nature of dreaming as experience, outlined earlier, in which dreaming, in its constitution, is understood as referring to a vantage point within this-world reality.

I propose that dreaming, (culturally) deemed as an experience during, or intrinsic to, sleep, is *representational knowledge*. I argue elsewhere

(Riches 1985) that representational knowledge has an ideological function: through representational knowledge people interpret their participation in events in an acceptable moral light. The ideology of dreaming is something I shall explore, later in the chapter, with reference to both Western and non-Western culture. The point to recall now is that, at another level, dreaming may be approached as operational knowledge and, at this other level, the pertinence of dreaming can be different. This tacit, or 'situational', level may unequivocally relate to the waking moment. From this perspective dreaming is the *sensing of images at the moment of waking which are recognizably human social events*. I commented earlier that, in contrast to representational knowledge, which is normally culturally relative, operational knowledge may well be universal knowledge. In the remainder of the chapter dreaming as social process will be explored in this operational sense.

Before moving on it is worth dealing with the fact that Western lay and scientific understandings were for long confident that their appreciations of dreaming were addressing a human universal inherent to sleep because of the existence of universally occurring REM (rapid eye movement) periods during sleep, coupled with the fact that, upon being wakened during an REM period, the individual reports dreaming occurring. (REM phases in sleep are periods when the sleeper is in a relatively acute state of physiological arousal.) However, the inference that REM reflects dreaming actually going on has recently come to be questioned within the scientific community itself (Foulkes 1985: 201–2). And this, in turn, given that most animals display REM, has implications for whether or not dreaming is uniquely human – I think it is. The likelihood is that reports of dreaming when people are awakened from REM sleep have to do with the moment of awakening rather than REM sleep itself, and that the latter functions merely in regard to the purely physical aspects of the boundary between sleep and awake (see Snyder 1966). One notes that philosophers of dreaming seem never to have been particularly convinced by the so-called REM evidence (e.g. Squires 1973; Dunlop 1977).

DREAMING AS SOCIAL PROCESS

From the standpoint of Weberian sociology what is uniquely human is that people engage in purposive social action. What is experienced as dreaming very commonly – often strikingly – incorporates the imagery of social events, and this being so, a provisional supposition is that the function of dreaming (in an operational sense) has something to do with social action in general and with an associated arena of social relations. As to what such a function might be we have been invited to attend to the *moment* at which dreaming is consciously experienced – the moment of waking. I shall presume that the moment of waking is a problematic occasion in the overall flux of human experience, and that dreaming in some way relates to, or resolves, such an occasion. In short, dreaming relates to the boundary between a certain 'other-world' experience and 'this-world' experience; this boundary, one surmises, importantly implicates the flow of social action. When I speak of 'dreaming as social process' I have these issues in mind. Note that this statement is built around the fundamental assumptions, outlined earlier, that people (everywhere) know of a distinction between asleep and awake, and also experience a reality shift corresponding with the moment of awakening.

Before starting the account of dreaming as social process it must be accepted that, in the event, dreaming is qualitatively different from (this-world) social action: it might incorporate the imagery of social events but even as it is consciously experienced it is not willed. (I discussed this earlier.) Moreover there is another difference. A (waking) experience of dreaming may be an entirely private experience (see Binswangen 1984). People may or may not report their dreams, and their decision in this regard is a mix of cultural and motivational influences, but the point is, unreported dreaming is no less valid than reported dreaming: speaking personally, I know that dreaming is a salient experience even when I choose not to disclose it. The analysis of dreaming in this chapter precisely revolves around people's experience, and therefore such 'private dreaming' cannot be discounted. The upshot is that dreaming will have to be treated *as if* it is social action. This means that analysis will proceed first by construing dreaming as social action, and second by correcting the account thus provided for the fact that, in certain important respects, it is not. Therefore the remainder of this section is effectively in two parts.

Dreaming, which we may now construe (by way of definition) as the waking experience of just-occurred social action, is, for human beings, a distinctive experience. It is different in kind from the 'this-world' experience that succeeds it; it is also different in kind from the 'other-world' experience (sleep) which precedes it. Recall that within our framework of operational knowledge we are resisting saying that this preceding experience and dreaming experience are one and the same. We may be confident that the individual knows that there exists such an 'other-world' experience simply through observing others sleeping, and by having been told that she or he sleeps. Conceivably, such sleeping experience is totally empty, but it is certainly different from that which *it* follows (awakeness) and from that which succeeds it (i.e. dreaming). To put it bluntly, the individual, by simple observation, distinguishes the states of asleep and awake and from personal experience knows of a brief intermediary experience corresponding to (awakening) dreaming. Parallels with the tripartite scheme of rites of passage come to mind at this juncture, especially if we insist (a little boldly) that awakening dreaming is in some sense, for all humans, a *remarkable* experience.

To review in very basic terms: rites of passage classically mark occasions in the life cycle when a person formally comes to take up new rights and responsibilities and to drop others; the person whose standing is thus being changed is the focus of the ritual. Going through the ritual amounts to a brief interruption in the person's incumbency in normal social statuses. As is well known, van Gennep adduced three distinct phases in virtually all rituals of this sort: a phase of separation, a phase of segregation and a phase of incorporation. Separation and incorporation respectively symbolize the initiate's removal from a previous social status and his or her implantation in a new one. Meanwhile segregation symbolizes a logical, sacred interim when the initiate is, so to say, statusless. Turner developed this. In his view, in the segregation phase, characterized by him as exemplifying a state of liminality, the experience is briefly given of 'communitas', the primeval sociality which makes the very constitution of society possible (van Gennep 1960; Turner 1969). There is, it may be proposed, a formal parallel between, on the one hand, awakening dreaming and, on the other hand, rites of passage in general and the segregation/liminal phase in particular.

The salience of the rite of passage in human society must be explored, and it is important for the argument about dreaming that at least some anthropological wisdom be laid out and questioned. This can be done in very simple terms. Certain received views about rites of passage reflect the methodology of structural-functionalism. Without the rite of passage, this perspective avers, there could be confusion at crucial times over precisely which standing in society a given person enjoyed. Specifically, in the context of change in social status, rites exist in order to obviate conceptual ambiguity in the individual's social position, in the segregation phase symbolically rendering the individual 'statusless' at the very instant of change. However this argument is not convincing. In particular, such is the complexity of human society that in the run of everyday affairs confusion over people's social standing is, in fact, both unceasing and inevitable: the art of social conduct precisely revolves around being able to pick up cues by which someone's social position (or, more often, the relevant position from among the many in which the individual could be incumbent) may be figured out. In any event, in some societies, people shift to a completely fresh status without the ritual marking, and chaos does not ensue.

The very nature of the activities to which people submit themselves in rites of passage, especially in the segregation/liminal phase, suggests an alternative account. Not only are these activities 'time out' from the flow of everyday affairs, they are also typically spectacularly so. The adolescent initiates of an African community, due to be secluded for a period in the bush, abruptly disappear from the village *en bloc*. At harvest ceremonies, marking the passage of time, men and women swap roles. Noise, movement, colour are commonly extravagant. From this, it may be suggested that rites of passage exist not specifically, or totally, to organize the passage, but as a medium of public communication: through the rite the community at large is being *made* to know that the social position of one or several people is being radically altered. Broadcasting and public relations purposes are being served: through the ritual's extraordinary and compelling events, a change in status is, by cultural fiat, advertised far and wide. This interpretation means that the supposed logical relation between a rite's three phases may be illusory: the separation and incorporation phases may stand as a pair, probably, indeed, representing the change in status; meanwhile, superimposed on this duality is the 'segregation' phase, triumphantly announcing that the deed is being done.

Dreaming, as an experience (of the waking moment) is, we are bold to say, a 'time out' experience where the extraordinary occurs. From what has been said it effectively stands between two unexceptional, though arguably fundamental social statuses – asleep and awake. This being so, the question arises as to whether the theoretical discussion about rites of passage can generate a hypothesis of why dreaming occurs. Not directly, it must be insisted, for, the moment an explanation of dreaming is asked for, dreaming's proper status, as potentially private and partially unconscious behaviour, must be conceded. In other words, once the question is posed, the treatment of dreaming as if it were a 'normal' experience, albeit of a particularly distinctive type, has to be abandoned. To be productive in the argument, as soon as the focus shifts to dreaming as such any proposition about rites of passage in human society has to be transformed. Fortunately the discussion (above) about the theoretical possibilities of rites of passage allows just such a transformation to be mooted. Where the explanation of dreaming is concerned, the notion that rites of passage serve to publicize, advertise and communicate certainly cannot hold: whatever people announce afterwards (if they choose), the experience of dreaming, as it occurs (at the waking moment), is closed and private. I suggest that, if dreaming is to be deemed as in some manner analogous to a rite of passage, it may be worth reverting to the ideas inspired by structural-functionalism. I propose that dreaming functions to obviate confusion – a personal and private confusion – relating to the passage from asleep to awake. The transformation logic behind such a proposal is:

- *Rites of passage* facilitate widespread public awareness of something which the intitiate, acceding to a new status, knows well.
- *Dreaming* facilitates an inner private awareness of something which the awakener, rising from sleep, knows barely at all.

In the case of dreaming we must ask, then, what it is that the awakener knows barely at all.

Here we attend to the nature of the dreaming experience, and to the evident paradox about dreaming, in operational knowledge. Albeit that dreaming is a (momentary) waking experience it evokes a string of events proceeding through time and culminating in the waking moment. The question arises as to why the liminal moment between asleep and awake should be marked by specifically this sort of evocation. The evident correlation between the evocation (of time flow) and the observable fact of sleeping (which consumes time) suggests that, on behalf of the awakener, dreaming performs a symbolic function: it represents the passage of time during sleep. (Note: I am not saying here that dreaming is *in* sleep; this is part of most cultures' representational knowledge of dreaming, which I consider later.)

As to what it is that the awakener, arising from sleep, knows barely at all, and to which this symbolic function of dreaming may respond, we draw out the *social* nature of the states of asleep and awake. The key point here is that sleep, as is known from observing others, is a time of social uncertainty – at least, social uncertainty in relation to this-world reality. One's sleep is a time when others are potentially socially active.

Here I am arguing that the relation between awakeness and sleep is context for the relation between sleep and dreaming. Sleep amounts to 'time out' from the awake world, and this has implications for effective social strategy. In the interim between successive periods of awakeness the 'world' will have moved on – others have probably gained advantage. The 'time out' nature of sleeping (as against the awake) means that, potentially, the awakening sleeper has no sense of this passage of time; indeed the awakening sleeper may not even realize that she or he has been asleep. An individual is ill placed beneficially to interact with the social world who, upon waking, is unable to appreciate that a stretch of time, potentially crammed with events, has been missed. I argue that dreaming as social process has as its function to obviate such social disadvantage. In its symbolic relation to sleep, dreaming, thanks to the strung-out images it enshrines, connotes the period of time elapsement and so, in the consciousness of the awakener, signals his or her immediate social predicament: the individual recognizes both that sleep has occurred *and* the social implications of this occurrence.

DREAMING AND DREAMS

Dreaming, then, socially orients the person in respect of the waking moment and on behalf of the this-world experiences that immediately follow. Three familiar properties of *dreams* are consonant with this hypothesis. The first relates to the fact that, since dreaming fulfils functions in relation to the waking moment, once that moment has passed its job is done. Cultures may variously resist or encourage it, but there is a psychological propensity for dreams rapidly to be forgotten, or, indeed, to be only subliminally known (this corresponds with the fact that upon waking people quite commonly declare that they have not been dreaming – see note 3). Second, what is dreamed in dreams must tally with this. So that *immediate* practicalities relating to this-world events be inherently neither directed nor diverted by dream occurrences, these latter will, upon waking, be rapidly recognizable as chaotic, fantastic and far fetched; in short, notwithstanding the meanings, including meanings on behalf of future action, which in some societies may be read into dream images, dream occurrences must be recognizable as that which they are – as dreams. Third, what is dreamed in dreams must, at the same time, be significant to the waking individual: dreams must *be* recognized. The dream is remembered as fantastic, but for it fully to command attention the person of the dreamer must, in dreaming imagery, be centre stage; dreaming imagery will feature momentous *personal* occurrences (D'Andrade 1961).

These remarks about the nature of *dreams* imply dreaming as *context*: dreaming provides a rationale in terms of which dreams – at least, certain aspects of dreams – may be explicated (see later for further discussion on this relationship). But can one say any more? – for example about the specifics, rather than the broad properties, of dream imagery, i.e. about why particular dream images crop up? What one should say about the specifics of dream imagery is that they are 'doubly private'. Dreaming itself, as mentioned earlier, is a private experience in that, as it occurs, it is valid as an experience even when unreported; yet, it has also been said, such privacy is tempered by the fact that everyone knows that everyone else has 'dreaming ability'. It is this dreaming ability, as a general experience, that this chapter has addressed. However, with specific dream images, one cannot begin to second guess another person's experiences as they are occurring. Thus the specifics of dream imagery is not something which an interpretive anthropology can address: an interpretive anthropology relies on the anthropologist empathizing with the informant's experience. As to where this leaves an understanding of specific dream images as such, this is something I briefly look at in the final section. Of course dreamers quite often report the specifics of their dreams, replete with cultural gloss. But this is another matter from why particular dreams crop up. In any event, dream reporting occurs in an ideological context which controls the manner of the reporting, as we shall now see.

REPRESENTATIONAL KNOWLEDGE AND DREAMING

I have argued that dreaming, an experience of the waking moment, connotes the sleep that has gone on and the events that have been missed.

Thus construed dreaming reflects operational knowledge – knowledge that is tacit and which has, one might say, a pragmatic function (see above); the capacity for such knowledge, we suspect, is universal to humankind. But in my culture I am told that dreaming is different from this: dreaming is something intrinsic to sleep – dreaming is an inherent component of what sleep is. I argued (again, in an earlier section) that this amounts to representational knowledge, and that such knowledge, varying strikingly from culture to culture, has an ideological function. When people, upon reflection, report their dreams in glorious detail – which one supposes they do for strategic purposes, if only to convey something about the sort of person they are – it may be assumed that this ideological function is crucially the context in terms of which the dream's non-private meaning should be read.

But what precisely is the ideological function that dreaming, as representational knowledge, fulfils? I have argued elsewhere (Riches 1985) that representational knowledge (in general) comprises knowledge in terms of which individuals may put a positive moral gloss on the actual or anticipated outcome of events in which they have participated or will be participating. This being so, we can say that dreaming as representational knowledge, as a culturally-mediated enunciation, reflects some aspect of a moral appreciation of the human social situation.

Here the interesting contrast is between societies such as my own, for which dreaming is *intrinsic* to sleep, and those others for whom dreaming occurs *during* sleep. The salient point about this contrast is that, in the former, dreaming, at least at first glance, is culturally construed as fantasy, that is to say, as of no great significance with regard to people's relations to one another in this-world reality. Such a construction is underpinned by the fact that sleep, itself, is deemed to be a period of social inertness – as, effectively, an empty reality. (Simple observation of others sleeping can rather easily support this sort of interpretation of sleep.) With the latter type of society we are dealing with the well-known notion that dream imagery reflects the experience of the soul as, during sleep, it is lost to the body. In such circumstances the soul is considered to be able to secure knowledge and/or influence events to the individual's advantage, an activity which to others, in this-world reality, is completely invisible. Research would no doubt tally up the one ideology of dreaming with a particular mode of social organization and the other with another, rather different mode. To ideologically construe dreaming as mere fantasy officially announces that during sleep social activity is suspended, whilst the opposite is the case when dreaming denotes notions of soul loss. The circumstances of my own society, specifically its individualistic ethos, invite the proposition that dreaming construed as fantasy is to be connected to the moral idea that competitive activity ostensibly invisible to others is inappropriate. It follows that dreaming construed as soul loss may reflect an apprehension of competitiveness in societies where individual-ism is ethically downplayed.

DREAMING AND CONSCIOUSNESS

The aim of the chapter is to indicate where, with regard to the study of dreaming, a rapprochement with the interests of science might lie. Unfortunately, Western scientific approaches are embedded in a peculiarly Western cultural appreciation of dreaming (as something intrinsic to sleep), so I want to develop a 'scientific' perspective which at least does not take in this assumption. The anthropological account of dreaming as social process, showing that dreaming is adaptive with regard to social action, basically deals with the psychological experience of dreaming (in this chapter, *shared* operational knowledge pertaining to dreaming is not shown to contradict the individual's *personal* experience[4]). Therefore I am led to develop a scientific account which focuses on the relation between dreaming and consciousness itself. The context to this discussion is the Weberian notion that a defining feature of what human beings do is purposive social action, and that such purposive social action is therefore the function of consciousness. As a preliminary we must briefly return to the distinction between dreaming and dreams, and deal with the ques-tion, more than once anticipated earlier, of the priority between them. Here I reiterate that dreaming is context for dreams: the experience of a (general) sense of dreaming is a precondition for specific dream images. The reverse cannot hold. The general category of 'dreaming' (as opposed to 'sleeping', or 'being awake', or whatever) cannot derive, via the human propensity to classify, from the accumulated experiences of dream images, since the general category is required in order that dream images may be recognized as such. Therefore a scientific account of dreaming and dreams should ultimately explicate them as separate entities, and incor-porate this priority.

The discussion begins with the generally relativistic nature of conscious-ness itself: consciousness is a relation between an identity and a reality. An individual's sense of engagement in what they do (consciousness), their self awareness (identity) and the world they take for granted (reality) are all, in this sense, mutually defining – and so inherently shifting and ungrounded. I suggest that dreaming in fact provides the required grounding, and therefore is a condition of consciousness.[5] We shall see that this suggestion is inspired by theoretical argument in soci-ology and anthropology which states that one's identity is determined in opposition to some 'other'.

The reasoning about the significance of dreaming is founded in the fact that dreaming reality, unlike other forms of reality, is biologically, and unitarily, given. It therefore provides a bedrock reality against which other (waking) realities (including, and especially, this-world reality) may ultimately be defined and contrasted. Experientially valid upon waking, yet not inherently contaminating subsequent realities, dreaming anchors other realities, and therefore identity and consciousness.

But a defining feature of dreaming is that it incorporates imagery which is recognizably of human activity – importantly, often *social* activity. The explanation of dreaming, as relating to a capacity for consciousness, does not yet specifically account for this, and will be fully convincing only when it does. Here I suggest that dreaming, if it is to make possible a capacity for consciousness, must convey the rationale for consciousness, namely purposive social action. Dreaming as social process, where dreaming incorporates social imagery, precisely does *convey* such purposiveness. In its social imagery dreaming *comprises* purpose – that of socially readying the awakening sleeper. Being embodied as a process which brings strategic reward, dreaming enhances a capacity for consciousness which is *appropriate* to that which is constitutive of human social life – social action.

We finally explicate dreaming and dreams as separate entities (with dreaming prior to dreams), and to do so propose, on the basis of the argument offered in this chapter, an evolutionary scenario. This incorporates a sequence of selective logic pertaining to the development of dreaming as a bedrock reality on behalf of consciousness. Note, however, that an *evolutionary* scenario, which argues for a specific type of relation between dreaming and dreams, requires that these concepts be recast a little. The synchronic account of the relation between dreaming and dreams, provided so far, allows the notion of dreaming to take in some of the features of dreams (e.g. imagery of social action) – in order that, through the general category 'dreaming', dreams may be recognized as such. An evolutionary account, where dreaming has priority, cannot admit this. I suspect that the evolutionary relation between dreaming and dreams, which I now lay out, may illustrate a general process by which, in human cognition, categories are developed – through metaphor. This links into the work of J. Fernandez (e.g. 1986).

1 The development of consciousness selects for individuals with a capacity, upon waking, to *sense* the elapsement of a passage of socially relevant time. Such a sense of elapsed time is realized through a linear sequence of striking images which may be purely visual in nature. This experience may be called dreaming. To label dreaming a liminal experience (see earlier) is rather appropriate in view of its fundamental evolutionary significance.

2 The worth of being able to sense that socially relevant time has elapsed during sleep selects for individuals with the capacity to experience a string of striking *social* images which *correspond with, and connote, this*

sense. In this chapter these images have been called dreams. Here the notion of 'select' underscores the supposition that the development of dream imagery is causally independent of the capacity to 'sense' time elapsement during sleep; therefore, one might say, in this evolutionary context, that dreams are *symbolic* of dreaming. It may be that the evolutionary precondition for a capacity for both (awakening) dreaming and dream imagery is the human's capacity for physiological excitement during sleep manifest already in the REM phases of sleep.

If the view of dreaming offered in this chapter is fundamental in the evolutionary manner just sketched, it is plausible to assert that other theories of dreaming, specifically the scientific approaches I have briefly (and indequately) touched upon, are contingent on this view, i.e. that the other approaches address processes in the human being which are epiphenomenal in relation to the 'social' and 'consciousness' worth of dreaming outlined here. Leaving aside the Western cultural assumptions unsurprisingly built into these scientific approaches, we may want to say that dreaming as, for example, facilitating a capacity for information processing, or dealing with overload in the brain, is supplementary to its purpose relating to a capacity for consciousness. In this way there may well be complementarity between these scientific approaches and the view of dreaming offered here.

NOTES

1 Kuper's demonstration that dreams have mythic structures and so may be amenable to *structuralist* dismemberment is a fascinating piece – anthropological, yet within the scientific genre. But his concern, in any event, is not centrally with why people dream.

2 A side issue: this does not prevent the heading, 'dreams'/'dreaming' being deployed to label discussions on the content of dreams. This is an entirely different concern from the one in this chapter which is about the phenomenon of dreaming itself.

3 According to virtually all theories of dreaming, including the one offered in this chapter, dreaming is in some manner fundamental for the human constitution; so it follows that everyone dreams, even if, in the case of not a few people, the experience is commonly, or always, a subliminal one.

4 Under the heading of cognition, Bloch has discussed what, in my opinion, is effectively operational knowledge, and, by reference to discussion in developmental psychology, has argued for its universality (Bloch 1985).

5 At this level of argument there are certain parallels, worth further research, with Foucault's idea that dreaming is a condition of imagination and a centre of becoming (Foucault 1984).

REFERENCES

Binswangen, L. (1984) 'Dream and existence', *Review of Existential Psychology and Psychiatry*, 19(1): 79–104.

Bloch, M. (1985) 'From cognition to ideology', in R. Fardon (ed.) *Power and Knowledge*, Edinburgh: Scottish Academic Press.

Caillois, R. (1965) 'Logical and philosophical problems of the dream', in G. von Gunebaum and R. Caillois (eds) *The Dream and Human Societies*, London: Cambridge University Press.

Caws, P. (1974) 'Operational, representational and explanatory models', *American Anthropologist* 76(1): 1–10.

Crick, M. and Mitcheson, G. (1983) 'The function of dream sleep', *Nature*, 304: 111–14.

D'Andrade, R. (1961) 'The effect of culture on dreams', in F. S. K. Hsu (ed.) *Psychological Anthropology: Approaches to Culture and Personality*, New York: Dorsey Press.

Dunlop, C. (ed.) (1977) *Philosophical Essays on Dreaming*, Ithaca: Cornell University Press.

Fernandez, J. (1986) *Persuasions and Performances: The Play of Tropes in Culture*, Chicago: University of Chicago Press.

Foucault, M. (1984) 'Dream, imagination and existence', *Review of Existential Psychology and Psychiatry* 19(1): 19–78.

Foulkes, D. (1985) *Dreaming: A Cognitive and Psychological Analysis*, Hillsdale, NJ: Erlbaum.

Jedrej, M.C. and Shaw, R. (eds) (1992) *Dreaming, Religion and Society in Africa*, Leiden: Brill.

Kuper, A. (1979) 'A structural approach to dreams', *Man*, 14(4): 663–83.

Riches, D. (1985) 'Power as a representational model', in R. Fardon (ed.) *Power and Knowledge*, Edinburgh: Scottish Academic Press.

Riches, D. (1991) 'Aggression, war, violence: space/time and paradigm', *Man*, 26: 281–98.

Snyder, F. (1966) 'Towards an evolutionary theory of dreaming', *American Journal of Psychiatry* 123(2): 121–42.

Squires, R. (1973) 'The problem of dreams', *Philosophy*, 48: 245–59.

Tedlock, B. (ed.) (1987) *Dreams: Anthropological and Psychological Interpretations*, Cambridge: Cambridge University Press.

Turner, V. (1969) *The Ritual Process: Structure and Anti-structure*, Harmondsworth: Penguin.

van Gennep, A. (1960) *The Rites of Passage*, London: Routledge & Kegan Paul.

Chapter 6

Trance and the theory of healing
Sociogenic and psychogenic components of consciousness

Andrew Strathern

INTRODUCTION

British and American anthropological theorists have found a new meeting ground in the study of concepts of personhood and the processes by which these are negotiated in social practice. However, the old problem of the relationship between the psychic and the social, stemming equally from Durkheim and Freud, remains. It must also be faced in any discussion of 'questions of consciousness'. In referring to components of consciousness as psychogenic and sociogenic I clearly appeal to the old dichotomy, but in focusing on consciousness as a concept that encompasses both I intend to transcend that dichotomy.

Consciousness is a term which has been employed from time to time in anthropology but hardly as a systematic tool or analytical concept. I trace its current prominence to the recent convergence of interests on personhood. Whatever else personhood implies, it must include at least the idea of a thinking, intentional entity that therefore possessed agency and the capacity to choose certain forms of action as against others. Such a conglomerate idea cannot fail to depend on an idea of consciousness. Consciousness has also been a leading theme in the development of cognitive science and the study of the brain, where it appears usually in conjunction with theories of evolution and the emergence of humanity and thus fits into another stream of anthropological theorizing. When we attempt to utilize the term for cross-cultural ethnographic purposes, however, we face the question of variation: consciousness, agency and so on may be viewed very differently in different cultures. There is a further difficulty, also, in the fact that consciousness appears to be a mentalistic concept and as such is to some extent bound up with our own local historical concepts of mind versus body. To counter this tendency anthropologists have adopted the term embodiment, and there is currently a kind of post-personhood explosion of works which deal with the body and embodiment in diverse ways, all designed to redress an earlier mentalistic bias. Since trance and spirit possession are obviously examples of 'embodied mentality' it is clear that embodiment must rank along with consciousness as one of the key concepts to be deployed. Embodiment, also, sometimes functions as the replacement in discourse for the unconscious; yet its dynamic is more sociogenic than psychogenic in the Freudian or Jungian sense. Consciousness, the body and embodiment thus represent a domain of ideas where the psychogenic and the sociogenic meet and overlap.

The same is true for the concept of historical consciousness which I found to be important when I turned to specific ethnographic cases of spirit possession. Bourguignon (1973: *passim*) has pointed to differences in the incidence of trance with and without possession, linking the former to more hierarchical social contexts. While her distinctions and refinements of them are important in general (Shaara and Strathern 1992: 45ff.), I shall assume here that possession is based on trancing and that the ability to experience trance is widely shared around the world (Winkelman 1990: 309). Taking the psychogenic here as the universal, then, trance is the basic phenomenon in psychogenic terms, and we can suggest features of it relevant to healing that can operate cross-culturally. Spirit possession, by contrast, is the locus of historical specificity. What is embodied in such possession behaviour is both a universal capacity and a specific realization of it. Trance also occurs only in specific cultural forms, so we cannot take instances of it simply as evidence of the psychogenic. In general, my position is that psychogenic and sociogenic are terms which appeal to certain theoretical viewpoints; they belong to the contrasting rhetorics of psychology and sociology/social anthropology. In practice, the phenomena which we study demand that we take both frameworks into account without necessarily giving primacy to either. It does not follow, for example, that because trancing is a universal capacity it always enters into the healing process in exactly the same way. However, we may argue that some features of it do so enter, for example, by making a sufferer from sickness more suggestible to the idea that recovery from sickness is possible.

The ethnographic cases which I explore in this chapter are chosen because they lend themselves to an elucidation of interplay between factors in the study of healing. More specifically, I show that while in all cases an ethnotheory of the person intersects with trancing in the production of healing therapies, the forms of historical consciousness which accompany this process vary with other features of the social context. Spirit possession is not only linked with hierarchy, as Bourguignon pointed out, but also with the complexities of historical experience which it encodes. The examples, then, are chosen to show both different modalities of healing and different modalities of historical consciousness. At the end of my ethnographic tour,[1] I will return to the triadic set of terms, embodiment, agency and consciousness, which emerge from the different cases. All three terms clearly both function as potential 'universals', thus giving us a comparative way of looking at personhood, and at the same time are likely to be inflected as 'particulars' in concrete cultural cases.

The cases I have chosen stretch from South-East Asia to Africa. Obviously no rigorous grid or scheme of comparison-making is intended. However, the movement of the tour is from politically simple to politically and historically complex cases. I start here with the case of the Temiar people, who live in the rain forests of Malaysia.

CASES

The Temiar: blowing *kahyek*

Marina Roseman (1991) has stressed the healing qualities of sound for the Temiar. Such healing is also bound up with their theory of 'souls' in an animistic cosmos, in which the souls of people interact, blend and differentiate themselves from those of animals, plants and the landscape. A pervasive distinction is made between upper and lower or outer and inner souls; in humans the distinction is between head and heart souls, and the head soul in particular becomes unbound from the body during dreams, in trance and in illness. It may encounter the soul of another entity, which then gives it a song and offers itself as the person's spirit guide, showing pathways for healing. A healing specialist, or medium, is one who has garnered healing songs in this way and can use them to heal others. The songs express an ability to move the heart and the spirits. Roseman calls them 'sonic icons of the heartbeat' (p. 15), which also 'set the cosmos in motion and effect the transformation of Temiar trance' (p. 16). Fundamental to all this is the Temiar ethnotheory of 'being', resting on the notion of multiple souls. The head soul is the 'vital, animating principle' (p. 25), and is a focal point of illness and of healing. It can be referred to as a 'plant shoot'. In trance it is said to be broken off like a snapped twig; as also when a person is startled. Temiar take great care not to startle others, yet illness may be traced to mild startling or angry words even if spoken indirectly, the more so if accompanied by pronouncing the autonym of the person at whom the words are directed. The head soul also goes out in the voice, especially in singing (p. 29). The head souls of spirit guides show themselves as *kahyek*, 'a cool, spiritual liquid likened to the colourless sap of plants, the clear waters of mountain streams, and morning dew' (p. 30). Mediums blow *kahyek* into patients' heads to heal them, drawing it from inside their own chests.

The head soul is not the seat of consciousness, which is found in the heart soul; the latter is also the locus of memory, including the memory of healing songs. If head soul represents vital substance, then heart soul manifests vital agency. The heart also experiences emotions. Anger, for example, heats and compacts the heart (p. 32), and can lead to illness. The odour of a person's body, particularly in the lower back, is also important. Cutting across someone's personal space can unbind their odour and again cause illness. Finally, there is also a shadow soul, which leaves the body at death. Roseman relates all of these concepts together as 'multiple, detachable components of self' (p. 45), but goes on to say that they constitute the Temiar 'person' (p. 46). (Self and the person are thus brought into relation: selves are multiple but the person is a unity.) Insightfully, she notes that there is a tension between egocentric and sociocentric components:

> Temiar interactions with one another and the cosmos are driven by a dynamic tension that, on one hand, celebrates the potential detachability of self, and on the other, guards the integrity of self. The cultural subscript of sociocentric interdependence, then, is the continual reinstatement of an independent, bounded self.
>
> (Roseman 1991: p. 47)

Health may involve the reinstatement of a boundary, a recovery of substance. Or it may involve the passing on of substance in exchanges between people by means of which they guard each other's head souls. But a broken promise or a gift denied, as well as an excessive gift, can all cause illness.

So far we see the following: (1) a theory of souls which also provides a theory of trance, song and healing; (2) a theory of exchange as a means of guarding health; (3) a theory of personhood which stresses the dialectics of establishing and passing across boundaries.

In the healing process, the spirit guide takes over vocalizing power from the medium. 'Temiar mediums describe the displacement of their own self while the spirit guide sings through them as "one's heart is elsewhere" ' (p. 115). Besides displacement there is an inversion: the spirit guide comes as a child to the medium, but it is the medium's teacher (p. 115). The singing draws *kahyek* into the medium and also into the medium's patients, making a cooling force for healing. Mediums are mostly men, but their spirit guides, sometimes seen as their consorts, are often female (there is a parallel with the Kaluli, Etoro and Duna of Papua New Guinea; see Schieffelin 1976; Kelly 1993; Stürzenhofecker 1993).

Illness results from the transformation of agents inside the body or from the drawing of the head soul out of a patient. The agents come from mountains, fruits and rivers, and the medium mobilizes the spirit guides from these same sources to combat the agents of illness. The medium is in trance while he heals the patient, and supporters around him also go into trance. The patient need not be in trance. However, since he or she has either lost the head soul or become invaded by the souls of illness agents, it is clear that in Temiar terms a 'displacement' has occurred. What the medium does is to treat 'his patient in the context of a cere-monial performance that reframes reality' (p. 147). The songs do this by referring elaborately to souls of things in the environment itself and bringing their essences to bear on the patient through the creation of sung images. What Roseman calls 'disembodied voice' becomes trans-formed into embodied *kahyek*, healing substance.

The healing songs are also a kind of history. As Roseman expresses it: 'a vibrant, continuous yet constantly reconstructed history of a people's relationship to their surroundings is encoded in the landscape' (p. 59). Furthermore, through singing, 'places become persons, landforms become specific locations' (p. 79).

The Temiar case shows that the songs of spirit mediums encode a history and thus constitute a mode of historical consciousness; and that healing is the invocation of that consciousness as a means of reframing the patient's experience. Whether the patient is in trance of not, the experience created rests on a heightened sense of embodied knowledge/practice concentrated in singing. From a cultural or sociogenic view, the key term here is the cosmos; from a psychogenic view it is that of reframing individual experience within the cosmos. Clearly, there is no contradiction between these views, since they come together in a single enactment.[2]

Wana shamanship: opening hidden realms

The Wana people of Sulawesi in Indonesia practise *mabalong*, a shamanic healing ritual in which drumming and singing play central parts. Shamans summon spirit familiars as Temiar mediums to spirit guides: there is more emphasis, however, on the power of the shaman to attract the familiar to him. The shaman's songs also define a local sense of community as well as encapsulating references to past history. They depend on a division of the world into the visible and the invisible or hidden: only shamans know how to enter the invisible realm. This realm is also the realm of the glorious past, the source of power. When the shaman invokes it his 'summons has the potential to be at once nostalgic and powerful: nostalgic because of its multiple allusions to past shamans and to an era of magic, powerful because the shaman conjures a potent concentration of hidden being around him' (Atkinson 1989: 76). At healing sessions, the shaman begins by summoning his own familiar to help him with the diagnosis of an illness and either to extract an object from the patient's body or to recover a part of the patient's 'being' ('soul'): for example, the body soul in the back, the dream agent, and the pulse points in the hands and feet

(p. 86). By invoking his familiars the shaman can augment his own vision with theirs and so perceive the hidden dimensions of existence, in a manner the Wana compare to dreaming (p. 92) and Atkinson suggests we might gloss as an altered state of consciousness (p. 92). The description is consistent with a state of light, self-induced trance.

Shamans are potentially ambiguous figures. They may control spirit familiars who are in fact liver-eating demons or vampires that possess X-ray vision. By implication they might use them to do harm. The shaman in his *mabalong* performances may 'assume the personalities and desires of his spirit allies' (p. 99), and if the audience do not indulge the spirits with their requests for special foods or other presents the shaman's soul may go off with the spirit in a huff.

The context of ideas about personhood within which shamanism operates is important. *Koro* refers to the living body, also to a 'soullike component of self' that resides in a person's upper back but may be absent in illness and survives death (p. 104). *Tanuana* is the dream-self, which can also be startled out of the body, again resulting in illness. Liver (*ate*), scalp skin (*pela mwo'o*) and brains (*uta*) are vital elements which may be stolen from the body and recovered by a shaman. In sum, 'the person ... is a fragile concatenation of hidden elements that are prone to disperse of their own accord or at will of external agents' (p. 114). Wana perceive a homology between person in this sense and polity and see shamans both as healing persons and as holding the community together (p. 118). *Mabalong* performances are as significant for the spectators in general as for the sick person, and Atkinson notes that the role of the actual patient 'is passive and usually minor' (p. 124). The patient does not engage in dialogue with the healer, and shows no signs of entering trance, but is drawn into the healing context through music and dance.

The second half of Atkinson's book is in fact concerned with the shaman's community role, and she compares shamans to the Melanesian 'great-man', since shamans unlike Melanesian big-men do not have direct control over production but rather over mystical power (Godelier and Strathern 1991). The shaman acts as a centripetal force in a small community through exercise of influence and by invoking spirits of mythology and of the periphery. He further creates an embryonic history based on a myth of nostalgia for a 'great' past in which power was putatively more centralized. The Wana shaman therefore defines a modal historical consciousness which implies discontinuity as well as continuity with the past as well as a greater political complexity than is found with the Temiar.[3]

The Mayotte: embodiment and objectification

Michael Lambek has elaborated an impressive cultural account of trance among the Mayotte people of Madagascar which builds successively on metaphors of 'text' and 'embodiment'. Lambek points out that spirit possession implies an elementary triangle of communication between a spirit, its host and a third party who must mediate between the first two, an intermediate consciousness that enables two different manifestations located within the same person to speak to each other. Implicit here is the idea that the host does not consciously hear what the spirit says and therefore cannot 'remember' what happens during the period of possession. Extrapolating a little, we can argue that possession intrinsically involves either blockage or contradiction or both and is itself a way of transcending contradiction.

In his latest work Lambek concentrates on experts who have learned to accommodate and manage a number of spirits, who impart to her or him their knowledge. Modifying the metaphor of text he used in the earlier work he writes:

> Possession is constituted by a practice and politics of voice rather than of text, of speaking rather than reading, of body rather than of intellect ... By its very nature possession finds the source of its authority in the embodiment of knowledge. A medium acquires and lays claim to knowledge by the public fact and personal experience of trance and by the coherence of his or her performance.
>
> (Lambek 1993: 306)

Embodiment is what makes the knowledge experientially real; its producer, however, has to objectify it in the personage of the spirit. There is therefore a dialectic of objectification and embodiment. Here Lambek directly follows Bourdieu, who applied his insight to the use of the body in culturally encoded space (Bourdieu 1977: 87). Lambek also draws inspiration from Fortes' work on taboo since taboos are embodied rules, transcending the gap between language and act. On these insights Lambek builds his own detailed picture of how a medium gradually builds up a coherent personality for the spirit who possessed him/her and uses this in practical life (= reframing). The communicative function is in prime focus and the context is sociogenic. Some questions of consciousness, however, remain.

If the host is in deep trance and does not remember what happens when possession takes place, how can the personality of the spirit be built up? Only through the mediation of others, whose consciousness therefore enters into the construction. This may help to explain how spirits become socially relevant. But in another sense it is possible to discern that by cultivating a range of spirits a medium actually acquires a level of individuation that would otherwise be denied. Through the spirits he/she can reveal aspects and desires that otherwise could not appear. Furthermore, we may suggest that the 'oppositional' character of possession is everywhere heightened as a result of the spread of Islam and the diffusion of gender ideology that goes with it. It is here that the question of historical consciousness also re-enters.

At Lombeni, where Lambek worked, two kinds of spirits were held to possess people, the *trumba* and the *patros* (1993: 310). Patros spirits are usually male and belong to a general type shared between the Near East and both East and West Africa. Senior *trumba* spirits represent deceased royal rulers of the Sakalava states of north-western Madagascar. Younger *trumba* represent nineteenth century social classes, e.g. warriors, sailors, slaves. They are not village ancestors. It is apparent that these spirits encode and are the sole current manifestation of a complex and partly pre-Islamic history. They are 'contradictory' to the present since they belong unambiguously to the powerful past. The contradictory character of these spirits, and their powerful aura, fits well with the contradictory way in which they stand for aspects of individuation that set possessed persons at odds with some aspects of their defined social roles. If this is correct the overall form of 'consciousness' that is at work is one that operates at two levels: historical/social and individual/psychic. Again, a homology between sociogenic and psychogenic components is found. That the one merges into the other can also be seen in the interesting fact that a child may take on its parent's spirits, in competition with and eventually as replacement for the elder generation: another locus for the dialectic of objectification and embodiment (see Lambek 1993: 324).

In his later work Lambek is not so much concerned with the question of illness. However, possession is seen initially as a kind of illness and cultivating the spirits is a kind of therapy. When it is recognized that a spirit is rising to the head of a patient a curer puts the patient into trance, listens to the demands of the spirit and negotiates with it (Lambek 1981: 47). The curer is also one who has spirits, who assist in extracting sorcery objects and in diagnosing illness generally. The curer relays the spirit's demands to the host. Feasts are held to placate the spirit until the host is able to have a stable relationship with it. The crucial point here is that the patient is first *put* into trance by a curer, and then later learns to *manage* his/her trance: thus there is an achievement of consciousness in control over trancing, a feature shared everywhere by mediums and shamans. Indeed, when we look at the phenomenon of possession, as opposed to trance without possession, it is clear that possession is frequently signalled by, or interpreted as, a form of illness (and vice versa), and that the cure for it is *not* exorcism, necessarily, but acceptance of an ongoing relationship. Such a perspective strengthens the idea that it represents a development of the consciousness of the host even though a formal separation between host and spirit is maintained based on the assertion of non-communication, i.e. on the ethnomodel of deep trance. It is equally evident that this separation is maintained by the position that the spirits involved are figures from the historical past. This latter point can be made more clearly from the final case, that of the Songhay.

Fusion of worlds, fission of the person: the Songhay

The Songhay people of Niger in West Africa have a long and complicated history, centred around the founding and dissolution of local dynasties or rulers, and their tributary relations to other kingdoms, for example, in Ghana and Mali (Stoller 1989). The Songhay themselves established an empire which flourished 1493–1591 and then declined through internecine rivalries. They remained a stratified patrilineal society with a strong distinction between nobles and slaves and a subordinate status for women generally. Finally, they were conquered by the French colonial army at the end of the nineteenth century. From the sixteenth century onwards they were also much influenced by Islam.

An equally complicated set of spirits can be involved in possessing mediums and their patients. For example, the Tooru spirits date back to the time of empire in the early sixteenth century; Genji Kawri spirits, from the same era, represent Islamic incursions; the Genji Bi represent indigenous peoples conquered by the Songhay; Hausa spirits reflect mercantile influences of the early twentieth century, and the Hauka are from French colonial times. 'Each spirit family, then, signifies a distinct historical period during which there occurred a sociocultural crisis' (Stoller 1989: 30). The Songhay case, therefore, offers a perfect example of tendencies observed in preceding instances: the preservation and representation of historical forces in the realm of spirit possession, and the relationship of possession not simply with hierarchy but with historical rupture and contradiction, crisis in Stoller's succinct term (cf. Kapferer 1992; 1986).

There is a pervasive theme, therefore, of the appropriation of power from the past and in a sense from the 'outside'. In a manner reminiscent of Mary Douglas' formulations, danger comes from the outside. But danger is also power, available to be socialized. The body as the medium for such power has also to be conceptualized as a mindful, intentional body, even though the prime image of possession makes of the host's body something apparently passive. According to Adamu Jenitongo, a Songhay seer and medium, the human body consists of flesh, life force, and the double (*bia*). Life force is in the heart, and it leaves at death. Spirit mediumship results from the displacement not of life force but of the double. The spirit is an invisible double which becomes visible in the host's body by displacing the host's double temporarily. As in the case of the Mayotte a person who wishes to become a medium must come to terms with the possession spirit. A *zima*'s (a medium's) children may become possessed by their parent's spirits, continuing a line of succession. Possession mediums must separate themselves from Islamic clerics, and to do so they wear black instead of white, noting that 'one foot cannot follow two paths' (p. 37). *Zima* therefore stand generally for indigenous Songhay values as against Islam. Although their activities cannot simply be classified as 'resistance' they do show an unmistakable oppositional character. Access to spirits of the past through trance-possession enables *zima* to validate their claims in the face of an Islamic hegemony. Their patients therefore participate in the same 'oppositional scenario' (a phrase I borrow from Schieffelin [1976], applying it to a different context).

Spirit mediumship also offers a contradictory and resistive role to certain gifted women, one of whom, Gusabu, Stoller describes in his Chapter Three (1989: 45ff.). Gusabu outlasted several husbands, was strong willed and picked out for favour by the spirits by their making her ill with possession sicknesses. Stoller explicitly notes that becoming a medium and/or entry into a possession troupe 'is a refuge from a social world in which women are powerless. Women constitute the majority of the spirit mediums' (p. 49). In turn spirit mediums become those who treat patients for 'resistant' illnesses that result from possession by spirits. The patients are initiated into the proper order of their spirits, and are thus cured of their sickness while permanently taking up a relationship with the spirits themselves. As in the Mayotte case, personal individuation and the regenesis of historical consciousness go hand in hand. The 'unconsciousness' of possession transmutes itself in the communicative triad into the 'consciousness' of an embodied role.[4]

The specificity, hierarchy and depth of historical experiences expressed in Songhay possession practices stand at the furthest remove, in this sense, from the Temiar case with which I began this survey. Yet in another sense, and in a different modality, Songhay ethnography doubles back on to the Temiar case since it is through music, melodic sound, that trancing is induced or healing encompassed. As Stoller writes:

> Sound is a powerful sensation in Songhay cultural experience. It is the only force that can penetrate the body – hence the emotive power of music in the world. Just as the sounds of words are important in the practice of sorcery and praise-singing in Songhay, so the sounds of certain musical instruments are central to Songhay possession ceremonies. These instruments are the monochord violin and the calabash drum.
>
> (Stoller 1989: 111)

The violin 'cries' to the people and its sound is the sound of the ancestors. 'We hear the sound and we know that we are on the path of the ancestors' (pathway as history) (p. 111). Thus 'the violinist is the human link between social and spirit worlds' (p. 113). Also the sound of the drums reminds the dancers, audiences, and spirits of the battlefield heroics of the Songhay past (p. 118). A poetics of nostalgia is turned into a poetics of power.

In addition, two genres, the Hauka and the Sasale performances, show the oppositional contexts of Songhay possession most clearly. Stoller describes Hauka as horrific comedy. Hauka is a Hausa word meaning craziness. Among the Songhay Hauka performances are funny, using obscenity as a challenge to colonially privileged characters. Hauka performers 'often wore pith helmets and carried swagger sticks. Sometimes they took the roles of European army generals who spoke to their troops in Pidgin French or Pidgin English. This frivolous burlesque makes impressionable children cringe and seasoned adults laugh' (p. 148). The Hauka in fact embodies the kind of parodic appropriation of the other which we often find also in colonial contexts in Melanesia and the wider Pacific region also (Keesing 1992; Thomas 1992).

The Sasale performances also use obscenity, this time specifically in the context of gender relations and in opposition to Islam. Hauka is connected to the rupture of French colonialism, Sasale to modernization in the twentieth century. Sasale prostitute spirits who outrageously challenge their spectators 'mock the practices of a neoconservative Islam that ... threatens the very foundation of Songhay society' (Stoller 1989: 169). Carnivalesque practices thus attempt to invert consciousness, to render ridiculous what has become normative, to show turbulence and negation beneath conformity, to emerge as spirits of protest against the perceived sickness of society.

DISCUSSION

Trance, healing and reframing

Trancing seems to play a variable role in the processes of healing exemplified in the cases I have looked at here. There is, for instance, the difference between cases where the healer enters trance, the patient does so, or both do. Indeed, it is difficult to be precise about the concept of trance itself, or to be sure that we are dealing with an altered state of consciousness as against a dramatic performance. Whatever the context, however, one feature seems to reappear, the reframing of experience. Trance facilitates such a reframing, as does spirit possession. At one end of the continuum we may be dealing with a new image presented to a patient, at the other with a whole new persona, an alter ego juxtaposed to the self. Either a metaphor or a historical figure may be in focus: in either case the result is an altered state of consciousness which whether trance induced or not conduces towards a patient's recovery, a process in which health and identity are brought into consonance with each other.

Ernest Rossi, in collaboration first with Milton Erickson and later with David Cheek, has developed a set of concepts, built into psychotherapeutic practices, that bear on this phenomenon in psychogenic terms (Erickson 1980; Rossi and Cheek 1988). Their psychotherapeutic work has focused to some extent on the recovery of traumatic memories, and hypnosis is used as a means of accessing such memories when suppressed. Memory itself is influenced by the state of the brain during an experience, expressible as a configuration of acetylcholine, catecholamine and serotonin systems. Endocrinal hormones and their peptide analogues 'are similarly involved in memory and modulation' (Rossi and Cheek 1988: 109). From observations such as these Rossi has developed what he calls the 'state-dependent memory, learning, and behaviour theory of mind-body healing in therapeutic hypnosis' (p. 109). Instead of regarding state-dependent learning as an exotic variant, Rossi proposes it as 'the broader, more generic form of learning that takes place in all complex organisms that have a cerebral cortex and limbic-hypothalamic system modulating the expression of Pavlovian and Skinnerian conditioning' (p. 109).

Physiological features of the body are also state dependent and obviously related to health and illness. Rossi has argued that the limbic-hypothalamic and other related systems are the means whereby information is transduced between the brain and the rest of the body. Accordingly, all methods of mind-body healing must operate by 'accessing and reframing the state-dependent memory and learning systems that encode symptoms and problems' (Rossi 1986: 55, quoted in Rossi and Cheek 1988: 111).[5]

These remarks can be brought to bear on trancing, as Rossi and Cheek intend. Trancing, whether through hypnosis or not, may enable a patient to recover memories encoded without conscious attention. Equally, it may enable new learning and new memories to be established. In trance, the patient is in a state of high receptivity. Exactly the same applies to the case where it is the shaman, not the patient, who is in trance. But in the ethnographic cases we have considered, the process of learning and reframing is not *confined* to trance episodes. What is revealed in trance is assimilated in other contexts and the holistic nature of experience is facilitated by the fact, according to Rossi and Cheek, that 'many of the sensory-perceptual languages of the mind ... are encoded like a map over the cortex ... [and] can be transduced or transformed into one another via the "cross-modal association areas" of the limbic system' (Rossi and Cheek 1988: 162). They go on to suggest in fact that such transduction can be termed consciousness. 'Consciousness [is] a process of self reflective information transduction' (p. 162). In other words it can be seen as a means of reflecting a state-dependent learning. Finally, such within-brain processes are closely linked to overall bodily states, since 'certain neurons within the hypothalamus of the brain convert the neural impulses of *mind* into the hormonal *information substances* of the body' (p. 163). The process of information transduction continues down via receptors to the cellular level. As Rossi and Cheek recognize, 'the current challenge is to determine just how and where hypnosis enters these cybernetic loops to facilitate mind-body healing' (p. 167) We could substitute 'trance' for 'hypnosis' in the above formulation.

This sketch of information transduction indicates that (1) there can be a complex translation from mental images into cellular modifications, and (2) consciousness plays a major role in facilitating such patterns. Such indications fall into line with the evidence of the communicative processes which surround trance and healing in the ethnographic cases I have examined. For these cases, however, we have also to extend the domain of consciousness further, since we have seen a consistent pattern in societies with complex histories for aspects of these histories to be encoded in possession-trance behaviour. It is as though the state-dependent theory of learning and memory had here been written large on the canvas of social history. Possession memory culturally encodes historical 'state-dependent' experiences, bringing these back also into alignment with individual experiences in a sliding scale. Such a work of 'analogous memory' has to be seen as both a creative act of consciousness and a recovery of suppressed and therefore unconscious experiences. In this way, the psychogenic and sociogenic again are seen to overlap.

Embodiment, agency and consciousness

Rossi's work significantly collapses the mind-body dichotomy, although it does give much primacy to brain-centred experience. Given this, what becomes of the concept of embodiment? Like many others we have used in anthropology, it too can now be relativized. Matters acted out through the body as embodied knowledge are also linked with brain transduction processes. Quite differently, ethnographic cases also show the relativity of the concept since mind-body concepts themselves vary cross-culturally. Is the head soul of the Temiar a part of the Temiar 'body' or not, for example? In Songhay spirit possession, the spirit double replaces the human double: is it a part of the 'body' or not? The concept of embodiment, like that of the body, is problematized, along with the concepts such as 'symbolic or metaphorical action'.

Just as Paul Stoller has insisted on a 'fusion' of the worlds' in his study of Songhay possession (Stoller 1989), so we may insist on a fusion of mind and body and of consciousness and unconsciousness in the kinds of expressions healers have invented in different cultures to achieve the reframing of experience. A good example of this is given by Kaja Finkler in her study of spiritualist healing in Mexico where she writes of Chucha, a women patient with chronic problems of chest pain. Chucha was told by her healer that her heart palpitations should be thought of as 'crystalline drops falling into an empty glass, the drops symbolising God's words transmitted during irradiations [spiritualist church services] and Chucha representing the empty glass' (Finkler 1994: 171–2). In this image, with its transposition from the body to the word via an extra-somatic comparison, we see exemplified again the general form of symbolic healing. Such images may calm the patient, aided by a mild condition of trance in which 'cortical excitation is diminished, the ergotropic system is less active, and the trophotropic system of the body is stimulated' (Finkler 1994: 164).

When we write in this way about psychological, physical and cultural factors, combined together in the reframing of experience, it is clear that we are far from espousing either an old-fashioned view of determination by the unconscious or a straightforward version of social determinism. The value of the concept of embodiment is that it can encompass both the psychogenic and the sociogenic. Bodily processes and encodings, which include brain signals and interpersonal communication, are the locus of information transduction and negotiation between people. If we see agency and consciousness as terms that tend towards a mentalistic framework for studying the person, the term embodiment can be used to express aspects of sociality which lie on the fringes of that framework. If we further put embodiment and consciousness together, we arrive at the idea of the 'mindful body' developed by Lock and Scheper-Hughes in the context of medical anthropology (1987), and thus at a concept both of the body and of the person which would easily be recognized by the peoples whose ethnotheories I have sketched above. We also arrive at the site of overlap between the psychogenic and the sociogenic, since the mindful body reflects both. Finally, since consciousness is included in the concept of the mindful body, it is apparent that we have also endowed it with the psychogenic and sociogenic components alluded to in my title. Aside from this point, it becomes important to recognize conceptual distinctions as well as overlaps between the terms I have used. Consciousness, agency and embodiment form a kind of triad which may exist simultaneously within the person or can be seen also as distributed within a set of social actions. In a healing encounter consciousness may belong especially to the shaman/healer embodiment (of a condition) to the patient, and agency may be shared by healer and patient in the action of healing itself. In all three concepts there is overlap with, but distinction from, the ethnotheory of the person which has provided a focus for many previous investigations. Particularly with consciousness there is an idea of the processual in addition to the categorical. Consciousness enters into events, creating, interpreting, modifying them and itself being modified over time. It is therefore a vital and central term in the anthropology of experience. In my treatment here, I have not been able to do justice fully to the dynamic and processual implications of the term, although these are present in the materials on the theme of individuation. Such a further exploration would require more space than I have been able to negotiate for the present 'tour'.

NOTES

1 This is how Nigel Rapport (pers. comm.) dubbed my peregrinations in the chapter, asking what the tour was supposed to show and whether it has an end. I am more clear that it does show some worthwhile 'sights' than I am that it comes to a point of completion, since I think of myself and others as still extending the tour itself. Meanwhile I thank Nigel also for the helpful signposts he provided in his overall comments on my chapter.

2 Temiar practice also conforms closely to James Dow's universal model of symbolic healing, with its four elements of a symbolic universe, legitimacy, attachment to a healer and the transformation of experience through the use of healing (Dow 1986). One might add that all healing in these terms contains 'symbolic' elements. A further point: my 'psychogenic' category here appeals to the 'individual/idiosyncratic' meaning of the term but *simultaneously* also to the 'universal' end of the continuum, since it conforms to the last element in Dow's general model.

3 The Trengganu of Malaysia show a further development of historical nostalgia in the world view projected by *bomoh* healers, combined with a theory of illness based on the idea of *angin* or 'inner wind', not found among either Temiar or Wana (Laderman 1991: 41–89). Laderman further suggests that her Trengganu materials offer 'the sole example in the ethnographic record of an indigenous non-Western method of non-projective psychotherapy existing within the context of a shamanistic seance' (p. 85). However, if we look outside shamanism, we can find parallels, for example in the Hagen people's use of the notion of *popokl* (anger) and the need to confess it if healing is to be achieved (see A. J. Strathern 1968; 1981; 1993; M. Strathern 1968; 1988).

4 The same point can be made in detail from the perceptive work of Janice Boddy (1989). In particular, Boddy develops a complex argument concerning individuation through possession. The Hofriyat women portrayed by Boddy are in fact bricoleurs of historical consciousness, exercising licensed reversal, carnival and parodic appropriation of the other. Roland Littlewood's discussion (this volume) of the different ways in which the issue of 'multiple personalities' is handled in American and British psychiatric practice essentially fits into the same frame as I have used here for possession-trance. What is at issue is whether the 'deviant' personality is accommodated or expelled. As we have seen, it is often in practice accommodated, so that a rule 'once possessed, always possessed' comes into play. Hofriyat women do this with a twist, since they embody spirits seen as 'not-self', while from the observer's viewpoint it is still their own 'individuation' that is at work (Lutz 1985; 1988).

5 My purpose in adducing the theories of Erickson and Rossi is not so much to inject their *specific* conceptions of hypnotism and trance into the data, but rather to utilize one of their main motifs at a phenomenological level. I am concerned, that is, more with the idea of state-dependent memory and learning than with wranglings about the specifics of trance as such. Critics have pointed out that Erickson himself was more of a practitioner than a theorist and that

Rossi has reinterpreted some of Erickson's work and worked into it his own perspectives. Weitzenhoffer (1989: Vol. 2, 180–293) also points out that Erickson's ideas on trance involved the following elements: fixation of attention, depotentiation of consciousness, an unconscious search, and multilevel communication. Erickson himself stressed the embodiment or *bodily* condition of trancing, a phenomenological viewpoint of considerable value to the ethnographic perspective. Similarly he recognized the positive contributions of the trancing subject to the emotional and symbolic work done in healing processes. Erickson's views thus fit reasonably well with James Dow's overall scheme (see note 2).

REFERENCES

Atkinson, Jane Monnig (1989) *The Art and Politics of Wana Shamanship*, Berkeley: University of California Press.

Boddy, Janice (1989) *Wombs and Alien Spirits*, Toronto: University of Toronto Press.

Bourdieu, Pierre (1977) *Outline of the Theory of Practice*, trans. Richard Nice, Cambridge: Cambridge University Press.

Bourguignon, Erika (ed.) (1973) *Religion, Altered States of Consciousness, and Social Change*, Columbus: Ohio State University Press.

Dow, James (1986) 'Universal aspects of symbolic healing: a theoretical synthesis', *American Anthropologist*, 88(1): 56–69.

Erickson, Milton (1980) in E. Rossi (ed.) *The Collected Papers of Milton H. Erickson on Hypnosis*, 3 vols, New York: Irvington Press.

Finkler, Kaja (1994) *Spiritualist Healers in Mexico. Successes and Failures of Alternative Therapeutics*, Salem, Mass.: Sheffield. (Originally published 1985.)

Godelier, Maurice and Strathern, Marilyn (eds) (1991) *Big-Men and Great-Men. Personifications of Power in Melanesia*, Cambridge: Cambridge University Press.

Kapferer, Bruce (1986) 'Performance and the structure of meaning and experience', pp. 188–206 in Victor W. Turner and Edward M. Bruner (eds) *The Anthropology of Experience*, Chicago: University of Illinois Press.

Kapferer, Bruce (1992) 'Review of P. Stoller', *Fusion of the Worlds'*, *American Ethnologist*, 19(4): 845–6.

Keesing, Roger M. (1992) *Custom and Confrontation. The Kwaio Struggle for Cultural Autonomy*, Chicago: University of Michigan Press.

Kelly, Raymond (1993) *Constructing Inequality. The Fabrication of a Hierarchy of Virtue among the Etoro*, Ann Arbor: University of Michigan Press.

Laderman, Carol (1991) *Taming the Winds of Desire. Psychology, Medicine, and Aesthetics in Malay Shamanistic Performances*, Berkeley: University of California Press.

Lambek, Michael (1981) *Human Spirits*, Cambridge: Cambridge University Press.

Lambek, Michael (1993) *Knowledge and Practice in Mayotte: Local Discources of Islam, Sorcery, and Spirit Possession*, Toronto: University of Toronto Press.

Lock, Margaret and Scheper-Hughes, Nancy (1987) 'The mindful body', *MAQ*, 1(1): 6041.

Lutz, Catherine (1985) 'Ethnopsychology compared to what? Explaining behaviour and consciousness among the Ifaluk', pp. 35–79 in Geoffrey M. White and John Fitzpatrick (eds) *Person, Self and Experience. Exploring Pacific Ethnopsychologies*, Berkeley: University of California Press.

Lutz, Catherine (1988) *Unnatural Emotions. Everyday Sentiments on a Micro-*

nesian Atoll and their Challenge to Western Theory, Chicago: University of Chicago Press.

Roseman, Marina (1991) *Healing Sounds from the Malaysian Rainforest. Temiar Music and Medicine*, Berkeley: University of California Press.

Rossi, Ernest L. (1986) *The Psychobiology of Mind-Body Healing: New Concepts in Therapeutic Hypnosis*, New York: Norton.

Rossi, Ernest and Cheek, David B. (1988) *Mind-Body Healing. Methods of Ideodynamic Healing in Hypnosis*, New York: Norton.

Schieffelin, Edward (1976) *The Sorrow of the Lonely and the Burning of the Dancers*, New York: St Martin's Press.

Shaara, Lila and Strathern, Andrew (1992) 'A preliminary analysis of the relationshop between altered states of consciousness, healing and social structure', *American Anthropologist*, 94(1): 145–60.

Stoller, Paul (1989) *Fusion of the Worlds. An Ethnography of Possession among the Songhay of Niger*, Chicago: University of Chicago Press.

Strathern, Andrew (1968) 'Sickness and frustration: variations in two Highlands societies', *Mankind*, 6: 545–50.

Strathern, Andrew (1981) 'Noman: representations of identity in Mount Hagen', pp. 281–303 in M. Stuchlik (ed.) *The Structure of Folk Models*, ASA Monograph No. 20, London: Academic Press.

Strathern, Andrew (1993) 'Keeping the body in mind', *Social Anthropology*, 2(1): 43–53.

Strathern, Marilyn (1968) 'Popokl: the question of morality', *Mankind*, 6: 533–62.

Strathern, Marilyn (1988) *The Gender of the Gift, Problems with Women and Problems with Society in Melanesia*, Berkeley: University of California Press.

Stürzenhofecker, Gabriele (1993) 'Times enmeshed: gender, space and history among the Duna', PhD thesis, University of Pittsburgh.

Thomas, Nicholas (1992) 'Substantivization and anthropological discourse: the transformation of practices into institutions in neo-traditional Pacific societies', pp. 64–85 in James G. Carrier (ed.) *History and Tradition in Melanesian Anthropology*, Berkeley: University of California Press.

Weitzenhoffer, André (1989) *The Practice of Hypnotism*, 2 vols, New York: Wiley.

Winkelman, Michael James (1990) 'Shamans and other "magico-religious" healers: a cross-cultural study of their origins, nature, and social transformations', *Ethos*, 18: 308–52.

Chapter 7

From the edge of death

Sorcery and the motion of consciousness

Bruce Kapferer

CONSCIOUSNESS, BODY AND WORLD

All human beings as active, living beings are conscious. They are, as Husserl says (1960; 1964; Muralt 1974), orientated within a life-world of other beings. They are present to the world and the world is present to them. Consciousness, in this regard, is not a thing in itself but a process, constituted through the motion of human being-in-the-world. Moreover, human consciousness takes its particular form – one which is in constant flux – from the integration of the human organism with its life-world. Consciousness, while always embodied and constituted and expressed through the action of the body, is formed, I stress, through its engagement with other human beings in the world. Human consciousness is not something that simply begins within the individual organism and then, in its awakening, moves out towards others. Consciousness takes form in the foundational fact of a unity of individual conscious human beings in a world already shared with others. To put it another way, individual consciousness emerges in a field of consciousness. It arises in a world of other conscious human beings who participate in the process of consciousness of any particular human being.

I should stress that my use of the term consciousness covers all aspects of the embodied awareness of human beings of their life-world and is not restricted to the action of reflective thought. Reflective thought emerges from within multiple dimensions of the consciousness of human beings, much of which is not grasped through acts of reflection. This, of course, is well accepted at least since Freud.

Individual action in the world is always, in my sense, conscious action and, furthermore, a consciousness continually changing within a field of consciousness. In this view, the life of persons as conscious bodies is inextricably and intricately bound up with the consciousness of others.

The perspective I pursue is consistent with a broad phenomenological position, one which embraces a diversity of directions and applications. The orientation parallels in some respects growing debate and research in the biological sciences concerning the evolution and nature of mind/ consciousness. These generally attack mind-body dualisms of the Cartesian kind, and insist on the fundamental biological and embodied ground of conscious being. A phenomenology, as also a growing amount of biological literature on the nature of the emergence of consciousness, insists on a grasp of the processes of consciousness in terms of its intentionality. In other words, consciousness while always embodied is also more than its embodiment or a reduction to processes within the inner regions of the physically bounded body.

Consciousness takes form in an intentional body, a body directed and oriented towards the horizons of its life-world. Furthermore, the dimensionality of this life-world and its horizons continually shift in the movement of the body towards its world.

Before I go any further, I emphasize that intentionality is not to be confused with the English word 'intention' or with the notion of motivation. Both words in their common usage imply some underlying reason or value. The term intentionality, as I use the term, merely refers to the directionality of all action, that action has a trajectory. This is not driven by any necessary or essential reason or value. In the distinction of intentionality from motivation, while all motivated action is intentional action all intentional action is not motivated action.[1]

This understanding of intentionality, which is central to the following discussion, and which I develop more elaborately elsewhere (Kapferer in press), is vital to an understanding of consciousness which (1) does not reduce the investigation of consciousness merely to the isolated individual organism and (2) does not seek to explore consciousness only through its second order cognitive reflections or concepts (themselves the constructs of consciousness) but through the intentional processes and the continually changing and emergent fields of consciousness from which such categories and constructs arise.

I extend the approach to consciousness outlined through a discussion of sorcery experiences among Sinhala Buddhists in Sri Lanka. Vital themes at the heart of the culture of sorcery in Sri Lanka and, I think, in sorcery practices as they have been recorded across the world, have implicit within them at least some of the notions I have presented about consciousness.

In Sri Lanka, sorcery (*kodivina*, also *huniyam*) is a force of human causation, and thoroughly ambiguous. It can augment life or destroy it, such possibilities being inseparably linked. Sorcery is usually viewed as immoral and negative action but the action to end sorcery's effects engages similar practice, although it will be legitimated and given its particular force as a righteous, justifiable, moral response. People can ensorcell others without their being reflectively aware of the fact. They can cause suffering through the force of their own intentionality, through the directionality of their glances, thought and speech (*asvaha, hovaha, kattavaha*). Intentionality is at the core of Sinhalese sorcery practices. These recognize the force of consciousness as originating in the body and leaping beyond its confines. They also acknowledge the force of sorcery as drawing its possibility and its potency from the fact that the conscious being of human beings is oriented to other human beings, participates in their fields of consciousness and by this fact can invade and overcome the very bodies of consciousness of others.

The key myths of sorcery elaborate the points. One of the more important concerns that of the first victim of sorcery, Manikpala, the queen of the first king, Mahasammata, or the Great Elect who creates the original hierarchical political ordering of the social world.[2] Manikpala comes within the gaze of Vasavarti Maraya, the World Destroyer, World Poisoner, Death, who then desires her.[3] Manikpala lives in the palace at the heart of the cosmic city or ordering of the world that Mahasammata creates.[4] The grand sorcerer breaks through all the barriers and limitations of the world order instituted by Mahasammata and attacks Manikpala located at the germinal centre of the protected spaces of the city/world order. The World Poisoner's assault is described as a cosmic rape. Vasavarti takes the form of a fire viper (*gini polanga*) and lodges in Manikpala's womb, consuming her from within. Vasavarti's thrust towards Manikpala images the destructive potency of intentionality, whose agent, Vasavarti, reproduces itself in the body of the other. I might add, of course, that Mahasammata is the generative aspect of intentional action which, in effect, is virtually inseparable from the destructive aspect. When he approaches Manikpala, Vasavarti assumes the shape of Mahasammata and is only revealed for what he is, at the last minute, by his viper's stench. The overriding intentional leap of the sorcerer, despite Manikpala's attempt to bar his way, negates Manikpala's own intentional capacity, her ability for action in the world, and she falls unconscious. The story goes on to relate how Manikpala is cured by a ritual of seven steps (the *hat adiya*) which retraces the intentional path of the sorcerer, progressively negating its destructive force. Simultaneously, of course, the retracing of the sorcerer's path is a process of the victim's intentional re-extension into the world.

This action is at the centre of the major anti-sorcery rite (the *Suniyama*) for the demon/god of sorcery, Suniyam. The rite effectively recentres the victim within cosmic processes and sets the victim in motion along the path towards the horizons of worldly existence. Indeed, the sorcery victim is made to traverse symbolically the entire span of existence and is oriented to the ultimate Buddhist goal of non-existence (*nirvana*). When reached, the victim returns reconstitutively, like a bodhisattva or the world-making King Mahasammata, and capable of self-recreation and of reconfiguring a world in which the life of the victim can be sustained.

The victim is restored as a being of intentionality and of embodied consciousness regenerate and regenerating. Obviously, these Sinhalese notions of sorcery build upon widespread cultural, religious and metaphysical reflections in the region stemming at least from Vedic times. The myths and events of the anti-sorcery rite, the Suniyama, to which I have referred, are strongly infused with Sinhala Buddhist adaptations and transformations of South Indian Hindu themes. While thoroughly acknowledging the cultural, historical and metaphysical specificity and underpinnings of sorcery practice in Sri Lanka, the ideas and notions which are engaged to the everyday and routine practice of sorcery might be described, in Husserl's sense, as 'secondary reflections' or a 'naive' grasping of the nature of human existence: a naivety which is profound.

The profundity of Sinhalese sorcery practice and, I suggest, most sorcery worldwide is founded in the implicit recognition that the consciousness of human beings is formed in-the-world. Furthermore, that the actualities of human beings are fundamentally affected by the mutual presencing of human being, that human beings are inevitably engaged in the webs of each other's intentional action: that the experience that human beings have of their worlds is of actualities of their construction. When the Azande assert such notions, as Evans-Pritchard (1937) describes in his celebrated ethnography, they are not being irrational or perverse – the tenor of some anthropological commentary – but are expressing what is the factuality of human existence in general. Moreover, sorcery practices, in Sri Lanka and elsewhere, mark the intentionality of human consciousness as simultaneously basic to the construction and destruction of the psychosocial worlds of human being.

Intentionality is at the root of social worlds, integral to what Sartre (1958) called the magicality of existential and social life, and sorcery practices mark it out as such. The leap of intentionality is potentially at the heart of the formation and ongoing process of life-supporting social relations as it may, too, be at the heart of their destruction. Sorcery is indeed concerned with the roots of being and consciousness in-the-world and, thus, in Sri Lanka its practice is replete with cthonic and originating cosmic imagery. The rites often take the form of reoriginating sacrifices in which cosmos, world and body are harmonically realigned. This is also a common ethnographically recorded feature worldwide of practices surrounding sorcery.

A broad point that I am making is that the exploration of sorcery practices, in Sri Lanka and more generally, reveals aspects of vital processes underlying the formation of the sociality of human beings. In much conventional anthropology, sorcery has tended to be discussed in relation to such issues as rationality, its use as a sanctioning force, as a representation of the contradictory and disordering processes of political and economic realities, and so on. There has been much focus on sorcery as some kind of false consciousness. I do not dispute the claims and insights of such perspectives. However, I draw attention to what might be regarded as the insights that practices of sorcery themselves reveal about the dynamics of human existence, possibly anywhere.

Among the more obvious is the insistence underlying so much sorcery practice that the actualities of human existence are fundamentally the constructions of human beings and that it is through the intentional consciousness of human beings, and the dilemmas engaged in such intentionality, that dimensions of human sociality emerge and collapse. The practices of sorcery are not just something to be understood and explained, the direction of so much anthropology, but, themselves contribute to and promote important understandings of the vital processes of human being.

In the rest of this chapter I focus on some aspects of the emotional and passionate experiences of sorcery. The stress is on the dynamics of fear and anger which manifest the retreat and extension of human intentionality and the birth and death of consciousness. The argument I present expands into a discussion of some of the main approaches in anthropology towards the emotions and their continuing dependence on a Cartesian mind-body dualism.

Such a dualism places the descriptive and explanatory emphasis on the cultural categories of experience and confines the grasping of experience and the formation of consciousness to the terms of these categories. This kind of approach sustains a rationalism that insufficiently grasps the import of the passionate forces that underlie the creation by human beings of the worlds that they construct and, possibly too, diminishes a fuller sense of their meaning in experience.

A CASE OF FEAR: THE CHAINING OF CONSCIOUSNESS

I outline an attack of sorcery involving a Sinhala man of about sixty, a housebuilder, who lives in the bustling market town of Matara in southern Sri Lanka. His sleep was broken by three terrifying dreams. The first was a dream in which he saw his father's brother (still very much alive) lying dead in a coffin. The experience was so intense that he could feel himself being overcome with grief as he 'saw' the body being lowered into the grave. Another dream started him awake: he dreamed that all his teeth were falling out. The third dream saw him attacked by monkeys who screamed and tore at his flesh. He saw these monkeys as manifestations of the Blood Demon (Riri Yaka) commonly associated with impending death. I shall not go into all the details of this case. But the housebuilder set about exploring all the circumstances of his social situation, discovering numerous indications of malevolence among kin and others living in his neighbourhood and among others, elsewhere in Sri Lanka, with whom he had some connection.

I stress some experiential aspects of the strange occurrences affecting the housebuilder which became increasingly marked as the evidence of sorcery. Thus, he described a terrible suffocating force bearing down on his chest and a great difficulty in breathing. His body grew cold and his limbs trembled and shivered. These symptoms culminated in the house-builder's collapse and being taken to hospital. Nothing physically wrong was diagnosed and he was soon discharged. But the fear of sorcery increased. He complained that both the food that his wife prepared and his house stank – indeed, he insisted, they reeked with the stench of the viper, of the demon of sorcery. According to the housebuilder's wife and other kin, he began to talk incessantly of death and dying. He refused to wash or to change his clothes. Imprisoned in his fear, he refused to eat. The housebuilder suffered a series of further collapses. His fear virtually immobilized him. He stayed indoors and refused to go out or meet with his friends, and he grew increasingly silent before his family. A doctor from a nearby clinic visited, and his wife called for help from numerous healers, including exorcists.

One marked feature of this case, as with many similar ones collected, was that the sorcery victim's initial terror expanded, and became increasingly immobilizing, as he and his relatives searched the world of their everyday life and the nature of their social relationships for clues as to the source of attack.

In instances of sorcery, the concern to comprehend, to interpret the meaning of experience, or to 'explain' the feeling and sense of embodied experience is particularly vital in the Sinhalese Buddhist context. It is one where the cultural emphases are quite explicit concerning the engagement of human beings in a complex weave of actions born of existence. The housebuilder was driven, I suggest, to grasp the meaning of his experience. Possibly, as with human beings everywhere, his experience exceeded the meaning, the reason, into which he could contain and structure it.

Dreams, or more appropriately nightmares, are a common indication that one is under attack by ghosts, demons and human beings. They are obvious signs of malevolence. These terrors of the sign build more fear. Such fear, its rising intensity which the housebuilder reported as his experience, is itself implicit recognition of the penetration of malignancy into the interior of the experiencing body. The body of fear is the ground upon which the symbols of evil affliction are the potential expressions: Manikpala invaded by Vasavarti or Queen Yawudagiri who is the mother of Oddi Raja, a sorcerer who manifests the major demon of sorcery.

The meaning of nightmares could be said to be the terror of their experiencing and what they seem to indicate. Their indices are integral to their terror (seeing death, experiencing the monkeys tearing at the body). However, the depth and intensity of the experience of nightmares, from all accounts, is packed with the portent which extends towards a meaning which is not yet. Nightmares, like most dreams, are at the edge of meaning, they indicate a world immediately present in the dreamer which flees comprehension. As a function of their fear, nightmares or horrible daydreams impel those who experience them to search for their meaning, to seek beneath the surface of ordinary life for that which is hidden. In this sense, terrible nightmares and day dreams, especially in their insistent recurrence, constitute experience as the extensions beyond meaning and sense, the overturning and upheaval of their structures. In this dynamic, there is a spiralling of fear (fear itself being the agent of its own expansion).

FEAR AND THE PLAY OF THE IMAGINATION

Through the terrible play of the vital imaginary the routine world of ordinary experience is broken down and its meanings and structures progressively dissolved. Alternatively, the gathering experience drives to the uncovering of more and more hidden meanings and possibilities of life. Meaning and structure become exhausted in the dreadful press of the experience of fear. As the housebuilder's action indicated, the experience of fear becomes all consuming. The expressions of the body, the disruptions of the senses, the chills, the shivering and the trembling, collapse and subsume meaning into the body of experience.

I note here the primordialism of the body in fear. Within it speech becomes silenced or, as the housebuilder's wife commented, speech drives out meaning and no longer becomes the means for acting in-the-world. The victim in fear refuses to eat and to dress.

Consuming fear, suggest the housebuilder and other sorcery victims, is a paralysis of the body. The senses of the body are reduced as the instruments of perception, the means for moving out upon the world. In the increasing immobilization of the body in fear, the senses are principally engaged in *reception* and become the means whereby that which is still without and around floods into and overwhelms the lived body. When this occurs the potential is there for any resistance of the body finally to be broken. The conscious body is submerged and like the housebuilder indeed loses consciousness.

The immobilizing of the body in fear progressively establishes the condition for a 'world-*within*-being' rather than a being-in-the-world. The imagination plays within the space of the experiencing body withdrawn into itself. Encountering no resistance or modification from others in the world towards whom the victim has ceased to move, the imagination of fear has no limitation apart from itself. Moving freely, the imagination draws the innumerable possibilities of external realities within the body of experience and *actualizes them within the lived experience of the body*. Different possibilities intermingle and merge in this creative play combining, perhaps, into a single fantastic and monstrous shape. At this point the imagination of fear may explode itself. The terror created in the dynamic of the imaginary either exceeds the experiential capacity of the body and/or the spin of the imaginary so consumes the realms of possibility that it virtually dies from lack of fuel. In other words, the imagining consciousness runs out of objects by which its energy is sustained. It is no longer intentionally directed out towards the world and is actively engaged in the subversion of such intentional process.

Sartre describes an aspect of the process of the imagination with reference to what he calls the 'chained consciousness' (1958: 308–59). He focuses on those moments between deep sleep and wakefulness as the period when the imagination seems to most of us to be fully at play. Sartre seizes on the point that at this time the body is virtually immobile. Consciousness within an immobile body is what he calls a chained consciousness. The imaginary is given up to itself and moves unchecked by anything outside itself or, rather, by the constant reorientations of perception effected by the motional body. The immobilization of the body in the progressive development of fear can be conceived of as a chaining of consciousness and further generative of the kind of all-consuming terror that I discuss. The Sinhalese exorcists who organize rites to overcome sorcery would seem to give such possibility full recognition.

The main anti-sorcery rite, the Suniyama referred to above, has a major event in which the victim of sorcery is literally bound with the poisonous hoops (snakes) of Suniyam. It comes at a high point in the rite after the victim has been purified of the sorcerer's intrusion upon his or her body. The victim is immobilized and it signifies, among other things, a binding in fear. The bonds of sorcery are cut, the victim is freed and is made to move out towards the world of existence once more.

The victim transcends the body in the world and is freed from a confinement to the body, to an interiority wherein the victim's consciousness consumes itself in the imaginative play of fear. In sorcery attack the bodies of victims become the expression of their belief. But, equally, sorcery, the way it is conceived in myth and ritual practice, is the expression of the experience and imagination of fear. The potential path of fear, for example, its regressive primordialism, its destruction of meaning and structure at life's surface through the revelation of subversive forces, the retreat into a world of inner despair and terror which appears to consume and exhaust meaning, find their parallel in the symbolism of Suniyam and in the symbolic events of his rites.

The fearful play of the imaginary links diverse, unsettling and disturbing experiences together. They live as the terror of the body not as some kind of coherent, organized or differentiated set of meanings but, I suggest, as an undifferentiated totalizing of experience congealed as the terror of sorcery. In effect, it is a world of non-meaning. This is the domain of the demon sorcerer which in rite and in myth lives outside the differences and structural arrangements of meaning, who cannot be incorporated within them and who breaks them down.

There is a relation here between the play of the imagination in fear and the play of the imaginary in fun and in comedy. Major anti-sorcery rites in Sri Lanka make the relation explicit and work on the distinction. Thus the event of being bound in the coils of fear in the Suniyama rite (consciousness confined and restrained in the body, consciousness in destruction, Death) is preceded by an extensive comic drama – the Vadiga Patuna (consciousness unrestrained and projected into the world, the re-establishment of Life).

The play of fear in sorcery and the play of comedy in the Vadiga Patuna express a totalizing dynamic. They are 'organizations' of discordancy, of disruption, discontinuity, of 'mis-rule'. However, each is ultimately oriented in an opposing direction.

The Suniyama comedy centres around the figures of the Indian brahmin-exorcists (*rsi*) who invented the cure for Manikpala's sorcery and who arrive in Sri Lanka to discover themselves in the midst of a Suniyama performance. They are startled at their discovery and confused by the strange language and setting. In the course of the comic events they begin to communicate with the Sinhala ritual performers and explore not just the meaning of the rite but the social and political world of the Suniyama. The process of this comedy is unrestrained. The actors move about the ritual arena, dart here and there and rush into the midst of the ritual audience. Much of the comedy concentrates on the dynamic of the reconstruction of language and the obscene mistakes of the foreign magicians generate much of the fun. The enjoyment expands as the magicians attempt to find names for actions and things. It is a play of a differentiating imagination which discovers and elaborates meaning. The very dynamic of the comedy is, in fact, from non-meaning to meaning. The actors in their motion around the arena shift perspective. The play of the comedy projects possibility upon the world and the actors move towards the possibilities of their construction which are either dissolved or sustained in the comic motion. The brahmins extend their consciousness into the world, a consciousness which through the comedy participates and grows as a function of such extension within a field of consciousness which itself is in flux.

The circumstance of the fearful imaginary, at least as expressed in the Suniyama and highlighted by the comic events, is, as I have described, a chained consciousness, one which, furthermore, is confined and imprisoned within the body. In a paradoxical sense, I suggest, consciousness is 'disembodied'. The body immobilized and restrained is no longer vital in the production of consciousness. It becomes the boundary of a consciousness given up to itself in virtual reverie, a dream-like world that projects back into itself and which has no context other than the actualities it spins through its play of the imaginary within the closure of the body. Not only does it exhaust meaning within itself, but also such a confined consciousness attacks its prison, the body itself, as the terrors of the body's destruction in the dreams of the ensorcelled indicate.

The major rites of anti-sorcery among Sinhalese aim to rebuild consciousness, one which is not given up to itself but which extends back towards the world through the motion of its body. In the Suniyama the sorcery victim comes to inhabit the space of a bodhisattva and like a bodhisattva is made to turn intentionally and recreatively back towards the world from which the victim has retreated in fear and which has flung the victim back to a primordial state at the brink of death.

A feature of the anti-sorcery rites to which I have been referring is that the emotional forces that might be integral to the experience of victims are appropriated into the structural processes of the rites. The victim is relatively inactive and subjected to the motion of the rite. This is relevant to the Buddhism of such rites which ideologically stresses the unplanned reactive dangers of action in existence. This extends an understanding of the relatively rigorous care of ritual proceedings in the Sinhala context, and rite as a reduction of risk. In the Suniyama, the action of the victim is tightly controlled and held within closely defined parameters.

The sorcery practices at the shrines refract more directly the vital passions of sorcery victims or the nature of sorcery as a statement of experience in the social and political world and, too, a reflective awareness of the nature of this world as it concentrates its force on victims. The activity at the shrines is far more under the control of victims. I explore some aspects of the activity at the sorcery, focusing on the dynamics of their reconstitutive anger and fury.

SPACES OF DEATH: SHRINES AND REFLECTIVE CONSCIOUSNESS

The main sorcery shrines are to a category of beings that I call demon/deities (*devatava/va*) and Suniyam is the chief among them. These demon/deities inclusive of Suniyam in their foundation myths are frequently described as divinized human beings. This underlines the pragmatism of sorcery and that the 'magicality' of sorcery (in Sartre's sense of the magical) refers to the magical world of a human-created world, a field of consciousness in which human beings are ultimately the potent intentional agents. The demon gods of sorcery are also simultaneously creative and destructive. They, like the sorcery they mediate, are Janus-faced and play back the malevolence against which they protect.

Two further features of the shrines may be noted. First, they are usually located at marginal points: at the edge of human habitation and/or at boundaries between different social communities or at places which mark the transition from one political locality (as defined in Sinhala historical tradition) into another. Some of the main shrines in Colombo are located in fringe areas, often areas of poverty. They are understood to be in zones of crime and general danger. The shrines are spaces of primal force and sites of fiery transformation. Second, the main shrines – and, especially, those where the cursing and killing work is done – are often seen to be places of great filth. One famous shrine frequented by Sinhala Buddhists in the Kurunegala area and run by a Muslim priest is crowded with mangy-looking dogs. These are foul animals to Muslims and in this context are viewed as objects of disgust by the Sinhala Buddhist clients. At other shrines, rancid coconut oil and other objects of disgust are used in cursing.

These marginal or liminal qualities of the sorcery shrines (inclusive of their disgust and the images of total cosmic power and often terrible destruction which crowd them) mark them out as 'spaces of death'. The qualities of these death spaces are integral to their power and fuse with the anguish of those who come in supplication to them. The sorcery shrines are places where death and life are in vital conjunction and the forces dynamic within them are critical in thrusting the supplicants back into the world.[5]

I give an example of an act of supplication before a sorcery shrine. Although the supplicant, a woman I call Babynona, addressed her own specific problems to the demon/deity of sorcery, the manner of her supplication is similar to numerous others that occur every day at the shrines.

The fury of Babynona

When Babynona approached the shrine to Suniyam, the shrine priest (*kapurala*) asked her what problem had brought her. This information is important as the priests typically insert aspects of their client's problems into their exhortations and plaints before the demon gods. Babynona explained quickly that her house landlord had demanded that she and her husband leave within three months. But they had no place to go. The deadline had passed and the landlord had sent his hired thugs to beat Babynona and her husband. 'Did you go to the police?' asked the priest. 'No,' she replied. 'The landlord is a friend of the OIC [Officer-in-Charge of Police]. He will never help. This is why I have come to Suniyam.' The priest asked the landlord's name. He then invoked Suniyam's attention (*kannalavva*) and uttered his curse (*vas kavi*) on the woman's behalf. The priest's powerful voice boomed and reverberated both invocation and curse around the chamber of the shrine.

I give homage to Iswara and to Rama
Homage to the mighty army of Skanda
Homage to the gem at Vadiga's neck
Homage and gifts to Oddisa
. . .
Oh! God who rules in Sri Lanka
Who carries the Vadiga sword in his right hand
The sword that severed the heads of the Asuras
Who carries the burning pot of fire in his left hand
Look upon this woman
. . .
The landlord [name inserted] has hired thugs
Oh! God, the thugs have beaten everyone in the house
This blameless woman cannot go to the police
The police do not help the poor, they are friends of the landlord.
God look upon this woman. Let her family live in peace.
Break the limbs of the thugs. Cut off their legs.
Burn the thugs into ash.
Oh! God who has destroyed the Asuras. Kill the landlord and destroy his thugs.
Oh! God, may you become a future Buddha for carrying out this punishment.

The priest then instructed Babynona to break a coconut, now infused with the power of his curse, on a stone before the image of Ganesh (the Remover of Obstacles). Babynona stood motionless and spoke inaudibly into the coconut. Babynona breathed her anguish into this object of destruction. Lifting the coconut high above her head she flung it towards the ground. Smashing against the stone, the energy of the priest's curse and Babynona's own suffering anger burst towards the source of her anguish.

I asked Babynona to repeat into a tape-recorder what she had just whispered, what supplicants call their *dukganavilla* or 'suffering striking'. Quite possibly she added more but what she said, still in the heat of her helplessness, communicates some sense of the emotional force and the ground of its energy that Babynona explosively directed out to the reality of her experience:

Oh, God! Commander of the army that destroyed the Asuras. Grant me a boon. Our landlord has hired thugs. They have beaten me and my whole family. Even my baby girl. Bring honour to your name by punishing these brutal people. Please punish them. I will always worship you. Punish them in three days or after seven days. Break their bones. Smash their heads into seven bits. Cover their bodies in sores. Oh, God . . . you are the most powerful in the three worlds. Oh God . . . this landlord has made himself rich by politics. He beats his own servants. He cares nothing for the people. He has nothing but bad qualities. He is a criminal. He sells pork. He even eats the vehicle on which Suniyam rides. Oh God! . . . punish this cruel man. Don't miss this chance to punish this man who harms the people. He worships only money. Oh God can you see my poverty. We eat only one meal a day. My children are sick. We have nowhere to live. We are only servants to the rich. We suffer everyday. Give us your divine sympathy. Give us life. May you become a Buddha in the future.

Babynona's anger, born of the abject desolation of her class situation, the forces of which quite literally beat upon her and her family, intensified in the context of Suniyam's violent place. Many others who visit the shrines appear to manifest a similar experience, if for diverse other reasons. The supplicants at the shrines – men and women – are not passive in their anguish before the shrines. They are not frozen in fear or the still foci within an active field of force, as when they are the patient/victim at the centre of a small anti-sorcery cutting rite (*kapuma*) or the larger and magnificent Suniyama. They express through the priest and within themselves that which presses upon them and gnaws inside. This is an externalization of the world that is consuming within, an externalizing or objectifying of a reality which has assumed malignant shape in relation to the supplicant. In these senses, victims distance and hold before themselves in reflective consciousness the dimensions of their distress. And then they cut it. This is the import of the anger of both priest and of supplicant.

The anger of the supplicants is far more than an expression of distress or even of cathartic release, though the notion of catharsis as purgation rather than a release of tension has bearing on this discussion.

The anger is powerful as anger. It acts directly on the body of the victim and on the way victims are oriented in their world and, too, upon that world as it is oriented towards them. Thus, the energy of the anger severs from the victim's body those destructive, or obstructive, qualities which are experienced as inhabiting or forcing against the body. The victim faces or turns back upon the world in a move which regrasps and reaffirms, in the very energy of its anger, an active and reconstitutive relation of the victim to a life-world. The motional force of the anger at the shrines might be understood as a radical unchaining of consciousness, a radical break with its own confinement and leap into the world to once again take part in the fields of force of human intentional being.

EMOTIONS AND THE BODY IN CONSCIOUSNESS

Anthropologists in their culture of relativism assert the crucial import of the cultural categories and the social constructions of emotion and emotional meaning (e.g. Lutz 1988; Lutz and Abu-Lughod 1990; Rosaldo 1980; Lynch 1991). They are critical of those physicalist or psychological perspectives, for example, which treat the emotions as 'things' located in the body, which define them in an essentialist, universalist and unproblematic way, and which fail to see them as the very stuff of social relations, or as the affects which have effect.[6] Broadly, a cognitive view is preferred which paradoxically can manifest a Cartesianism of a kind which many anthropologists currently contributing to emotion research would appear to reject.[7] My difficulty with such approaches and criticisms is that for all their concern to escape a Western bias, they reproduce it. Thus they compartmentalize, dichotomize and separate out processes which should be taken together and in relation. The very categories of a Western social science, its divisions into 'psychology', 'sociology', 'anthropology' and so on determine the way the field of enquiry is carved up and debated. The anthropologists I have cited, while I agree with much of what they say (e.g. their anti-essentialism, the importance of cultural meanings, etc.), nonetheless disembody experience and locate it externally to the body in social and cultural definitions of the emotions. They then in a parody of Descartes make the consciously reflected categories of the nature of experience, here the emotions, the form and content of the experience. In other words, thought determines being and action in the world!

Experience grasped through its cultural categories is already moving out towards such reflective apprehension. The emotions, fear, anger and love, for example, are already being lived in the course of their coming to conscious awareness. They assume the shape of a 'thingness', as an object penetrating inside from the outside and moving out again, in the process of beginning to perceive oneself through action in the world. This inner perception, or acute self-consciousness, is emergent in 'fearing' as an action anterior to its being recognized as fear. The inner perception takes shape in the individual's movement through the world in the process of which a particular awareness of the body is constituted. The victim's body in such movement becomes aware to the victim as his or her body and, furthermore, a body given over to the senses, the body 'in itself'. The victim's senses become objects to the victim, things in themselves, simultaneously pointing to disturbances in the world of the victim as a disturbance of the victim's own organism. Thus, the housebuilder, of whom I wrote earlier in this chapter, living his situation of fear in a world, was already experiencing its trembling before his apprehension of it as the trembling of his body significant as sorcery attack. The point I am making is that emotional experience is a process which is at once in the world and embodied, 'physical', 'psychological' and 'sociological'. This is the direction of Sinhalese 'theory' and practice concerning the matter (see Kapferer 1983; forthcoming). Merleau-Ponty presents excellently my argument and one which the Sinhalese sorcery materials I have presented would appear to support.

> Both universality and the world lie at the core of individuality and the subject, and this will never be understood as long as the world is made into an object. It is understood immediately if the world is the field of our experience, and if we are nothing but a view of the world, for in that case it is seen that the most intimate vibration of our psycho-physical being already announces the world, the quality being the outline of a thing, and the thing the outline of the world.
>
> (Merleau-Ponty, 1962: 406)

Experience and the emotionality of experience is always more than the cognitive or language categories of its construction. This is self-evident in the contexts of sorcery. Sorcery, in Sinhalese cultural conception and performance, virtually exceeds its comprehension. It defies classification. The fear, fury and anger of the supplicants before the sorcery shrines appear as a gathering of experience to language and a moving through language beyond it. Thus, the poetics of cursing. The sorcery experience, its excess, is defeated and transformed by language which can also progressively confine it.

The movement to sorcery rite and to sorcery shrine is nothing less than that radical 'upsurge' of the individual in the world of which both Sartre and Merleau-Ponty write so brilliantly. This upsurge they argue, and the sorcery rites and practices echo agreement, is produced in the resistances, ruptures and threats to existence in the world. The upsurge is that emergence of the individual consciousness aware of itself:

> only in those extreme situations in which it is under threat: for example, in the dread of death or of another's gaze upon me. The consciousness which conditions language is merely a comprehensive and inarticulate grasp upon the world, like that of the infant at its first breath, or of the man about to drown and who is impelled towards life.
>
> (Merleau-Ponty 1962: 404)

The pathos of the pleas at the sorcery shrines and the intense examination of self-experience and the context of experience by sorcery victims manifests this urgency to life. The victims express themselves as the fundamental points of contingency in a world they did not create, which in fact constitutes them in its density, but towards which they must establish an original relation. The violence of the shrines is the violence of reorigination and, too, of rebirth which is also a major metaphor of the rites. In the sacrificial structure of the Suniyama, described earlier, the recreation of the consciousness of the sorcery victim, as a being capable of actively constituting the world of the victim's existence, is equated with the first act of human ordering will, the creation of the original order of political society by King Mahasammata (see Kapferer forthcoming).

THE INTENTIONALITY OF CONSCIOUSNESS

I have concentrated on sorcery and its passions because they are quintessentially intentional. Intentionality and its dynamics are at the centre of an understanding of human consciousness and the emotions are the passionate expression of the intentional direction of human beings into their life-worlds. The relatively extreme emotional manifestations of human intentional consciousness (a consciousness which is enduringly passionate or sensible in the world) that I have discussed indicate how the dynamics of conscious experience are affected by radical changes in intentional processes. Basic to this approach is that consciousness is always rooted in the body, and always experienced as a motion of the body. This phenomenological orientation is directed to overcome mind-body dualisms of the Cartesian kind. Such dualisms are not easily disposed of, even in recent perspectives being developed towards the study of mind and consciousness in biology, psychology and other disciplines. For example, some approaches in cognitive psychology, as Fodor argues (1983), demonstrate what can be called a neo-Cartesianism. Recently, Edelman (1994), pursuing a Darwinian evolutionist approach to brain/consciousness, and alive to an intentionalist perspective, nonetheless recreates a Cartesianism in a brain/consciousness and body divide. In his reaction to approaches that do not ground consciousness in foundational biological processes, Edelman overlooks some advantages of an intentionalist perspective. The approach insists on the fact that consciousness is grounded in the body and in the world and that such a unity is dynamic (and therefore consciousness is constantly dynamic and shifting its character). The unity of body and world is through the process of intentionality.

The difficulty in escaping Cartesian dualism or, what Dennett (1991) refers to as the 'Cartesian theatre' perspective, is not merely, I suggest, a function of Western cosmological assumptions grounded in the history of Western philosophical and scientific thought. The intentionality of consciousness, its leap towards the world and its further development within a field of consciousness, the space of intersection of the intentionalities of other human beings, can create the suggestion within embodied experience that consciousness is something separate from the body. Such experience, including, perhaps, 'out-of-body' experiences and the Eve or multiple personality phenomenon (see Kenny 1986; Littlewood this volume), is testimony to the intentionality of consciousness.

Some experiences manifest an overriding or overwhelming of consciousness, in which consciousness appears to be dramatically free and even disembodied. Dreaming is an example and I have discussed the fearful imaginary in sorcery experience which includes the sensation of consciousness as something alien to the body that crushes against it and invades within. I have understood certain aspects of these processes in terms of a notion of the 'chained consciousness'. This occurs in the situation of the immobilized body which nonetheless maintains its motility in the intentional thrust of consciousness. It might be said that the fundamental motional unity of body and consciousness in the activities of fully wakeful life is disrupted. The intentionality of consciousness comes up against the factuality that the body of consciousness is chained. In this condition, perhaps, an intentional consciousness enters into a 'frenzy' of movement, strains against the motionlessness of the physical body, sometimes exploding it into wakefulness or, else, exhausting itself in a fury of images of that experiential world to which it extends and which is integral to the constitution of consciousness; occasionally attacking that which has become its limitation rather than the engine of movement, the very body of consciousness.

Aspects of Sinhalese sorcery practice have been engaged to pursue an argument that draws very freely on perspectives within a Western philosophical phenomenology and existentialism. This does not mean that such approaches have authority in the understanding of sorcery. In my view a phenomenology sets out in more abstract terms what already is richly exfoliated in sorcery beliefs and practices: possibly especially so given the South Asian context of the ethnography, a world whose cosmologies are widely agreed to explore notions that a Western phenomenology may be seen to have reinvented. However, this aside, I stress the authority which Sinhalese sorcery practice, and what is defined as sorcery more widely by anthropologists, has in the understanding of such complex issues as the nature of human consciousness and the circumstances of its formation. Sorcery practices implicitly and often most explicitly develop their understanding of human experience on the basis of the embodiment of human consciousness and that this consciousness is intentional. Furthermore, it is an intentionality that has effect and is affected and effected by its motion and participation within a field of consciousness. Consciousness, in other words, while embodied, nonetheless extends beyond its physical confines into the world which is fundamentally and inseparably part of the dimensionality of consciousness. Sorcery beliefs and practices are cultural constructions on the historical worlds of those who live them. But more than this, they express what I take to be the factuality of the experiential consciousness of human being, that it is intentional. Sorcery beliefs and practices in the sense I am pursuing here are not merely representations of historical worlds, an historical consciousness. Also, they reveal dynamics at the heart of the emergence of human consciousness and experience which, indeed, are active in the creation and destruction of those actualities which sorcery beliefs and practices often so marvellously reflect or refract.

NOTES

My thanks to Buck Schieffelin, and to my students at University College London, for their criticisms.

1 Searle (1983; 1984) discusses consciousness and mind through a similar approach to intentionality. However, he chooses to give little attention to the pioneering work of Husserl and other phenomenologists on the matter. His notion of intentionality includes motivation and value which are excluded from my usage.

2 This story is a folk extension of a story in the Buddhist textual tradition concerning the origin of the world known as the Agganna Sutta.

3 Vasavarta Maraya in local traditions is often associated with Devadatta, the cousin of Gautama Buddha who abandoned the Buddha's teaching and became his enemy.

4 Elsewhere (Kapferer forthcoming), I interpret Mahasammata as the embodiment of the collective consciousness of human being to create the order of the political world.

5 Most of the shrines to the demon/deities, and Suniyam in particular, are of relatively recent origin. The Suniyam shrines began to grow up in the capital of Colombo early this century and expanded after the Second World War following considerable migration from peasant and smaller urban areas, largely in the south of the island. Their priests (*kapurala*) are usually persons without a family tradition of shrine work and have often come into practice after a series of existential problems encountered in ordinary life (e.g. see Obeyesekere 1981; Gombrich and Obeyesekere 1989). Their ideas are often highly distinct from those of *adura* (exorcists) who generally come from low castes in the Sinhala hierarchy and belong to family traditions of sorcery and other healing practice (see Kapferer 1983). Nonetheless, shrine priests and *adura* occupy the one diverse cultural field and their ideas and innovations are mutually influential. In many ways, the often highly original practices of the shrine priests 'naively' reproduce the more systematic and ritually worked out arguments engaged in the sorcery rituals, such as the Suniyama, conducted routinely by *adura*.

6 In *Encounters* Goffman (1958) demonstrates how outbursts of emotion are strategically used to transform the situations of interaction.

7 Lynch produces a useful survey of approaches to the emotions. He states, 'Cognitivism, as an approach to the study of emotion, has developed into many variations, some of which retain a universalist perspective. One variation of cognitivism, social constructionism, is particularly influential in anthropology. Social constructionism modified by insights from deconstruction is the theoretical perspective within which most essays in this volume must be understood' (Lynch 1991: 8). This approach is overly dismissive of others. This derives, I think, from its thorough relativism founded in a perspective (of cultural categories of cognition) which no amount of appeal to 'deconstructionism' will modify adequately.

REFERENCES

Dennett, D. (1991) *Consciousness Explained*, London: Penguin.

Edelman, G. (1994) *Bright Air, Brilliant Fire: On the Matter of the Mind*, London: Penguin.

Evans-Pritchard, E. E. (1937) *Witchcraft, Oracles and Magic Among the Azande*, Oxford: Clarendon Press.

Fodor, J. (1983) *The Modularity of Mind*, Cambridge, Mass.: MIT Press.

Gombrich, R. and Obeyesekere, G. (1989) *Buddhism Transformed*, Princeton: Princeton University Press.

Husserl, E. (1960) *Cartesian Meditations*, trans. D. Cairns, New York: Collier.

Husserl, E. (1964) *The Idea of Phenomenology*, trans. W. Palston and G. Nakhnikian, The Hague: Martinus Nijhoff.

Kapferer, B. (1983) *A Celebration of Demons*, Bloomington: Indiana University Press.

Kapferer, B. (forthcoming) *The Feast of Power: Sorcery, Sociality and Violence in Sri Lanka*.

Kenny, M. G. (1986) *The Passion of Ansel Bourne: Multiple Personality in American Culture*, Washington, DC: Smithsonian Institution Press.

Lutz, C. (1988) 'The domain of emotion words in Ifaluk', *American Ethnologist*, 9: 113–28.

Lutz, C. and Abu-Lughod, L. (1990) *Language and Politics of Emotion*, Cambridge: Cambridge University Press.

Lynch, O. (ed.) (1991) *Divine Passions: The Social Construction of Emotion in India*, Los Angeles: University of California Press.

Merleau-Ponty, M. (1962) *Phenomenology of Perception*, trans. C. Smith, London: Routledge.

Muralt, A. de (1974) *The Idea of Phenomenology: Husserlian Exemplarism*, Evanston: Northwestern University Press.

Obeyesekere, G. (1981) *Medusa's Hair: An Essay on Personal Symbols and Religious Experience*, Chicago: University of Chicago Press.

Rosaldo, M. Z. (1980) *Knowledge and Passion*, Cambridge: Cambridge University Press.

Sartre, J.-P. (1958) *Being and Nothingness*, trans. H. E. Barnes, London: Methuen.

Searle, J. R. (1983) *Intentionality: An Essay in the Philosophy of Mind*, Cambridge: Cambridge University Press.

Searle, J. R. (1984) *Minds, Brains and Science*, London: Penguin.

Chapter 8

The return of multiple consciousne

Decadence and postmodernity in the specification of psychopathology

Roland Littlewood

As with any other social fact, we can interpret an illness as somehow characteristic of the particular society in which it is found. Such specificity has been a particular problem for comparative psychiatry: can we argue both local specification as well as membership of some more universal psychopathological category when a 'behavioural syndrome appearing in widely differing cultures takes on local meaning so completely that it appears uniquely suited to articulate important dimensions of each local culture, as though it had sprung naturally from that environment' (Good *et al.* 1992)? Alternatively we can start from the idea that where some general category of 'illness' or other loss of personal agency is locally recognized, this category is then shaped and deployed, through fluctuating popularity and social contingencies, and through the immediate interests of therapeutic networks, their experts and victims (Lloyd 1990). European anthropology has turned from interpreting the 'total social fact' to a recognition that institutions are constructed through instrumental actions, and that rather than take these actions just as reflections of mentalities or political processes of society at large, we should examine in closer detail the practical power which is available to individuals at particular historical moments.[1] In this chapter I consider the reemergence of the phenomenon of multiple personality – *double consciousness* as it was described by the neuropsychiatrists of the late nineteenth century.

DOUBLE CONSCIOUSNESS

The diagnosis of double consciousness – in which two different personal-ities coexist in association with a single physical body – became fashion-able in France and America between 1880 and 1900, collecting together a multitude of other phenomena: catalepsy, fugue and trance states, mediumship and spiritism, demonic possession, visions and dreams, tel-epathy and automatic writing, somnambulism, crystal-ball gazing and other forms of divination, the automatism of urban crowds, conscripted soldiers and criminals, religious conversion and stigmata, revivalism and folk panics; and, centrally, hypnotism and its earlier manifestations, mes-merism and magnetism. Magnetizers had discovered that their subjects could be placed in a state akin to sleep and then induced to perform actions of which they had no memory when they later 'awoke'. Under the influence of two French neurologists, Jean-Martin Charcot and Pierre Janet, the hypnotic state was elided with *hysteria*, a term deriving from the Hippocratics which by the late nineteenth century included a number of phasic phenomena: the hysterical patient, usually young and female, returning at intervals, generally within hours, to her normal state appar-ently ignorant of the episode. Symptoms included amnesia, blindness, anaesthesia, hallucinations, excited and inappropriate behaviour, together with fits and paralyses which did not conform with anatomical knowledge but rather with popular conceptions of what it was to be amnesic or paralysed. Charcot distinguished hysterical fits from epilepsy in that they were 'caused by ideas'. There was already widespread popular and medico-legal interest in whether murder could be committed by a sleeping or hypnotic double. Was the patient then to be considered responsible? In placing hysteria together with other instances of the 'narrowing of the field of consciousness', Charcot called attention to the *aboulia* – the loss of will – which characterized all these patterns; though apparently pur-poseful in avoiding or forgetting unpleasant experiences, the patient could not be held to be fully aware or responsible for their hysteria. Conscious-ness[2] was somehow 'dissociated', to use Janet's term, and the patient seemed blandly indifferent or even unaware of the impact of her symp-toms upon others.

From the 1830s it had been recognized that double consciousness, the most dramatic form of hysteria, could emerge either spontaneously or in the course of hypnotic treatment for nervous complaints (Ellenberger 1970: 129–31). The patients were typically young women who seemed to alternate between two states: the first recalling the original personality as recognized by her family, sick, inhibited and quiet, often a prim martyr who complained of being 'possessed by something' (Kenny 1986: 150). By contrast her second state was flirtatious, untamed and irresponsible. Characteristically there was one-way amnesia, the second 'personality' (as the state was recognized in the more extended cases) being aware of the first. A third or subsequent personality might then emerge which had variable knowledge of the earlier personalities. With practice the experi-enced physician could summon or dismiss these through hypnosis or simply by firmly instructing the patient. The extent to which he might recognize and name the emergent personalities as separate individuals is well illustrated by Morton Prince's (1905) treatment of Miss Beauchamp, a patient in 1890s Boston. As the different personalities emerge during the medical consultation, they write letters to each other and to Dr Prince, spy and play tricks; they have different appetites, musical abilities and susceptibility to illness. Yet they seem unified enough to present a single public front outside the consulting room, to travel and run a household. Prince pursues 'the real Miss Beauchamp', eliciting the help of one personality against another, intriguing, making and breaking pacts, yet constantly deceived by the emergence of new personalities and half-personalities or the elision of the existing ones. He attempts to fuse or else 'kill off' some personalities. In their struggle, both personalities and doctor frequently evoke the idiom of demonic possession, Dr Prince threatening to send the lesser personalities 'back where they came from'. His account also recalls a farcical comedy of errors with the personalities either on or off 'the stage' (Prince 1978: 7) and he begins to wonder if he is really treating a family as he addresses separate letters to each. (Regrettably they steal and read each other's mail.) Prince labels the personalities B1, B2 and so on, and develops increasingly complicated diagrams to illustrate their relative knowledge and control over each other. Meanwhile his gripping reports on the progress of the case in medical conferences have become well known, and one of Miss B's personalities herself develops an interest in clinical psychology. The personality Prince eventually identifies as 'the real Miss B' reads his final manuscript before publication, marries one of his colleagues, and her published case is soon made into a popular play.

To see, as we might now do, Dr Prince as blithely avoiding his patient's conflicting aspirations, concretizing her possible identities as fascinating serial phenomena, with Miss B herself continually outwitting her physician, leading him on, teasing, fighting under the guise of *aboulia* with the weapons at her disposal, is tempting, but it is to impose our own commonsense assumptions (and her doctor's) of a unitary self somewhere 'behind' all the personalities. Medical interpretation of multiple consciousness assumed that in the general run of things there is a single bounded volitional self, which shares a biography with the body, reflecting and directing its experiences, with a characteristic and enduring identity of personal sentiments, abilities and memories, which are experienced and perceived as hanging together.[3] But this hanging together becomes unstuck in dreams, or in the usual processes of forgetting and inattention, such that chunks of past experience cannot necessarily be recalled simultaneously; and under appropriate conditions (brain damage, inherited constitution, emotional trauma, hypnosis) the split-off fragments might be so extensive as to constitute a parallel secondary personality (Janet 1925; Ellenberger 1970: Ch. 3). But it was uncertain how much the latter should be seen as split off from an integral unitary consciousness to which it then became generally inaccessible, or else regarded as clusters of actually existing subpersonalities which always underlay (or even constituted) the conscious personality of everyday life. In either case, their appearance was generally taken as a diminution in 'nervous energy'

(Janet) occasioned by hereditary vulnerability and various traumata, including industrial and railway accidents, unpleasant news, sexual violence and sexual frustration, and conflicting moral demands. Whether this energy itself had physical existence akin to that of magnetism and of the presumed communication between the newly discovered cells of the brain was arguable: in the 1890s French neurologists attempted to transfer hysterical symptoms and even personalities from one patient to another by means of powerful magnets or telepathy, but it became increasingly accepted that 'magnetism' was an analogy for something rather less concrete.[4]

Janet argued that narrowed consciousness had a practical function in hiding traumatic memories from awareness. Like Ribot, he argued that double consciousness refuted Kant's transcendental self, for consciousness was evidently generated in experience. Ellenberger (1966) has suggested that this dynamic model of hysteria owed much to the Catholic notion of the pathogenic secret in which purgation of guilt for secret crimes, incest or infanticide, resulted in physical and spiritual healing. For Protestants, the pastoral 'cure of souls' provided an increasingly secular and explicitly psychological alternative, confession being reframed as a cathartic recall to awareness of the guilty act. The neurologists of the French Second Republic claimed that they had uncovered the clinical underpinnings of clerical superstition and popular credulity: the guilty secret life of the gambler, criminal and eccentric now being recognized as the ludic secondary personality. Romantic and symbolist literature too were preoccupied by this notion of a shadow or double (Hoffman, Goethe, Hogg, Poe, Dostoevsky, Stevenson, Wilde), now less a demonic familiar or changeling than some deeper and amoral persistence in the mind of an earlier evolutionary and mythopoeic epoch. Many of the New England psychologists who remained close to transcendentalism and even spiritualism retained a more ambiguous attitude to the supernatural, allowing it entry to the physical through certain extreme bodily states in a dualist metaphysics by which mind and matter came together and separated under particular conditions.[5] They attempted with professional mediums the same hypnotic experiments as with their neurasthenic patients. As an organized body of ideas, following the widely reported experiences of the Fox sisters in 1847, spiritualism swept the United States. Spontaneous communications with the other world became standardized through gifted female mediums, together with the increasingly routinized phenomena of automatic writing, seances, table rapping and messages from the dead; the other world less a distant paradise than a cloudy Homeric underworld populated by somewhat banal spirit guides. Spiritualists saw themselves as establishing a natural religion free from clerical obscurantism and dogmatism; they were enthusiasts for biological evolution, for the emancipation of slaves and women, for social welfare and public health: American perfectionists whose ideas and membership overlapped with Christian Scientists (who denied the reality of sickness) and Transcendentalists (who denied evil and eternal punishment). Spiritualism has continued to wax and wane, the contacts on the other side being variously understood as congealed *psychic energy* or taking distinct personalities as named *controls, guides, spirits* and (in the orientalist groups) *masters.*

Between 1900 and 1910 double consciousness suddenly disappeared from the medical literature. The diagnosis had unified what we might now distinguish as neurological and psychological interests; after Charcot's death the two diverged, to come close again only in the 'cognitive science' of the 1980s. Charcot's successors concentrated research on those psychological conditions which presumed an underlying biological disease; they hinted that his working-class patients had been rewarded with a pension, that they had deliberately faked double consciousness and hysteria, and had seduced his medical students. Leading in the opposite direction, Freud's psychoanalysis had followed the Parisian and Bostonian move away from hereditary suggestibility to emphasize the meaning for the patient of the symptoms, to develop a dynamic psychological model in which our lower instincts and appetites, like the *controls* of the spiritualists, sought to translate themselves into higher forms. A more developmental 'biology-up' unconscious (rather than a working down from the unitary consciousness of everyday experience) explained the popular recognition that at some level people might act against what seemed to be their real interests, moral agency being thus more complex than allowed for in clinical medicine. Psychoanalysts took Janet's idea of a distinct subconscious personality simply as a part of normal functioning, and the 'self' they elaborated was now less unified and enduring; that it could compete with other selves of the same order, each bearing proper names and associated with the same body, became increasingly implausible. Opponents of Freud criticized his psychology for reifying its subpersonal mechanisms (ego, super-ego, id) as if these were distinct personalities, but psychoanalytical emphasis on the integration of the moral personality, together with a greater interest in the relationship between doctor and patient, seem to have avoided any proliferation of new personalities in the course of treatment. Psychoanalysis divorced itself from the clinical dramas of the public hospital, becoming an increasingly interpretive procedure, its patients bourgeois, the setting private, the clinical relationship contractual.

MULTIPLE CONSCIOUSNESS AND THE ETHNOGRAPHY OF SPIRIT POSSESSION

Citing parallels between psychotherapy and popular healing, Janet traced a development from medieval witchcraft and spirit possession, through magnetism and spiritualism to the neurological clinic (Janet 1925). Double consciousness he took as purely intrapersonal; and thus its Western expression as something 'psychological' rather than 'spiritual' more truly reflected its origin, as did the new clinical treatment which argued for the integration of what were subjective phenomena. (For consciousness is now more real to us than the spirits.) Similarly, those anthropological models of mediumship and possession influenced by psychiatry argued that the spirits represented the personified externalization of standardized psychological conflicts which went along with a generally animistic reading of the natural world. The contemporary Western representatives of this primitive psychology were hysterics and women, regressing back to an earlier evolutionary level of suggestibility and magical thinking.

The anthropological debate on primitive mentality need not be traced here, except to note its shift from a psychology of mechanism to a sociological reading in which 'indigenous psychologies' represent particular cultural sentiments and histories through categories of personhood, autonomy, moral agency, character, responsibility and the like; and that these categories are pragmatically deployed in certain situations. The theoretical language now adopted is less clinical and of a higher order of generality, allowing incorporation of less obviously medical concerns: affliction or invidia rather than psychological trauma, alternative phases of consciousness rather than hysteria and possession states, creativity rather than pathology. But the scholarly consensus on the psychophysiology of spirit possession and multiple personality remains not unlike that elaborated in the 1890s: people have the ability to dissociate their mental processes and do so the whole time – through changing moods, selective attention and putting unpleasant issues 'out of mind', through fantasy and dreaming. Some of these private experiences are not easily remembered, because they are hardly significant enough to remark upon, because memories of them have faded, or else because they are unpleasant or painful in some way. Immediate awareness fluctuates, dependent on what we recognize as intended perception; the quality of our will being variable, dependent on our immediate interests and customary procedures: you can eat an apple whilst riding your bicycle but you are not equally 'in' each activity at any one moment, nor are you generally aware of switching from one to the other deliberately for your stream of awareness appears a seamless web. To be conscious is to focus attention on something, bestowing reality on perception: a neocortical disposition selected in evolution which enables the organism to engage flexibly with different situations (Campbell *et al.* 1925: 1–12; Ornstein 1985); and our ability to dissociate is adaptive in switching attention, in avoiding sensory overload and physical pain, or terrifying and conflictual situations.

Dissociation is thus the necessary flip side of consciousness: it allows a private system of representation and self-monitoring, permitting reflection, anticipation, planning, creative imagination, recognition of another's motives and identification with them, acting and deceit: requirements for our formulating complex programmes of social action. Under certain conditions such as hypnosis, or particular types of sensory patterning, deprivation or overload, hyperventilation or the ingestion of psychoactive substances, dissociation can be facilitated to enhance or diminish concentration, to daydream or meditate, as a sense of community or 'out-of-body experience', as hallucinations, anaesthesia or paralysis. Because of their distinctive physiological facilitation, these experiences, like religious conversion or artistic inspiration, may be recognized as something external through our cultural schema of a bounded self as the usual locus of experience and volition with our particular notions of external reality, causality and personal subjectivity; and they are realized through standardized practices. They may cease to be recognized as our own processes, to become personified as human-like entities, whether benign or malevolent.[6] Out of the alternative modes of human consciousness a culture selects its 'ordinary consciousness', its 'characteristic and habitual patterning of mental functioning that adapts the individual ... to survive in his culture's consensual reality' (Tart 1980: 249).

This standard model leaves certain problems. Its emphasis on the more extensive type of dissociation privileges a prior physiological state over the local psychology which explains it; particularly in the generally unremarked fluctuations of our daily awareness it is difficult to make this distinction, thus rendering everyday consciousness and moral agency relatively unproblematic and fixed. Nor does it allow for less verbalized schemata for a multiplex self: particularly through pregnancy, but also lactation, menstruation, masturbation, coitus, dance, play, pratfall, violence, blushing, feeding, excretion, disease, sleeping and dreaming.

The similarity between subpersonal elements in rather different psychologies has often been remarked. Horton (1983) notes the convergence between the psychoanalytical schema (ego, id and super-ego processes) and certain West African psychologies (the individual having 'agencies' derived from a unique soul, from nature, and lineage).[7] These elements are not generally experienced or identified as separate centres of awareness, for by and large, our everyday 'self'[8] does seem fairly unitary, with the development in early life of an internally consistent awareness as the locus of biographical experience (Laughlin et al. 1992), and which is recognized by others as an entity continuing through time and morally accountable for its past actions: a centre of narrative gravity, as Dennett (1971) puts it. Both psychoanalytic and West African schemata are accounts which reconcile our understanding that we are indeed unique, self-aware and volitional individuals yet we share something of our identity with animals and with our fellows. In circumstances where everyday identity does not hang together in the expected way, when our taken-for-granted boundary between action and contingency is radically disrupted by dispute, disaster or sickness, we may emphasize such available distinctions and give the elements a greater degree of personified autonomy such that moral relations between them serve for an immediate causal explanation.

Yet our experience of an enduring self is multifaceted. We generally 'occupy' a variety of roles, titles, offices and statuses, without these obscuring some continuing personal identity. We are not distinct individuals in each, and usually these identities do not conflict too much, yet we adopt a different comportment and social character (persona) in each, context dependent yet drawn from and representing an enduring individual, even if in certain circumstances we identify more fully with one or other. The selves of multiple personalities or possessing spirits may advertise a particular social status, often one to which we do not usually have access. For, against the nineteenth century neurologists, we might argue that alternative personalities are not simply an existing part of us which is then split off, but rather new potentials, ambitions, strategems, perversities and imagined identities, which we try on to see how they fit, whether aspiring to adopt them permanently, or just in game-playing masquerade or private fantasy. And there are all sorts of options and uncertainties along different continua: play acting, glossolalia, personae nominalized through social standardization as representing personified values, historical or cosmological figures.

MULTIPLE PERSONALITY RETURNS

Reportings of double consciousness declined in Europe and America from 1900. Sporadic cases occasionally appeared, and the popular image of the good/bad double was continually replayed through films based on the classic Gothic novels but also through the cinematic popularization of psychoanalysis itself, where in an accessible linear narrative personal conflicts were represented as variant personifications or dreams of the same individual. In the late 1970s, following public concern about widespread sexual abuse of female children, cases of multiple personality began to emerge again in the United States. As before, questions of authenticity and medical suggestion were immediately raised. The psychiatrist who had treated Christine Sizeman (well known through the film based on *The Three Faces of Eve* [Thigpen and Cleckley 1957]), argued that spontaneous multiple personality was rare. After the film made him famous he was besieged by *multiples*, as individuals with multiple personality disorder (MPD) were now called: of the thousands of patients he saw in the thirty years after Eve, only one he regarded as genuine, that is spontaneous and prior to medical intervention (Burne 1993).

MPD differed from nineteenth century double consciousness in the sheer number of personalities who now appeared. Sybil, the first well-publicized case attributed to repressed memories of sexual abuse, developed sixteen personalities.[9] Eve, who had retired from public view presumed cured, now returned with twenty-two personalities, to chair the recently formed International Society for the Study of Multiple Personality. An increasingly vocal activist group, Speaking For Ourselves, criticized doubting doctors (Kenny 1986), whilst sympathetic psychiatrists provided public legitimation with a supportive new journal, *Dissociation*. Significantly, they now ascribed to each personality proper names by which they were addressed in therapy. The spontaneity of the syndrome has continued to be argued in the medical press, particularly as to whether lost memories could be accurately recalled to awareness decades later (Aldridge-Morris 1989; Friesen 1991).[10] Some doctors maintain that MPD can be identified in 10 per cent of psychiatric patients whilst popular self-help manuals argue that half the female American population have been sexually abused. The question of induction through mass publicity or through the particular therapies used (hypnosis, guided imagery, body massage) is countered with the argument that genuine MPD is the consequence of a hidden trauma in which the pain is so intense that the self 'leaves' (Crabtree 1985): its public recognition simply enables multiples to seek professional support or to recognize the condition in themselves.

Over a hundred different secondary personalities (*alters*) associated with the same physical body have been identified, many with consistent differences in handedness, facial expression, cerebral bloodflow and EEG recordings, up to 60 points difference in IQ scores, with their own characteristic visual abilities, handwriting, vocabulary, speech patterns and immunological responses, with different memories, personal and family histories, different ages, genders, ethnicity; they are often suicidal, self-mutilating, self-hating, and sometimes violent.[11] Compared with their nineteenth century predecessors, not only do larger numbers of personalities emerge but these seem generally more aware of each, coming and going relatively freely outside clinical sessions, conversing together as they scheme, quarrel, choose their different wardrobes or obtain spectacle prescriptions consistent with their various ages. Medical treatment of the new epidemic initially recalled that of the last century: hypnosis and persuasion to discharge the pathogenic secret and reintegrate the alters with the original self. As before, the secondary personalities objected to being killed off. But now, with the appearance of the multiple activists on television shows, and through well-publicized court defences that the personality in the dock was not the same one who had committed the crime (the defendant when giving evidence being sworn in separately under their different personalities), the alters have gained a public voice and demand their legal right to life. They are now accommodated not exorcized; killing them off is regarded by the multiple movement as murder, as the concealment of one crime by another (Hacking 1991). The preferred therapy is to keep all the personalities in play, to encourage 'mutual awareness and communication' between them in what has increasingly come to resemble family therapy. Hypnotherapists encourage the patient to meet and comfort their abused earlier self, or to 'come out and play' only in dreamtime. Drama therapists enable each individual in their group to take on and role-play one of the personalities elicited from one of their number.

In the 1890s doctors sympathetic to spiritualism had sometimes accepted secondary personalities as visiting benign spirits. This interpretation too has returned but now in a demonic variant. Sexual abuse of children in both Britain and America has been linked with satanic cannibalism and child sacrifice (Sinason 1994). The idea has been encouraged among teachers and social workers by charismatic Christian networks which practise exorcism and generally favour a diabolical interpretation of human malevolence.[12] One Harvard psychiatrist argues that the sexual abuse is carried out not by the child's family but by extraterrestrials who abduct and then return the victim. The multiple selves are variously taken as the possessing aliens themselves, as the psychological representation or psychic reincarnation of the human perpetrator, as living or deceased family members, as new attempts at self-healing, or as the lost person of an abusive childhood (Crabtree 1985). Christian psychiatrists describe them as incubi, as congealed ancestral vices or as the vengeful spirits of aborted foetuses.

The spontaneous occurrence of MPD has recently been challenged. Seven thousand people have joined an anti-MPD group, the False Memory Syndrome Foundation. Legal suits by adults against their parents for having sexually abused them as children, and against doctors for having failed to diagnose their MPD, have been met by counter-claims against the individual's current doctors for inducing a 'false memory syndrome' in distressed individuals who are persuaded to recall nonexistent sexual abuse, backed up by 'survivors' manuals' and the widespread publicity on MPD. (Damages against the parent for sexual abuse have been of the order of up to $5 million.) The question of legally establishing the existence of abuse is confused by the absence of clear physical signs and the obvious questions as to the suggestibility of child or patient as a potential witness (Horn 1993).

THE FLANEUR AND THE CYBERPUNK: DECADENT AND POSTMODERN SPACES

Double consciousness and MPD have sufficient resemblance to each other to justify our comparing them under the common rubric of multiple personality.[13] Contemporary multiples regard both manifestations as the same pattern and are familiar with the earlier literature. Whether we read the pattern as an idiom of distress, as a psychological defence or as a creative fantasy, whether we grant it some existence as a distinct psychophysiological state, socially induced or requiring public acceptance to bring it into the open, its local context and meanings are significant. Can either wave be related to a coherent group of professional interests, or to some more diffuse susceptibility of the times? We can recognize in both epidemics a committed network of expert doctors and psychologists who accept the phenomenon as a legitimate matter of interest, diagnosing it where others fail, and who are identified with it through newspaper articles, publicized case histories and, in the second wave, cinema dramatizations and television shows.

Expert groups maintain the necessity of their therapeutic activities by offering an illness as emblematic of the current preoccupations, 'the national disease', 'the sickness of our age', 'our number one mental health problem': a prototype to which other ills are referred or into which they are subsumed. (Young [1983] has proposed post-traumatic stress disorder – of which MPD is often taken as a variant – as originally a medical exculpation for the guilt of Vietnam War veterans, a diagnosis that has then become available for taking on other vexed questions of the attribution of personal or institutional responsibility.) It is not too difficult to devise such homologies between individual and society, the experiencing self offering a microcosm of wider issues, the dissociation of the individual standing for the dissociation of the collectivity, now less a hierarchy than a contractual network.[14] It is less easy to show how such models plausibly motivate personal experiences. That the self is a mirror of society is itself a local psychology: Europeans may see it that way, or they may not, or more likely they see it that way in certain situations.

In the United States, during the late nineteenth century as much as now, personal failure requires less some sense of bad luck than of the malevolence of others or of competitive disadvantage – with recourse to legal redress or to the sort of 'positive' transformation, eliding religious conversion, self-knowledge and managerial presentation, exemplified by Dale Carnegie or Vincent Pearle. The United States has always taken itself as the site of strategic self-fashioning, by which diverse immigrant groups realize themselves as Americans as they move to higher status jobs, improve their education, as they change residence, neighbourhood, profession, friends, spouses, political affiliation, leisure activities, voluntary associations and even their name and religion, with associated changes of mannerism, comportment, language and dress. Their identity is achieved in the very process of transformation, in fulfilling some inherent potential, both as the normative expectation of what it is to be genuinely American and as a practical possibility, articulated for men in popular manuals of self-help and entrepreneurial psychology, for women through remodelling their bodies by dieting and plastic surgery; realizing one's 'personality' in the marketing of it, articulated through a politico-thera-peutic language of communication, growth, space, realization and sin-cerity. Psychology is the American cultural idiom, one which argues for individualism and self-sufficiency, for personal choice and instrumental action, for attaining self-knowledge. What might be regarded elsewhere as an extreme response to current dissatisfaction with personal circum-stances – voluntarily disappearing from one's present neighbourhood and family to emerge elsewhere with a new name and a new identity – is facilitated by a publishing house which has produced over thirty manuals to teach something British psychiatrists might recognize as a hysterical fugue.[15]

I am aware that this is a European image of the United States which since Trollope and Toqueville has seen America as anomic and neotenic, its emphasis on personal self-transformation as an avoidance of the recog-nition of class conflict, its institutions sustained by periodic moral panics and social dramas, its citizens unable to agree on what constitutes reality without recourse to legal or medical expertise. Yet America's 'obsession with self-awareness' (Kenny 1986: 2) is well recognized by its own cultural critics (Kenny 1986; Lasch 1978). Self-realization through pulling on one's bootstraps has always been central to what it is to be an American – from the frontier regeneration of the Great Awakening and its transform-ation of self and nature, to transcendentalism, pragmatism, progressivism, 'little man' populism, to boosterism and soroptimism: a quest for sincerity, for achieved rather than ascribed status, a fundamentally optimistic view that time and space still lie unlimited before us. Upward social mobility and perfectionism are hardly limited to America, and it is easy to identify in any society a concern with rapid social change, the breakdown of family life and traditional interpersonal ties, as did the European pessimism of Herder, Gissing, Pater and Musil, but it has seemed integral to the American way of life to regard incompleteness as the accepted state of affairs.

In any period of perceived change, society and self may each be seen as fragmented or double, estranged from the past to face an uncertain future.[16] If George Gissing bemoaned the end of the nineteenth century as 'decades of sexual anarchy . . . with the laws governing human identity, friendships and sexual behaviour breaking down', now our 'radical demo-cratisation of the personal' (Giddens 1992), our fragmented and commodi-fied performance of alternative selves, may be argued to be especially part of the late modern condition (Wilson 1988). With the decline of Calvinist moral imperatives, American individualism has become, as Lears (1983) puts it, 'weightless and unreal'. Is there anything more specific about contemporary *fin-de-siècle* America, endlessly self-creating, poly-phonic, ludic and multiplex,[17] which suggests closer parallels with late nineteenth century France? – that other daughter of the Enlightenment which perceived itself as preoccupied with artifice and representation, recognizing the commodification of sex and marriage, anxious about the sexual exploitation of children and about female emancipation; another legalistic republic characterized by the detachment of the voyeuristic boulevard flaneur posing in the rootless *spleen* of the anonymous urban crowd; new and impersonal urban stores; increased opportunities for mobility and travel; enthusiasms for bodily transformation and athletics; with the intermittent emergence of variant sexualities, and the loss of traditional clerical authority under the governments of the Third Republic: public concerns ambivalently countered by a response which Ellenberger (1970: 279–83) has characterized as 'Neo-Romantic' – irrational, narcissistic, decadent and primitivist, positivism's images of boundless technological progress and limitless material prosperity now foreclosed, shot through with pessimism and a sense that time was running out with the century, the race exhausted, its vigour dissipated, with a quest for secular myths and new heroes, or else for mystical continuities with a natural world that at times seemed exhausted too, with a return to religious orthodoxy or else to domesticated variants of Eastern religions. In the United States the brief resurgence of Protestant fundamentalism in the 1980s required public figures to declare that they had been 'born again': recalling the earlier fate of double consciousness, this demand for testimonies of spontaneity collapsed in religious scandals and cynical accusations of feigning; we might wonder if the demands for 'born again' testimonies should be taken as a response to the perceived fragmentation of personal identity (as argued by its protagonists) or simply a manifestation of it.

It would be easy to delineate a multitude of parallels between the end of the French nineteenth century and the end of the American twentieth. More specifically we might note a shift in the contemporary self, not so much dissociation as relocation, the external physical frontiers becoming more congested and foreshortened so that our bodies turn in on themselves, self-sufficient through dietetics and 'body consciousness'. We are both lesser than we thought, as simply elements in a natural world which is indifferent to human interests; and greater, in that we recognize this world only as refracted through our cognitions. Multiple personality was once attributed to the introduction of the photograph, the phonograph, the telephone and the X-ray (Ellenberger 1970).[18] Where then did the telephone conversation take place? We might argue – in what we now term emergent 'cyberspace' – in the virtual architecture of electronically-sustained memory which we enter through our personal computer, in interactive television (and more recently virtual reality), in electronic mail, Internet, multidimensional graphic user interfaces and hypertext, in 'personal' marketing profiles generated by credit card use, video conferencing, Minitel and teledildonics: a global technology which questions individual work, property, value and ownership, and which radically resituates the location of our taken-for-granted physical experience and interactions in a post-industrial and post-corporeal global space. As do the 'transferable' elements of our human body shop – sperm, egg, embryo and organ banks, fertility drugs and multiple births, cerebral implants of foetal tissue, electronic prostheses and gene splicing. For women these are particularly significant in the debate on foetal personhood – the obvious embodied schema for two beings housed in one body. Like the medieval mechanical clock, the computer has become our 'defining technology' (Bolter 1986), a model for the self now seen through an idiom of inputs and outputs, the body as hardware, consciousness as software. But computers are not just an available metaphor or fetishized technology, for the computer circuit actually embodies rather than merely represents symbolic logic in a virtual space which in each generation of computers seeks to grow ever larger in relation to the physical space of its linear circuits and available telephone bandwidth. Cyberpunk literature, like the not dissimilar 'hard AI' and Artificial Life arguments, offers more than a fantasized model of the self – rather a model for a virtual self which has no inevitable locus in the physical body. Human minds have become serial virtual machines implemented on parallel hardware, and MPD just a different program run on this same hardware. 'Cyberspace becomes another venue for consciousness itself . . . Animism is not only possible, it is implicit . . . To the body in cyberspace we are the mind. By a strange reversal of our cultural expectations, however, it is the body in cyberspace that is immortal, while the animating soul, housed in a body outside cyberspace, faces mortality' (Benedict 1991: 124, 240, 241).

I do not want to make too much of this: dedicated on-line computers are just the latest reshaping of embodied individual agency in an historical progression that includes tools, speech, clothing, residence, figurative representation, silent reading, autobiography, linear perspective, the novel, pornography and mechanized transport; each progression may well be experienced as a 'dissociation of sensibility'[19] (although Eliot located that in the sixteenth century). But if the problem for nineteenth century philosophers lay in the disintegration of the self, current interest lies in the opposite – in the apparent synthesis of our subpersonal elements; now it is not altered states of consciousness that are problematic but our illusive experience of unitary consciousness itself. The notion of a multiplex self as a flexible network is available not just in theoretical psychology (state-specific memory: Martingdale) and neurophilosophy (Sperry, Fodor, Gardner, Dennett, Edelman), but in the more accessible 'human potential therapies' which emphasize the realization of all our 'selves' appropriately recognized under a multiplicity of names.[20] Akin to the earlier manuals of self-perfectioning and managerial efficiency, such human technologies employ not only a popularised psychoanalytical idiom of untapped levels of consciousness (as in EST, scientology and transcendental meditation) but of potential selves which are to be serially realized, in which transformations of identity have fruitful economic implications; in which selves are neither transitory masks nor imaginary novelties but the realization of something authentic, of which we rest unaware until therapeutically liberated from our past, purged of atavistic memories, lower stages and hypocritical obligations; less a Puritan struggle for arduous refashioning than freedom for what was already there to assume its natural place. The decisive therapeutic step in concretizing these potentials into MPD seems to have been in personalizing them with a proper name. Despite its affinity with the pluripotent roles demanded by post-industrial capitalism, multiple personality is not a phenomenon which happens by itself but rather one elaborated in certain expert relationships; and now in a medico-legal commerce which places the sources of affliction beyond a unitary self which feels constricted as it seeks to reappropriate its 'personal space'.

REALITY, TRUTH, POWER

What might constitute the medical reality of multiple personality? Presumably that it exists independently of the willed intention of the protagonist, and can be objectively demonstrated as a distinct state independent of any local meaning, recognition or therapeutic intervention. As with certain other contemporary syndromes (post-traumatic stress disorder, myalgic encephalomyelitis, total allergy syndrome), the medical debate on multiple personality mobilizes supporters and opponents who argue for its validity or otherwise; inauthenticity variously being that the pattern is induced by doctor or simulated by patient (this sliding into unconscious motivation), or less commonly that the whole phenomenon is a duplicitous joint fabrication which neither takes for actuality.

Both protagonists and critics require an essentialist dualism: either it happens to you or else you do it (e.g. Friesen 1991; Kenny 1986). Each 'it' is a rather different sort of thing: disease versus masquerade. In a number of recent publications I have argued rather for a conventional dualism; that we can understand ourselves and the world as a consequence of cause and effect processes, generally independent of, but potentially accessible to, human awareness – the naturalistic mode of thought. Yet we can understand the same matters personalistically – as the motivated actions of agents employing such characteristically human attributes as intentionality, anticipation, representation, identification, promise and deceit. And that whilst we conventionally allocate one or other area of interest to the naturalistic or the personalistic, perhaps objectifying them as separate domains (nature: culture :: body:mind), we can apply either mode to any phenomenon. The self may be a machine, the natural world may be animate. Psychiatric considerations of such phenomena as parasuicide (a symptom of depressive illness? or an attempt to die?) or myalgic encephalomyelitis (disease process? malingering?), like medico-legal debates on criminal responsibility (mad? bad?), continually slip between one and the other, for only one mode can be correct at any one time. (The pragmatic legal categories of tort and diminished responsibility generally duck any attempt to examine their mutual relationship.) Neither can be demonstrated as completely true, or false; we always live with the two options.[21]

Psychoanalysis attempted to reconcile this antinomy through a subpersonal psychology which showed how intentionality emerges dynamically from naturalistic subpersonal structures. Its notion of fantasy (not empirically true, yet not exactly fabricated) elided the duality for multiple personality. That the professional acceptance of psychoanalysis seems inversely related to the recognition of multiple personality argues against reading the current wave of MPD simply as our postmodern consciousness, for its enthusiasts insist on the objective reality of both the syndrome and of its invariant cause, child sexual abuse, a signifier with an all too real signified. And opponents too generally revert to a pre-Freudian positivism in denying its existence: no reality to MPD because no causal trauma. This goes along with a reshaping of the balance between our two modes of thought in the last fifteen years in both Britain and the United States, in a generally more personalistic direction – towards an emphasis on individual responsibility for unemployment and poverty, and on the rights and responsibilities of the mentally ill, with a diminished place in a contracted natural world controlled by self-sufficient individuals for 'accidents' – which remain real events but now as violating traumata occasioned by the mischief or negligence of others, autonomous agents whom we hold legally accountable.[22]

Access to an experience we might gloss as a diminution of everyday agency has appeared in rather different cultural and political contexts, available to certain individuals through altered brain physiology (naturalistically) and through their perceived situation (personalistically); and this can be occasioned by experienced conflicts and traumata understood through conventional bodily techniques and notions of the self – 'this isn't happening to me, this is happening to someone else' (Kenny 1986: 17); and by its social consequences. The everyday locus of our immediate experience and action remains a generally unitary and internally consistent individual, bounded, autonomous and fairly undifferentiated, coextensive with a physical body and with that body's history: whether we assume that such unity is given in the body's neural make-up, or else that the idiom of a single rather than a multiplex self has proved more successful in our biologically adaptive and cultural history.

Such a unitary individual may recognize herself or himself as losing will, coherence and responsibility, whether at times of self-doubt or radical social change, through diseases of the brain, or in situations standardized as dance, violence and sorcery, as ecstasy, glossolalia, spirit mediumship, hypnosis, hysteria and multiple personality – occasions when our local representations of the self may then provide operational models for multiplicity or fragmentation through mind–body distinctions, psychological faculties, humours, evolutionary or topographical levels, multiple souls, spirit familiars and powers, hidden doubles, guardian angels, consubstantial deities, twins and other products of unnatural fecundity, the differentiation of kin, onomastics and the avoidance of homonyms, personifications of the foetus, the dead and the dreamer, the subpersonalities of West African psychologies and the human potential movement, and now the cyborgs and extraterrestrials of the computer technovisionaries. The loss of volition and control may be recognized as temporary or permanent, as partial or total, as a conflict, penetration, rape or theft; or we may identify our moral agency completely with the intruding other, simultaneously or serially, whether aware of seeking such an identification or just finding it happen – as sought or involuntary possession. Context, expectation, access to a particular schema, and the example and response of others organize a variety of standardized patterns, tentative essays, partial stages, elisions and the like, which in turn demonstrate the experiential reality of our local cosmology (Laughlin *et al.* 1992). Different social positions allow access to particular patterns; thus we might argue that hysterical fugues, like shamanic vision quests and 'central possession cults', are generally more available to men (going with male access to a more extensive geographical and social space with anticipated movement into a new social persona), whilst 'static' dissociations, involuntary (peripheral) possession and multiple personality are just more available to women's restricted mobility or with their experience of pregnancy (Young 1984) and something like a sick role.

To take these patterns simply as personalistic, as always strategically motivated, as a role-play which the participants themselves prefer to recognize as involuntary (Spanos 1989; Hacking 1992), assumes that the very articulation of the two modes is voluntary; but as Kirmayer (1992) points out, the currently fashionable 'top-down' notion of role-play in anthropology recapitulates the public assumptions through which hypnosis and MPD now emerge: the particularly Western idea of the centrality of a directing self. Reading it however in a naturalistic 'bottom-up' way alone leaves us with the contrary problem – that our loss of volition is necessarily non-volitional: this medical idiom is limiting, not only because it is in the immediate clinical context that these patterns are legitimated in Western societies, but because of the difficulty in making the customary distinction between aetiology, pathology, symptoms and treatment.

Why women? At a high level of generality, the pattern identified as the eventual psychopathology by doctors is a reconfiguring of the position ascribed to subdominant individuals (Littlewood and Lipsedge 1987; cf. Kapferer 1979); if the female is sickly and fearful, vulnerable to demons, controlled by others or lacking in moral will, performing rather than transforming, carrying another being within her, then her illness will embody these characteristics – usually an extension of them, sometimes a compromise with them (Littlewood and Lipsedge 1987; Kapferer 1979). And MPD is perhaps an extreme variant of those other patterns by which women can negotiate through the characteristics ascribed to them by men; for all illnesses involve some identification with an image of ourself as being ill. Last century the neuropsychiatrist Benedikt wondered if women were more prone to hysteria because they had more to hide (Ellenberger 1966); and in the sense that women's muted voice, to use the Ardeners' terminology, argues for a double-voiced tradition, both inside and against the public way of seeing things, double consciousness seems an apt representation (and practical deployment) of their situation. Like the intruding spirit (Kapferer, this volume), a disease is something which limits our moral agency; and recognition of an external cause, whether spirit or disease, compels others to legitimation and restitution; it is in the slippage between naturalistic and personalistic that MPD (and the spirits) emerges. Sexual abuse, like disease, is something that seems to happen to us, against volition; the recognition of the violation of female children, the sense that nothing can ever be enough to recompense that child, powerfully compels acceptance of the reality of the abuse and of its consequences. If illnesses are taken as mirrors of their age, then MPD acknowledges a new and rawer manifestation of male domination, an opening up of our society's terrible secrets. If the spirits of *shango* and *vodu* present standardized historical identities (Strathern, this volume), and the secondary personalities of the nineteenth century hysterics were taken for earlier levels of evolutionary development, then the fragmented alters of the current epidemic now offer us an unstable multiplicity of ambiguously welcome children, fantasized selves and wounded healers.[23]

As with certain other illnesses in European societies, women with MPD join together in groups which play down the role of the doctor, sororities through which the symptom is accommodated as a testimony to oppression. As in the non-Western analogies (anthropology's cults of affliction), sufferers in Alcoholics Anonymous or Speaking For Ourselves come together to affirm their illness, to strike a contract with it and dedicate themselves to its power, often to gain a sense of heightened control. Through this accommodation the sodality then takes on other, wider, 'non-therapeutic' tasks, in which affected individuals market their experience as emblematic, their suffering as achievement, their recovery as expert knowledge.[24] Some nineteenth century women reframed the existing power of the medical hypnotist over suggestible unmarried woman, to reaffirm such female weakness as now privileged access to a higher knowledge, the medium establishing for herself a professional career which offered wider solutions to the problems of others, and for the social reformers of the period a demystified and natural religion (Owen 1989). As contemporary multiples affirm the moral legitimacy of their several personalities, they have aligned themselves with the movements for ethnic and gender redefinition and for sexual choice, the stigma of rape becoming the means of transcending their origin, the ascribed now translated into the achieved, the pathological becoming a marketable realm of political authenticity.

NOTES

I am grateful to the Nuffield and Leverhulme Foundations and to the Institute of Social and Cultural Anthropology, Oxford University, for research fellowships during which this chapter was first drafted; and for observations from Bill Fulford, Maurice Greenberg, Paul Jackson, Sushrut Jadhav, Jean La Fontaine, Laurence Kirmayer, Murray Last, Ioan Lewis, Bill Watson and Allan Young. This chapter owes something to conversations with Godfrey Lienhardt in the weeks before his death in 1993. I miss what would have been his customary acerbic comments: *kene wun akec wetden tieng.*

 1 To maintain the Durkheimian idiom, to something closer to his transient 'social currents'; to Moscovici's social representations, Dawkins' memes, Sperber's epidemiological representations, or Foucault's micropractices.
 2 The French noun *conscience* denotes psychophysiological state (consciousness) as well as moral identity (conscience). There were a number of similar terms for the more developed instances (*conscience dissociée*) involving idioms of doubling and multiplicity, alternation, narrowing, dissociation, fragmentation, disintegration, decomposition, deaggregation, splitting off, or simply variation, depending on the extent of one-way or mutual amnesia (Campbell *et al.* 1925: 195; Ellenberger 1970: *passim*).
 3 As Geertz (1983: 59) puts it in his account of the Western self, a 'bounded, unique, more or less integrated motivational and cognitive universe, a dynamic centre of awareness, emotion, judgement and action organised into a distinctive whole and set contrastively both against other such wholes and against a social and natural background . . .'.
 4 'Nervous energy' was a naturalistic reading of 'will' as a function of the number of brain cells (Campbell *et al.* 1925: 91). Freud's unpublished *Project for a Scientific Psychology* attempted to reconcile the physical passage of energy through neurons with their consequent organization into structured channels which then facilitated the same mental patterns (an idea that goes back to Descartes' canalization and is also found in Prince's 'nets' or 'neurograms'). His abandonment of the manuscript in 1895 is often taken as Freud's move from the physicalism of Helmholtz and Brücke towards a purely interpretive dynamic (purposive) psychology. Edelman's recent (1992) 'neural Darwinism' proposes something remarkably similar: rather than simply enacting a genetic programme, the connections between cells in the developing post-natal brain are influenced by inputs from their environment and respond correspondingly, actively competing against and colonizing the organization of

other groups of cells in relation to their outside world. To an extent, then, their 'design-fixing' repertoires approach what may be termed representation – intentionality in the philosopher's sense. Putting Edelman's theory together with Dennett (1991) and Dawkins' (1982) notion of the brain being 'colonized' by memes (the anthropologist's collective representations) argues for one way into the naturalistic-personalistic antinomy (p. 167).

5 Panpsychism. The British psychiatrist McDougall (Rivers' colleague on the Torres Straits expedition) regarded the subselves as held together by telepathy, and took one of Miss Beauchamp's personalities elicited by Prince for an autonomous spirit (McDougall 1911: 367).

6 As 'passiones' (Lienhardt 1961: 151): 'A diviner is a man in whom the division is permanently present; a Power, or Powers, are always latent within him but he has the ability to dissociate them in himself at will, letting them manifest themselves in him. While thus dissociated, the diviner *is* a Power, for which his body is host.'

7 I am grossly simplifying Horton's instances for which McDougall's 'animism' offers an academic psychology closer than Freud's, his elements having greater autonomy, more of a 'vertical' split.

8 Mauss (1950: 61). Mauss of course restricts the term *moi*, conventionally translated as self (or person), to the social and moral representation, not as I have done here to the operational and embodied 'I': *cf*. William James' 'empirical me', or the 'private self' of Lienhardt and the 'biological individual' of La Fontaine: both in Carrithers *et al.* (1986). Yet these must be fairly isomorphic, or at least not too disconsonant, with the social self. In Creole Trinidad where individuals may describe themselves as comprising a physical body plus various combinations of soul, spirit, a mind, shadow and guardian angel, they do not recognize themselves as fragmented except in certain situations where everyday unity is called into question (generally responsibility for otherwise inexplicable or antisocial actions) or during personal cogitations on how to reduce pain or discard undesirable vices (Littlewood 1993). No more does the Christian Briton generally worry about whether the mind or the soul is in charge except for moments of temptation, guilt, religious doubt or conversion.

9 *Sybil* (Schreiber 1973) was followed by: *The Five Of Me* (1977), *Tell Me Who I Am Before I Die* (1977), *The Flock* (1991), and a male case, *The Minds of Billy Milligan* (1981).

10 MPD (dissociative identity disorder) is recognized by the American Psychiatric Association (in DSM-IV) and the World Health Organization (ICD-10).

11 These are characteristics of the notoriously vague diagnosis of personality disorder. I recall a patient admitted to University College Hospital last year after taking an 'overdose' who told me of the recent murder of her boyfriend, the deaths in car accidents the previous week of both her identically named twin sister and her nephew, and a gripping life history of sexual abuse, incest, mistaken identity, satanism and a millionaire father who was a well-known 'television personality'.

12 Why teaching and social work? Both are low status, poorly paid professions, with a high proportion of women, and a good deal of publicly defined responsibility and personal commitment, yet with little independent authority, no consistently accepted intellectual rationale or body of accepted practice, and constantly vulnerable to sudden swings of public policy. MPD itself has been described as common among female social workers and nurses who are also identified with the not unrelated pattern of Munchausen's Syndrome by Proxy:

the induction of symptoms in their children by isolated mothers in establishing a parenting relationship together with a male doctor (Littlewood 1991).

13 By the 1920s 'personality' had become synonymous with 'consciousness' (e.g. Campbell *et al.* 1925: 246), perhaps as a particularly American idea of the self as psychological type rather than moral character, yet 'personality' has long · been associated with agency: 'For a time he loses the sense of his own personality, and becomes a mere passive instrument of the deity' (1655: cit. OED).

14 As in the Durkheimian approach of Douglas, in which loosely organized polities (the United States?) parallel and somehow facilitate individual dissociation and spirit intrusion. Similarly, psychologically orientated anthropologists and cultural critics (e.g. Lasch 1978) take individual conflicts as the microcosm of wider social fragmentations: 'The current popularity of multiple personality is the product of the disorder of our times' (Kenny 1986: 180).

15 *Times*, London, 11 September 1993. For example Martin (1993).

16 James Thompson's 'I was twain, two selves distinct that cannot join again'; Dickens' 'two states of consciousness which never clash, but each of which pursues his separate ways as though it were continuous instead of broken'; Stevenson's 'man is not truly one but truly two'. Inspired by the literature on hypnotism, modernism developed a more fractured individual (Doestoevsky) whose apparent linear consciousness either congealed into temporary consistencies (Joyce, Woolf) or was accessible to an enduring self (Pirandello). Descartes' argument that one cannot think there is no 'I' has become increasingly implausible.

17 Warhol's and Oldenberg's multiples, body counts and mass disaster statistics, serial killers and multiple births: the sheer *absurdity* of multiplication, as Benjamin put it.

18 The phonograph was a common image of the unconscious (Campbell *et al.* 1925: 318), the telegraph of the medium (Kenny 1986). Clinical engagement with the elusive secondary personalities recalls not only the practice of the medium but of the telephone operator: 'Later in the course of the same interview Chris [another personality] was obtained. The same questions were put to her' (Prince 1978: 32).

19 Jameson's (1991: 44) postmodern *hyperspace* – an 'alarming disjunction between the body and its built environment'.

20 As internalized parents or children, as underdogs, types, archetypes, potentials, personalities, subpersonalities, voices, selves, subselves, possible selves, ego states, images, imagos, doubles, clusters, roles, parts, scripts, actors, figures, prototypes, polarities, schemas, subsystems (to take a few from Rowan [1990]).

21 An ironic simultaneity (Littlewood 1991; 1993). Their very distinction may be seen as naturalistic (the distinction in our experience and actions between the involuntary and voluntary nervous system, as Merleau-Ponty noted) or as personalistic (given by cultural history as, for example, in the dualism of Judaeo-Christianity refined by the mechanical science of the Renaissance).

22 Heelas (1981: 50), like Haraway (1988), argues from locus of control experiments that where there is a strong emphasis on the autonomous self, there is a tendency to see one's body as other and to attribute undesirable deviations to some discrete agency external to this self, such as a malevolent spirit: Kenny's (1986: 26) 'paradoxes of liberty'. Underlying this is an issue which informs much of this volume: how the flux of experience becomes congealed into hypostasized entities – a process surprisingly ignored by cognitive psychologists but which has been variously addressed by Marxists, Kleinians and

Buddhists through the idea that nominal categories are less ambiguous than experiencing, and under problematic circumstances we shape a fetishized world following our own intense recognition of ourselves as physical beings. Early in life we start to perceive the world as nominalized – as composed of entities of recurrent invariance (Laughlin *et al.* 1992), and such reification is fundamental to social categorization, giving ontological status to the experienced world (Lakoff 1987). We might approximately map the shifting locations of agency along the phenomenological dimensions of *aboulia*-intentionality and self-other (cf. Heelas):

```
                        O
                        |
    Aliens              |    Social roles
    Twins               |    Accessed computers
    Spirits             |    'Faces'
                        |    'Masks'
                        |
A -------------------------------------------------------- I
                        |
    Souls               |    Virtual reality
    Subpersonalities    |    Personality
    Archetypes          |
    Faculties           |
                        S
```

And plot medical evaluation of the traumatic memory along the probably more useful aetiological dimensions of naturalistic-personalistic and internal-external:

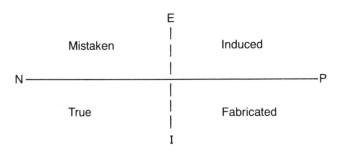

```
                        E
                        |
    Mistaken            |    Induced
                        |
                        |
N -----------------------------------------------------P
                        |
    True                |    Fabricated
                        |
                        I
```

23 As if with the 'self as a reflexive project' (Giddens 1992), modernity is unable to sustain the attempt to unify time, place and action, yet cannot cope with flux alone, and retreats to concretized simulacra of an embodied individual.
24 Lewis (1969), Janzen (1982). And then attract recruits who had not previously regarded themselves as sufferers.

REFERENCES

Aldridge-Morris, R. (1989) *Multiple Personalities: An Exercise in Deception*, London: Erlbaum.
Benedict, M. (ed.) (1991) *Cyberspace: First Steps*, Cambridge, Mass.: MIT Press.
Bolter, J. D. (1986) *Turing's Man: Western Culture in the Computer Age*, Harmondsworth: Penguin.
Burne, J. (1993) 'One person, many people', *Times*, 4 March (London).

Campbell, C. M., Langfield, H. S., McDougall, W., Roback, A. A. and Taylor, E. W. (eds) (1925) *Problems of Personality: Studies Presented to Dr Morton Prince*, London: Kegan Paul, Trench & Trubner.

Carrithers, M., Collins, S. and Lukes, S. (eds) (1986) *The Category of the Person*, Cambridge: Cambridge University Press.

Crabtree, A. (1985) *Multiple Man: Explorations in Possession and Multiple Personality*, New York: Praeger.

Dawkins, R. (1982) *The Extended Phenotype*, San Francisco: Freeman.

Dennett, D. C. (1991) *Consciousness Explained*, New York: Little, Brown.

Edelman, G. M. (1992) *Bright Air, Brilliant Sun: On the Matter of the Mind*, New York: Basic Books.

Ellenberger, H. F. (1966) 'The pathogenic secret and its therapeutics', *Journal of the History of the Behavioural Sciences*, 2: 29–42.

Ellenberger, H. F. (1970) *The Discovery of the Unconscious: The History and Evolution of Dynamic Psychiatry*, London: Allen Lane.

Friesen, J. G. (1991) *Uncovering the Mystery of Multiple Personality Disorder*, San Bernadino, Calif.: Here's Life Publishers.

Geertz, C. (1983) 'From the native's point of view: on the nature of anthropological understanding', pp. 55–70 in C. Geertz (ed.) *Local Knowledge*, New York: Basic Books.

Giddens, A. (1992) *The Transformation of Intimacy: Sexuality, Love and Eroticism in Modern Societies*, Cambridge: Polity Press.

Good, B., Good, M.-J. D. (1992) 'The comparative study of Graeco-Islamic medicine: the integration of medical knowledge into local symbolic contexts', in C. Leslie and A. Young (eds) *Paths to Asian Medical Knowledge*, Berkeley: California University Press.

Hacking, I. (1991) 'The making and molding of child abuse', *Critical Enquiry*, 17: 253–88.

Hacking, I. (1992) 'Multiple personality disorder and its hosts', *History of the Human Sciences*, 5: 3–31.

Haraway, D. (1988) 'The biopolitics of postmodern bodies: determinations of self and other in immune system discourse', Wenner Gren Foundation Conference on Medical Anthropology, Lisbon.

Heelas, P. (1981) 'The model applied: anthropology and indigenous psychologies', in P. Heelas and A. Lock (eds), *Indigenous Psychologies: The Anthropology of the Self*, London: Academic Press.

Horn, M. (1993) 'Memories lost and found', *US News and World Report*, 19 November: 52–63.

Horton, R. (1983) 'Social psychologies: African and Western', afterword in M. Fortes, *Oedipus and Job in West African Religion*, Cambridge: Cambridge University Press.

Jameson, F. (1991) *Postmodernism, or, The Cultural Logic of Late Capitalism*, London: Verso.

Janet, P. (1925) *Psychological Healing*, London: Allen & Unwin.

Janzen, J. M. (1982) 'Drums anonymous: towards an understanding of structures of therapeutic maintenance', in M. W. De Vries, R. L. Berg and M. Lipkin (eds), *The Use and Abuse of Medicine*, New York: Praeger.

Kapferer, B. (1979) 'Mind, self and other in demonic illness: the negation and reconstruction of self', *American Ethnologist*, 6: 110–33.

Kenny, M. G. (1986) *The Passion of Ansel Bourne: Multiple Personality in American Culture*, Washington, DC: Smithsonian Institution Press.

Kirmayer, L. J. (1992) 'Social constructions of hypnosis', *International Journal of Clinical and Experimental Hypnosis*, 11: 276–300.

Lakoff, G. (1987) *Women, Fire and Dangerous Things: What Categories Reveal About the Mind*, Chicago: Chicago University Press.

Lasch, C. (1978) *The Culture of Narcissism: American Life in an Age of Diminishing Expectations*, New York: Norton.

Laughlin, C. D., McManus, J. and D'Aquili, E. (1992) *Brain, Symbol and Experience: Towards a Neurophenomenology of Human Consciousness*, New York: Columbia University Press.

Lears, T. J. J. (1983) 'From salvation to self-realisation: advertising and the therapeutic roots of the consumer culture, 1880–1930', in R. W. Fox and T. J. J. Lears (eds) *The Culture of Consumption*, New York: Random House.

Lewis, I. M. (1969) 'Spirit possession in Northern Somaliland', in J. Beattie and J. Middleton (eds) *Spirit Mediumship and Society in Africa*, London: Routledge & Kegan Paul.

Lienhardt, G. (1961) *Divinity and Experience: The Religion of the Dinka*, Oxford: Oxford University Press.

Littlewood, R. (1991) 'Gender, role and sickness: the ritual psychopathologies of the nurse', in P. Holden and J. Littlewood (eds) *Anthropology and Nursing*, London: Routledge.

Littlewood, R. (1993) *Pathology and Identity: The Work of Mother Earth in Trinidad*, Cambridge: Cambridge University Press.

Littlewood, R. and Lipsedge, M. (1987) 'The butterfly and the serpent: culture, psychopathology and biomedicine', *Culture, Medicine and Psychiatry*, 11: 289–335.

Lloyd, G. E. R. (1990) *Demystifying Mentalities*, Cambridge: Cambridge University Press.

McDougall, W. (1911) *Body and Mind: A History and a Defence of Animism*. (Republished Boston: Beacon Press, 1961.)

Martin, J. (1993) *Scram: Relocating Under a New Identity*, Washington, DC: Loompanics Unlimited.

Mauss, M. (1950) *Sociology and Psychology*, trans. 1979, London: Routledge & Kegan Paul.

Ornstein, R.C. (1985) *The Roots of the Self*, San Francisco: Harper.

Owen, A. (1989) *The Darkened Room: Women, Power and Spiritualism in Late Victorian England*, London: Virago.

Prince, M. (1978) *The Dissociation of a Personality: The Hunt for the Real Miss Beauchamp*, with an introduction by C. Rycroft, Oxford: Oxford University Press. (Originally published 1905.)

Rowan, J. (1990) *Subpersonalities: The People Inside Us*, London: Routledge.

Schreiber, F. R. (1973) *Sybil*, Chicago: Regnery.

Sinason, V. (ed.) (1994) *Treating Survivors of Satanist Abuse*, London: Routledge.

Spanos, N. P. (1989) 'Hypnosis, demonic possession and multiple personality: strategic enactments and disavowals of responsibility for actions', in C. A. Ward (ed.) *Altered States of Consciousness and Mental Health*, Newbury Park, Calif.: Sage.

Tart, C. (1980) 'A systems approach to altered states of consciousness', in J. M. Davidson and R. J. Davidson (eds) *The Psychobiology of Consciousness*, New York: Plenum Press.

Thigpen, C. H. and Cleckley, H. M. (1957) *The Three Faces of Eve*, New York: McGraw-Hill.

Wilson, E. (1988) *Hallucinations: Life In The Post-Modern City*, London: Radius.

Young, A. (1983) 'Reading DSM-III on PTSD: an anthropological account of a core text in American psychiatry', Conference on Anthropologies of Medicine, University of Hamburg.

Young, I. (1984) 'Pregnant embodiment: subjectivity and alienation', *Journal of Medicine and Philosophy*, 9: 45–62.

Part III

Chapter 9

The inarticulate mind

The place of awareness in social action

Kirsten Hastrup

Time past and time future
Allow but a little consciousness.
To be conscious is not to be in time
But only in time can the moment in the rose-garden,
The moment in the arbour where the rain beat,
The moment in the draughty church at smokefall
Be remembered; involved with past and future.
Only through time time is conquered.
(T. S. Eliot 1935)[1]

Questions of consciousness entail endless other questions, and to address them one enters an indeterminate field of enquiry. Indeterminacy is no reason to sidestep any question, however, but provides a particular challenge to find one's own way in the hope that it leads to and through places of general interest. The ambition, of course, is eventually to reach a clearing where the mind may rest and remember the moments of insight.[2]

The resting mind is not a consequence of having achieved a perfect understanding of things real. The illusion of the mind as a carbon paper doing nothing more than faithfully registering the facts of life is broken. Rather, the mind is a dynamic zone of contact between embodied knowledge and contested evidence. It is a space of interaction between habituation and flexibility, between immediate knowing and unprecedented understanding. The mind, therefore, is only partly articulate. Only a proportion of the knowledge stored or challenged by the mind can readily be called forth in discursive statements; the rest remains silent and hence partly inaccessible to others. The definition of knowledge propounded by Descartes: 'All knowledge is certain and evident cognition' (1988:1), has long since been abandoned in anthropology, well aware that cultural knowledge is more often expressed in action than in cognitive declaration (e.g. Bloch 1991). Without discarding language as an important vehicle of expression, we can claim it neither to be transparent, nor to be the only store of cultural knowledge. Both language and body function as depositories of deferred thoughts that may be recalled in particular situations (Bourdieu 1990: 69). This is an important premiss for the following discussion of awareness in social action.

The discussion takes off from two ethnographic cases, one from Egypt, the other from Brazil. The first case is the one of the Awlad 'Ali Bedouins presented by Lila Abu-Lughod (1986; 1993). These people are caught, it seems, in apparently contradictive discourses on their life that illustrate an important distinction between consciousness and awareness in my argument. The Brazilian case is owed to Nancy Scheper-Hughes (1992), whose concern with the silence of the poor inhabitants of a shanty town, and their apparent resistance to articulating their sufferings, provides a kind of parable for the inarticulate mind with which I am concerned in this chapter.

In both cases, I am seeking to combine ethnography with an argument on collective consciousness, exploring at least a figment of the relationship between human agency and articulation, so eloquently dealt with in philosophy by Charles Taylor (e.g. 1985a; 1985b). In order to 'anthropologize' this agenda, I ground my exposition in particular social realities. In the process, the focus sharpens on the place of awareness in social action.

Rather than a presentation of results, this chapter evolves as an argument. I therefore privilege the itinerary over the map as my guide to matters of consciousness. The map presents us with a plane projection of observations on place, while the itinerary gives us a discursive series of operations and movements in space (de Certeau 1988: 117–19). Generally, I would suggest that itineraries be redeemed as valid guides for journeying in the territory of knowledge. In contrast to maps, they have a truly directive force. A map helps you situate your position, but the itinerary spells out the goal and the relevant places of reference. It is, therefore, a travellers' guide *par excellence*: it is only by knowing where you are going that you can know who you are.

The sites that we shall visit on our way from the general discussion of consciousness and awareness to a fuller understanding of the mind are those of veiled sentiment, delirious experience, habituated persons and desirable orders. The clearing where we shall hopefully find some rest is that of the ethics of inarticulacy.

CONSCIOUSNESS AND AWARENESS

With such terms as consciousness and awareness we are on slippery ground. We are still squarely within social reality, of course: these are features of the real world (see Taylor 1989: 69) and provide us with means of explaining people's actions. But they require conceptual clarification.

I would suggest that one operative distinction between consciousness and awareness can be made in terms of relative explicitness: awareness refers to an explicit understanding, while consciousness is largely an implicit vector of knowing.[3] Explicitness is also that which makes awareness social, rather than individual, since explicating something, if only to oneself, of necessity involves particular cultural schemes and values. There is no 'explication' outside a conversational community, whether this is actually addressed or not in the particular instance. While meaning is certainly always emergent rather than prior to events or phenomena, it must still in some sense be shared.[4] 'Mad' acts cannot, by definition, be understood (Vendler 1984: 209). The semantic features of language are public features: 'What no one can, in the nature of the case, figure out from the totality of the relevant evidence cannot be part of meaning' (Davidson 1984: 235).

Awareness is emergent and collectively premissed, like meaning; it projects itself outward and becomes entangled in other projections. Not unlike the 'ecstatic body' described by Drew Leder (1990), awareness can be suggestively seen as a feature of the 'ecstatic mind', connecting the self and the world. By contrast, the 'recessive body' has an analogue in a 'recessive mind', that is the unknowable processes of understanding that takes place within the self.[5] The recessive mind is part of habitus. 'The *habitus* – embodied history, internalized as a second nature and so forgotten as history – is the active presence of the whole past of which it is the product' (Bourdieu 1990: 56).

This connects to another feature of the distinction made here between the notions of awareness and consciousness, viz. that of temporality. As suggested by T. S. Eliot in the lines quoted above, one may claim that to be conscious is not to be in time. In other words, consciousness belongs to a timeless dimension of knowing the world and the self. I would suggest that, by contrast, awareness is in time. It relates to the historically specific moment, whether in the rose garden or in the shanty town. It belongs to a time-bound dimension of understanding.

In order to clarify this distinction we may liken it to the relationship between recollection and memory, following Søren Kierkegaard. Recollections are outside time, eternally present in one's life; their imprint cannot be erased. It is the active if voiceless presence of the whole past, forgotten as history and deposited as self-evidence. Memories, on the other hand, are extracted from history and placed in time; they are remembered, narrated, reinterpreted, sometimes rejected and often soon forgotten. Recollections are unmediated experiences. Memory makes a critical difference to these: in being remembered, experience 'becomes "a memory", with all that this entails, not merely of the consistent, the enduring, the reliable, but also of the fragile, the errant, the confabulated' (Casey 1987: xii). The process of making memory explicit, of foregrounding it from the archive of implicit recollection and habituated knowledge, has a parallel in the transformation of mere experience into *an* experience, as discussed by Victor Turner (1986: 35). This transformation is made by way of narrative expression; by telling we carve out units of experience and meaning from the continuity of life. An experience, therefore, has an explicit temporal dimension (Bruner 1986: 7). In real life, there are no absolute beginnings or ends to particular events; there are antecedents and successors to every moment. Yet we cannot but punctuate this in narrative.

Similarly, I suggest that we regard consciousness as indistinguishable from our continuous being in between time past and time future. Awareness cuts us loose from this; just like narrative punctuates experience, awareness constantly arrests the flow of consciousness – to make room for action, as it were. Relating the question of consciousness and awareness to agency is to seek a theoretical understanding of motivation, constituting the link between culture and action (D'Andrade 1992: 41). Motivation is the moving force between these (analytical) entities; as such it is timeless in itself, but by inducing movement it spills over into time and informs local action.

VEILED SENTIMENT: A BEDOUIN EXAMPLE

To give body to these words I shall introduce an ethnographic example. It is the case of the Awlad 'Ali Bedouins of Egypt, studied by Lila Abu-Lughod (1986; 1993). The Bedouins often sing or punctuate their conversation with poetry, thus switching from one discourse to another. The switch is not possible in all circumstances; poetry can be used only within an intimate social context. There are strict social barriers, mostly gender specific, to the use of the poetic mode. It belongs to a realm of secrecy, that cannot and should not be betrayed. 'Poetry is, in so many ways, the discourse of opposition to the system and of defiance of those who represent it: it is antistructure just as it is antimorality' (Abu-Lughod 1986: 251). As such it cannot be part of the articulate understanding of social life. It belongs to a separate register, and draws upon an estranged vocabulary. Here is a poem by a man whose wife had left him, much to his concern; she had returned, however. Publicly, he could admit only of anger at her ill behaviour. Privately, and with no small embarrassment, he confided a couple of poems to the inquisitive ethnographer:

Cooking with a liquid of tears
at a funeral for the beloved. . . .

Her bad deeds were wrongs that hurt
yet I won't repay them, still dear the beloved . . .

(Abu-Lughod 1986: 189)

His personal sentiments are harboured here; sadness, longing and love for the lost wife. Upon her return and after having confided in the ethnographer, he had her serve as an intermediary between himself and the wife. He asked the ethnographer to read aloud the 'talk of the other day' to his wife in his presence. He had to use this indirect means to communicate his sentiments to her. Poetry, then, is more than an obscure set of words. It is a performance. There is no way to understand Bedouin verse independent of the social context of its performance (see Baumann 1986).

The poetic mode is a way of expressing individual emotional experience in an idiom outside the ordinary conversational community of the Awlad 'Ali Bedouins, yet still within a shared medium of communication: it is culturally central (Abu-Lughod 1986: 32). The centrality of a poetry that must remain partly secret is not as enigmatic as it appears at first sight. It expresses a conscious feeling of life that lies beyond the strictures of the outspoken cultural code in which sentiment is denied and forbidden. For instance, a deep emotional attachment or, indeed, a felt lack of genuine affection between spouses that must pass unnoticed in ordinary conversation and social interaction can be expressed poetically, in words that derive their meaning from shared inner experiences rather than from the shared vocabulary of the social and moral system.

At the heart of the Bedouin moral system are the values of honour and modesty, values that shape individual histories (Abu-Lughod 1986: 78ff.). The supreme value of the honour code is that of autonomy; the weak and dependent who cannot realize this value can still achieve respect and honour through the alternative code, that of modesty. Men who admit of passion, and thus of dependence upon woman, are dishonoured.

> Greater contempt is reserved for the man who, not simply a slave to his passions, compromises his independence by admitting dependence on a particular woman. This sign of weakness permits the proper power relations between the sexes to be reversed. One old woman told me, 'When a man is really something [manly], he pays no heed to women.' 'A man who listens to his wife when she tells him what to do is a fool,' said a young woman.
>
> (Abu-Lughod 1986: 94)

In the public discourse on marriage and sexual relations it is the man who must control the woman. The code of honour demands explicit recognition of his autonomy, also on the part of those women who certainly 'know better'. On their side, they have to abide to the modesty code. Says one woman about her co-spouse, the husband Sagr's second wife:

> From the moment she arrived, she couldn't stand it. The first time she

came here she only stayed four days. This was twenty days after she married him. Even when she was a bride she had no modesty. She'd wander around the camp talking to people. When she saw him coming home she'd run back excited, 'Sagr has come! Sagr has come!' Why, in those days we women in the camp were so respectful of him that we wouldn't even say his name.

(Abu-Lughod 1993: 96)

Attachment and emotion must be publicly subdued. The community can have no collective and public awareness of such feelings. True sentiments must be veiled in non-literal poetry, from which part of the recessive mind's processing of implicit knowledge can be inferred. 'Poetry as a form provides a modest way of communicating immodest sentiments of attachment and an honourable way of communicating the sentiments of dependency' (Abu-Lughod 1986: 240). We have, then, two complementary discourses: one *on* emotions, and codifying these in terms of honour and modesty, another which is an emotional discourse, conveying an affective dimension of Bedouin life that is barred from immediate view (see Abu-Lughod and Lutz 1990).

Bedouin poetry thus is an important means of communication through which we (and they) may discover how individuals experience their life (see LeVine 1982: 293). The temporal mode of the poetic communication is ahistorical, quite unlike the temporal mode of the women's stories that are literal renderings of past events (see Abu-Lughod 1993). This reflects the distinction made above between mere experience and *an* experience, or between recollection and memory.

If ordinary, literal discourse frames social experience in certain ways, poetry is an alternative medium which 'reminds' people of another way of being and another kind of experience – deeply embodied. With poetry we are in the realm of linguistic indeterminacy; the language parallax of poetic creativity (Friedrich 1986) is not innocent with respect to experience, because expression and experience are dialectically related (see Bruner 1986; Rosaldo 1986). The difference is not one of language *per se* or of a particular kind of metaphoric reasoning. After all, metaphors are extremely literal and have no meaning beyond the *use* that is made of them (Davidson 1984: 245ff.). It is rather a matter of discourse, one allowing for articulation of awareness and collective codes of honour and modesty; the other for expression of a shared if implicit consciousness of suppressed sentiment.

Both of these discourses are part of Bedouin culture and inform agency. Agency and meaning have one thing in common: they are not accountable for in terms of the observable, physical features of the world (Vendler 1984: 207). They do not belong exclusively to the explicate world, even if most often explained discursively with reference to a particular awareness of context and intention. In actual fact, both the code of honour and the anti-structural mode of passion motivate action in Bedouin society.

DELIRIOUS EXPERIENCE: A CASE FROM BRAZIL

Nancy Scheper-Hughes has written a remarkable ethnography on the violence of everyday life in Brazil (1992).[6] It is called *Death Without Weeping*, thus immediately drawing our attention to an apparent silence in face of massive suffering. The people studied are shanty town dwellers in north-eastern Brazil, living in the shadow of sugar-cane, and of a feudal structure. The poverty of these people is immense, and among other things it results in a child mortality rate that makes one shiver.

In this community there are two 'generative themes' (Paulo Freire) in everyday talk: thirst and hunger. People see their lives as doubly cursed by drought and famine, both of which are the virulent consequences of the encroaching sugar-cane fields (Scheper-Hughes 1992: 69). Thirst and hunger seem to be 'master-motives' in the local hierarchy of motivation.[7] Most daily activities are related to the motive of relieving hunger. It is a conscious motive, outside time. It is ever present and serves as an experiential framework of almost any activity. Even the highly praised sexual vigour of the people is interpreted in relation to this scheme. Says one woman:

> Sure I'm hungry. Almost everyday my house is without food. My compensation is screwing. You asked me if I take pleasure in sex? Of course I do! How else am I going to know that I'm alive if I don't screw? At least in sex I can feel my flesh moving around and I know that hunger hasn't killed me yet.
>
> (Scheper-Hughes 1992: 165)

The delirious experience of hunger resonates with the sensuous experience of sex.

A common symptom and, indeed, a folk-diagnosis is *delírio de fome*, madness from hunger. It is the end result of prolonged starvation, the climax of the lived experience of hunger. The experience of starvation and the ethno-medical discourse fit together. *Delírio de fome* is a state of being which is part of the shared social experience, and to which no numbers, no calculations apply (see Hastrup 1993b). The facts of starvation in the shanty town are immeasurable; yet their hardness is witnessed and felt by the people, for whom they become part of the collective consciousness.

Deaths from undernourishment and dehydration among infants and children can be counted, of course, at least to the extent that they are reported. (For fear of organ thefts, parents often hasten to bury their children with only a minimum of bureaucratic intervention.) But the degree to which the shanty town dwellers are conscious of the omnipresent death from starvation is not a feature of numbers; it is a theme that infiltrates any communication. Even young children are often sadly aware of their living in a limbo between life and death. Once seven year old Edilson's mother told the anthropologist that the boy would probably soon join his dead siblings; the anthropologist advised her not to talk like that in front of Edilson, but the boy shut her up in defence of his mother: 'Hush, Mãe, hush. I'm not afraid; I'm ready to go there' (Scheper-Hughes 1992: 142). The readiness stems from a continuous experience with death.

The never-ending story of starvation frames local life; yet a new kind of narrative intervention has become increasingly pertinent during the twenty-odd years that Scheper-Hughes has been involved with the shanty town. It is a narrative intervention that punctuates experience in a new and different way as a result of the impact of Western medical science. The medical discourse is causal and curative and deals with bodies and minds as if separate entities. The result is that with the gradual medication of Brazilian society, the centre of gravity in the madness from hunger is displaced. Starvation cannot be cured, but madness may be relieved; with medication 'mad' acts have required a new public meaning. *Delírio de fome* gradually collapses with the folk-concept of *nervos*, and remedies are sought to relieve this. Hunger is still part of experience, but the narrative focus is on the theme of madness.

> The madness, the *delírio de fome*, once understood as the terrifying end point in the experience of angry and collective starvation, is transformed into a personal and 'psychological' problem, one that requires medication. In this way hunger is isolated and denied, and an individualized discourse on sickness comes to replace a more radical and socialized discourse on hunger.
>
> (Scheper-Hughes 1992: 169).

A new illness narrative (see Kleinman 1988) is constructed that breaks asunder social experience. Or, in the terms of the present argument, a public awareness of individual nervousness supplants the traditional and collective consciousness of hunger. This consciousness is outside time, it is an all-pervasive recollection, inescapably marking people's lives. Hunger was always a generative theme in the social talk, yet the stories never arrested the flow of that experience. They motivated no hope of relief. By contrast, the new medical awareness gives promise of curing, and people seize the opportunity to take fate in their own hands. The buying of useless medicines that leaves even less money for food than before has become an individual strategy to conquer the collective misery, however futile.

THE HABITUATED PERSON

To understand the specific impact of the Western medical discourse upon the Brazilian awareness of their suffering it is necessary to study its derivation. The medical discourse derives from a particular worldview, focusing on the individual and separating body and mind. With the insights gained – also from within medical science itself – scholars now seek to reunite analytically what was never ontologically separate (Hastrup 1994a). The body is in the mind (Johnson 1987); or, it is in itself 'mindful' (Scheper-Hughes and Lock 1987). Yet, the distinction between body and mind still seems all pervasive in the received wisdom on 'selves', and in medical language. As such it captivates the creative powers of the people in the shanty town and reframes their experience.

With the development of the first person standpoint in Western philosophy as a derivative of St Augustine's radical reflexivity, knowledge or awareness became that of an agent. This is not solely the matter of musing upon one's own experience, making it an object of contemplation. "Radical reflexivity brings to the fore a kind of presence to oneself which is inseparable from one's being the agent of that experience" (Taylor 1989: 131). This is what makes one a being that can speak of itself in the first person, and what made the language of inwardness irresistible. 'I think' somehow became an action outside the world, inside the self. 'Will' became located in the mind, and it was essential to rational action in the early modern period; 'weakness of will' became the ultimate failure however much we can now unmask it as a contradiction in terms (Davidson 1980: 21ff.).

With Descartes the moral resources, too, became firmly and explicitly placed within ourselves, and the entire inner/outer dichotomy took on a new meaning. Scientific explanation was cut loose from moral vision; the former became a question of correct representation, the latter of individual firmness of will. The very notion of 'idea' migrated from cosmos to person; its ontic sense was relocated to an intrapsychic world. The idea became something one had 'in the mind' (Taylor 1989: 144). There, it became a means for objectifying the world, including the body. As a cultural model it had its own motivating force. The distinction made by Descartes between *res cogitans* and *res extensa* provided rationale for the sharp distinction between mind and body, which we have since then had to straddle. It is also this metaphysical dualism which has ever since been reflected in the subject-object dichotomy as basic to our knowledge of the world (Bernstein 1983: 115–16).

This violates both the classical ontology and the ordinary experience of embodied understanding so vigorously demonstrated by the notion of *delírio de fome*. To understand, for Descartes, involved disengagement from our own material selves, those uncontrolled sources of error and moral vice. To achieve pure knowledge one first had to achieve self-purification; self-mastery became a matter of controlling the bodily source of error, rationality became a matter of instrumental control. The medical discourse epitomizes this. The shanty town dwellers seek to fulfil the demand for instrumental control by subjecting themselves to medication; their 'will' has taken the shape of a pill.

If the medical discourse now frames people's explicit understanding of their condition, they still *know* their real plight, of course. Hunger is all pervasive and not easily erased from the mind. It is only discursively that the perennial experience of starvation can be formulated as *an* experience of nervousness, calling for immediate medical intervention. There is a certain clash of discourses. The traditional talk of hunger resides beyond precise time, it has no beginning and no end; the talk of nervousness and the related curative discourse gives a hope of termination. Illness narratives must have a beginning and an end; the cure is willed.

Among the Awlad 'Ali Bedouins there is also a set of contrasting discourses. Their will is explicitly encoded in the discourse on honour and modesty; self-mastery is a highly praised virtue, leaving the modern idea of the 'disengaged self' in total control.[8] In poetry, however, veiled admission is given to the experience of bodily craving, of uncontrolled passion, and of improper sentiment in general; the wilful selves disintegrate. Agency springs from the comprehensive source of articulate public understanding and concealed intimate passion. Agency is a feature of continuing conversation in a community, embracing both a discourse on emotions and an emotional discourse. As we have seen, the conversation in the Bedouin camp as well as in the shanty town is firmly grounded in shared bodily experience and in the consciousness of affect and hunger. This is where agency takes off.

The anthropological concern with agency breaks away from the naturalism and behaviourism implied in the utilitarian perspective. To be a competent human agent is to exist in a space defined by distinctions of worth, not only by words and practical reason (Taylor 1985a: 3). Such distinctions are socially and historically constructed, and become part of the habitus of people. The disengaged self yields to the habituated person.

As observed by Scheper-Hughes, the displacement of the experience of hunger is not sufficiently explained by 'false consciousness' or metaphorical delirium (1992: 184). It rather points to a new form of embodiment, or body praxis. 'Embodiment concerns the ways that people come to "inhabit" their bodies so that these become in every sense of the term "habituated"' (1992: 184). The people of the shanty town have inhabited famished bodies for a long time; their minds embody this experience. The consciousness of hunger has become part of culture – as incorporated. Similarly, Bedouin women (and men) have a continuous bodily experience of passion. This is what makes their poetic anti-discourse central to an understanding of their lived experience.

The incorporation of culture implies a process of sedimentation (Leder 1990: 31–2). More and more knowledge is taken for granted. Culture crystallizes in the body and thus becomes part of the hidden faculties of the self. In this sense culture becomes naturalized in socialization and experience. It forms our habits:

> The phenomenon of *habit formation* sorts out the ideas which survive repeated use and puts them in a more or less separate category. These trusted ideas then become available for immediate use without thoughtful inspection, while the more flexible parts of the mind can be saved for use in newer matters.
>
> (Bateson 1972: 501)

The lived space of the shanty town people has become naturalized as one of starvation. The naturalness of the lived space is related to 'the way our own body is the vehicle, the stage, and the object of experience at the same time' (Hanks 1990: 5). The body is motivated by this experience, and as such it is the locus of agency (Hastrup 1994b). It allows for little flexibility; the consciousness of hunger in the shanty town has crystallized and is available for immediate knowing. It provides a motive for action beyond words. In a parallel fashion, the sensation of passion in Bedouin society cannot be admitted into ordinary language. By intimating immorality, the poetic discourse is illegitimate in the public domain (see Bourdieu 1991). The outspokenness of honourable social selves is complemented by secret sentiments to which persons are habituated.

THE DESIRABLE ORDER

The poetics of passion and the silence of starvation are strong motivational factors in the lives of the afflicted. Motivation is not found in the disengaged mind or in utilitarianism. We should distinguish between motives and intentions; the former are largely implicit frameworks for action, the latter explicit rationalizations of it (Pettit 1976). Intentions and motives relate to what Taylor has called first and second order desires (Taylor 1985a: 15). What makes us fully human is our power to evaluate our first order desires, and thus to act on the basis of relative worth. This introduces a distinction between 'weak' and 'strong' evaluation. With weak evaluations we are concerned with outcomes, while strong evaluations define the quality of our motivation (Taylor 1985a: 16).

There are no selves beyond a particular social context. Phrased differently, identity is intimately linked to orientation in a moral space (Taylor 1989: 28ff.). This implies that 'social actors not only acquire a sense of what is natural, they also acquire strongly motivating senses of what is desirable. They not only know, they also care' (Strauss and Quinn 1993: 3). In practical life, knowledge, so often isolated as cognition in theory, is not independent of emotion and evaluation.

Evaluation, or the sense of relative worth, infiltrates social action. Facts and values are two sides of the same coin (Putnam 1990: 135ff.). 'Facts' cannot be identified without an implicit scale of evaluation. Taking this a step further, we realize that experience and description are bound together in a constitutive relation that admits of causal influences in both directions: 'it can sometimes allow us to alter experience by coming to fresh insight; but more fundamentally it circumscribes insight through the deeply embedded shape of experience for us' (Taylor 1985a: 37). The lived experience of the famished circumscribes their insight into their powerlessness. The dislocated medical description of their delirium does not allow for an alteration of experience.

> Because of this constitutive relation, our descriptions of our motiv-
> ations, and our attempts to formulate what we hold important, are not
> simple descriptions in that their objects are not fully independent. And
> yet they are not simply arbitrary either, such that anything goes. There
> are more or less adequate, more or less truthful, more self-clairvoyant
> or self-deluding interpretations. Because of this double fact, because
> an articulation can be *wrong*, and yet it shapes what it is wrong about,
> we sometimes see erroneous articulations as involving a distortion of
> the reality concerned. We do not just speak of error but frequently
> also of illusion or delusion.
>
> (Taylor 1985a: 37–8)

Illusion or delusion may be the result of failure to revise the givens of culture: when too much is taken for granted, flexibility is at risk. Significance becomes distorted as meanings fossilize. This is one reason for the abatement of culture or for the fall of civilizations.[9]

Silence or secrecy may be imbued with value and thus with motivational force. The absence of direct and public articulation points not to lack of consciousness of the values or desires implied but to a lack of means to act explicitly upon it; in the face of enduring misery and practical impotence, an awareness of particular desires cannot be allowed to arrest the consciousness of the general order of the desirable.

All people are aware of their environment, and offer articulations of it. In so doing, however, they lay out different features of the world and of human action in some perspicuous order. Awareness, like memory, makes room for error or illusion; the experience of hunger may be confabulated as a psychological problem, and the desire to overcome it may be relieved by way of medication. By contrast, consciousness cannot be manipulated; the desirable order of things is collectively sensed, even when silence or secrecy prevail. If passion between men and women is non-existent in public speech, love is not easily denied in the collective consciousness of the Bedouins.

THE ETHICS OF INARTICULACY

It is one of the tasks of anthropology to reclaim the areas of silence as a basis for understanding human agency, and to seek a theoretical understanding of the parameters that may influence the relative publicizing of collective experience. It remains to be discussed why it is that anthropology can make a claim to a kind of higher order understanding than local knowledge. One way of evaluating different schemes for understanding is by their relative power to achieve more or less perspicuous orders of comprehension. A claim of this kind can, according to Charles Taylor, be made by theoretical cultures against atheoretical ones (Taylor 1985b: 150). The former invariably catch the attention of the latter when they meet. The success of Western scientific culture is a case in point, but certainly not the only one. If we replace 'cultures' with 'schemes' of a more general kind, we have a way of assessing the force of the anthropological argument in relation to local knowledge.

This is not a correlate of objective or absolute understanding versus subjective or relative knowledge. I agree with Bourdieu when he claims that this distinction is ruinous to social science (Bourdieu 1990: 25). Whether cast as objectivism or subjectivism, both are theoretical modes of knowledge, 'equally opposed to the practical mode of knowledge which is the basis of ordinary experience of the social world' (Bordieu 1990: 25).[10]

A prerequisite for theorizing in this sense is a degree of self-reflection which amounts to St Augustine's 'radical reflexivity', or perhaps to Paulo Freire's 'critical consciousness'. Theoretical knowledge implies an understanding of its own condition, as well as its possible impact upon practical knowledge. This is how anthropology may be said to have a dual legitimacy. Anthropology, after all, exists both 'as a field of knowledge (a *disciplinary* field) and as a field of action (a *force* field)' (Scheper-Hughes 1992: 24–5). Awareness and force are intimately linked in anthropology as well as culture; unlike argument, knowledge by itself has no power. The *raison d'être* of anthropology, be it conceived as a Western construct or a global paradigm, lies precisely in its being theoretically aware of the situatedness of local awareness, and its intricate relationship to social agency.

This is how anthropology may become a 'site of resistance' (Scheper-Hughes). Giving voice is not to force people to speak; after all, the anthropological vision may not reflect the native voice at all (see Hastrup 1993a). Nor is it a matter of replacing 'false' consciousnesses with correct ones. It is to respect silence and provide a theoretical context, including the historical situatedness, of whatever selective awareness people may have of their own situation. This may, then, be offered for the inspection of the people involved.

Individuals are not only defined by their space but are also its defining consciousness (Ardener 1987: 40). The anthropological interpretation may arrest the collective consciousness and place it squarely in time; a new awareness may result. People are never just victims of social forms, because social forms owe their shape partly to the fact that they are inhabited by people thinking about social forms (Hollis 1985: 232). And, as said above, thinking implies caring.

Transculturally, there is equity as far as awareness and rationality is concerned; or, in other words, people have equal reasons for assuming the correctness of their view of the world. This is no plea for a mindless relativism. While certainly, conceptual relativity is a feature of the world, in the sense that it may be understood by alternative reference schemes, this is not an argument for ontological relativity (Davidson 1984: 235). There are claims to relative truth to be made; transcultural insight pre-cisely provides a basis for judgement which blind ethnocentricity *and* relativism both negate. This is one, potentially controversial, reason for pursuing anthropology as a theoretical mode of knowledge. Likewise, it is the basis for refusing to accept moral relativism as the net result of the anthropological involvement with people (see Scheper-Hughes 1992: 21f.). No cultures are incorrigible, but 'correction' hinges on a higher order, contextual understanding than that provided within local aware-ness. As we have seen, articulateness is selective – for more reasons than I have been able to discuss here.

The ethics of inarticulacy imply that anthropology should seek to re-articulate the strong evaluations that have been silenced by unfortunate social circumstances or hegemonic historical positions, but which are, nevertheless, integral parts of local consciousness. Rearticulation in this sense means giving 'momentum' to consciousness by reinstating it in time:

Only through time time is conquered.

NOTES

1 The lines quoted are from the poem 'Burnt Norton', the first of Eliot's *Four Quartets* (London 1944: Faber & Faber Ltd, 1944: 25).
2 The present chapter is a companion argument to one presented in 'The Moti-vated Body' (Hastrup 1994b). It also provides a fragment of a position that has been more fully developed elsewhere (Hastrup 1995).
3 The analytical distinction between knowing and understanding is owed to Vendler (1984).
4 To see meaning as emergent rather than prefigured is part of the argument

made by pragmatism as against semantics in newer linguistic philosophy (see, for example, Lakoff 1987).

5 In Leder's terms the ecstatic dimension of the body comprises the senses, notably the gaze and the voice, by which we project ourselves into the world and 'take it in'. The recessive dimension, by contrast, refers to all the hidden faculties and processes of the body, which keep us alive and process the information received (Leder 1990).

6 My evaluation of Scheper-Hughes' monograph is that of an impressed reader, not an expert on Brazil. I am impressed by her will to combine objectivity and solidarity, and by her sensitivity to silence.

7 The notion of master motive is owed to D'Andrade (1992).

8 For an elaborate historical account of the emergence of the rational and disengaged modern self, I refer to Taylor (1989).

9 One example is provided by the virtual collapse of Icelandic society during the period 1400–1800, following the remarkable flourishing of the Middle Ages. Here the old terms on everyone's lips had a steadily decreasing bearing on the historical situation in which the Icelanders found themselves; the result was social disintegration (Hastrup 1990).

10 For an extended discussion of the interrelationship between social experience and anthropological knowledge, see Hastrup and Hervik (1994).

REFERENCES

Abu-Lughod, Lila (1986) *Veiled Sentiments: Honor and Poetry in a Bedouin Society*, Berkeley: University of California Press.

Abu-Lughod, Lila (1993) *Writing Women's Worlds: Bedouin Stories*, Berkeley: University of California Press.

Abu-Lughod. Lila and Lutz, Catherine A. (1990) 'Introduction: emotion, discourse, and the politics of everyday life', in Catherine A. Lutz and Lila Abu-Lughod (eds) *Language and the Politics of Emotion*, Cambridge: Cambridge University Press.

Ardener, Edwin (1987) 'Remote areas: some theoretical considerations', Anthony Jackson (ed.) *Anthropology at Home*, ASA Monograph No. 25, London: Tavistock.

Bateson, Gregory (1972) *Steps to an Ecology of Mind*, New York: Ballantine.

Baumann, Richard (1986) *Story, Performance, and Event: Contextual Studies of Oral Narrative*, Cambridge: Cambridge University Press.

Bernstein, Richard J. (1983) *Beyond Objectivism and Relativism*, Oxford: Blackwell.

Bloch, Maurice (1991) 'Language, anthropology, and cognitive science', *Man*, 26: 183–98.

Bourdieu, Pierre (1990) *The Logic of Practice*, Cambridge: Polity Press.

Bourdieu, Pierre (1991) 'The production and reproduction of legitimate language', in *Language and Symbolic Power*, Cambridge: Polity Press.

Bruner, Edward (1986) 'Experience and its expressions', in Victor W. Turner and Edward M. Bruner (eds) *The Anthropology of Experience*, Urbana and Chicago: University of Illinois Press.

Casey, Edward S. (1987) *Remembering: a Phenomenological Study*, Bloomington: University of Indiana Press.

D'Andrade, Roy (1992) 'Schemas and motivation', in Roy D'Andrade and Claudia Strauss (eds) *Human Motives and Cultural Models*, Cambridge: Cambridge University Press.

Davidson, Donald (1980) *Essays on Actions and Events*, Oxford: Clarendon Press.

Davidson, Donald (1984) *Enquiries into Truth and Interpretation*, Oxford: Clarendon Press.

de Certeau. Michel (1988) *The Practice of Everyday Life*, Berkeley: University of California Press.

Descartes, René (1988) in John Cottingham (ed.) *Selected Philosophical Writings*, Cambridge: Cambridge University Press.

Friedrich, Paul (1986) *The Language Parallax. Linguistic Relativism and Poetic Indeterminacy*, Austin: University of Texas Press.

Hanks, William (1990) *Referential Practice: Language and Lived Space among the Maya*, Chicago: University of Chicago Press.

Hastrup, Kirsten (1990) *Nature and Policy in Iceland 1400–1800. An Anthropological Analysis of History and Mentality*, Oxford: Clarendon Press.

Hastrup, Kirsten (1993a) 'The native voice and the anthropological vision', *Social Anthropology/Anthropologie Sociale*, 1: 173–86.

Hastrup, Kirsten (1993b) 'Hunger and the hardness of facts', *Man*, 28: 727–39.

Hastrup, Kirsten (1994a) 'Anthropological knowledge incorporated', in Kirsten Hastrup and Peter Hervik (eds) *Social Experience and Anthropological Knowledge*, London: Routledge.

Hastrup, Kirsten (1994b) 'The motivated body. The locus of agency in culture', in *A Passage to Anthropology*, London: Routledge.

Hastrup, Kirsten (1995) *A Passage to Anthropology: Between Experience and Theory*, London: Routledge.

Hastrup, Kirsten and Hervik, Peter (eds) (1994) *Social Experience and Anthropological Knowledge*, London: Routledge.

Hollis, Mark (1985) 'Of masks and men', in S. Carrithers *et al.* (eds) *The Concept of the Person*, Cambridge: Cambridge University Press.

Johnson, Mark (1987) *The Body in the Mind*, Chicago: University of Chicago Press.

Kleinman, Arthur (1988) *The Illness Narratives: Suffering, Healing, and the Human Condition*, New York: Basic Books.

Lakoff, George (1987) *Women, Fire, and Dangerous Things*, Chicago: University of Chicago Press.

Leder, Drew (1990) *The Absent Body*, Chicago: University of Chicago Press.

LeVine, Robert A. (1982) 'Gusii funerals: meanings of life and death in an African community', *Ethos*, 10: 26–65.

Pettit, Philip (1976) 'Making actions intelligible', in Rom Harré (ed.) *Life Sentences. Aspects of the Social Role of Language*, London: Wiley.

Putnam, Hilary (1990) *Realism with a Human Face*, Cambridge, Mass.: Harvard University Press.

Rosaldo, Renato (1986) 'Ilongot hunting as story and experience', in Victor W. Turner and Edward M. Bruner (eds) *The Anthropology of Experience*, Urbana: University of Illinois Press.

Scheper-Hughes, Nancy (1992) *Death Without Weeping. The Violence of Everyday Life in Brazil*, Berkeley: University of California Press.

Scheper-Hughes, Nancy and Lock, Margaret (1987) 'The mindful body: a prolegomenon to future work in medical anthropology', *Medical Anthropology Quarterly*, 1: 6–41.

Strauss, Claudia and Quinn, Naomi (1993) 'A cognitive/cultural anthropology', in Robert Borofsky (ed.) *Assessing Developments in Anthropology*, New York: McGraw-Hill.

Taylor, Charles (1985a) *Human Agency and Language. Philosophical Papers 1*, Cambridge: Cambridge University Press.

Taylor, Charles (1985b) *Philosophy and the Human Sciences. Philosophical Papers 2.* Cambridge: Cambridge University Press.

Taylor, Charles (1989) *Sources of the Self. The Making of the Modern Identity.* Cambridge: Cambridge University Press.

Turner, Victor (1986) 'Dewey, Dilthey, and drama: an essay in the anthropology of experience', in Victor W. Turner and Edward M. Bruner (eds) *The Anthropology of Experience*, Urbana: University of Illinois Press.

Vendler, Zeno (1984) 'Understanding people', in R. Shweder and R. LeVine (eds) *Culture Theory*, Cambridge: Cambridge University Press.

Chapter 10

Blank banners and Islamic consciousness in Zanzibar

David Parkin

INTRODUCTION

Durkheim's *la conscience* in *The Elementary Forms of the Religious Life* (1915), significantly translated into English as both conscience and consciousness (see, for example, G. Simpson, original translator of *The Division of Labour in Society* [Durkheim 1964] and J. W. Swain, translator of *Elementary Forms of the Religious Life*), is people's awareness of their religious sentiment as morality. It is countered by the structuralist and marxist notion of unaware or underlying religious self-mystification or false consciousness. These two descriptions of religious thought, one producing moral society and the other masked and exploitative social formations, may once have separated Durkheimian functionalism from structuralism and marxism. Nowadays the descriptions are popularly abridged media theories which seek elements of both the moral and the exploitative in many modern forms of collective religious enthusiasm. Thus, persons described by Western media as 'religious fundamentalists' (to take one epithet) carry a globally recognized designation, which is part of a transnational demarcatory vocabulary, and may themselves have been inspired in the first place by examples of moral renaissance reported and explained in the media, sometimes in terms of underlying politico-economic and social conditions. The 1940s and 1950s objectivist scholarship of, say, Sundkler's (1961) study of Bantu prophets in South Africa or that of Worsley on Melanesian cargo cults (1957) presented analyses of the complex interplay of spiritual and material deprivation from a metropolitan perspective and for a like readership. The issues they addressed have become subjectively compressed as globally purveyed news speak. Nowadays, religious participants, media readers and viewers alike communicate through example with one another: religious activists stress the fundamental, self-verifying truth of their mission, while non-participant media observers seek alternative explanations from outside the religion. Of the so-called world religions, the current claims for and about Islam are particularly focused.

Anthropological theory is implicit in comparative ethnographic description, and not explicitly formulated as in other social sciences, and so is easily appropriated by these latter without acknowledgement as in the recent concern with problems of 'culture', popular, global and otherwise. It is not a matter of regret that anthropological theory is then refashioned into a neatness that defies the original ethnographic complexity that inspired it. On the contrary 'their' explicit theorizing is what maintains the distinction, for anthropology needs to remain theoretically untidy. It follows that we ourselves need not use the now too well-honed if presumptive paradigm of individual versus social agency to resolve the problem of the inherent reification in a Durkheimian concept of religious consciousness (God is society and surmounts individual agency) or a marxist one of false consciousness (religion mystifies individuals' acceptance of society).

Anthropologists are at their best when metaphorically recasting concepts which are becoming familiar to others. Using theoretical untidiness as its starting point, I choose the metaphor of 'blank banners' (Ardener 1971: xliii, lxxxiii) rather than individual or collective consciousness to capture the broad range of sentiments, aims, causes and consequences of an Islamic movement. The metaphor is a visual one and I use it to suggest, in this example, that what we might otherwise call consciousness turns on issues of bodily concealment, adornment and exposure.

The Cartesian notion of consciousness, from which the Durkheimian and marxist versions derive, suffers the same problem as referential theory in linguistics. It privileges a socially decontextualized mental state in search of an object. But mental states do not seek objects: they are only ever *already* inscribed in the materiality of bodily form, action and encoded objects. If we are to transcend Cartesian dualities, we have to say that consciousness is not to do with abstract cognition but with intelligent or what I have elsewhere called animated materiality (Parkin 1993). Rather than ask what it is people are or are not conscious of, we can look instead at how they discuss, locate and present their own and others' bodily selves as the various and interlaced experiences of personal existence which make up popular movements. I here take a phenomenological view (see Parkin 1985 and Kapferer, this volume), extending it to the idea of a bodily aesthetics comprising rather than separating physical sensation from abstract cognition. Embodiment, which I take to be the consubstantiation of physical action, purposive design and unintended consequence, is therefore materialized thought.

If 'culture' is that long conversation between the generations about how to do things when, where, why and with whom, then consciousness can be regarded as a kind of meta-conversation occurring at times of heightened 'awareness' (see Hastrup, this volume): in the very course of what they are doing, persons here reflect on and justify, evaluate or condemn their action, affecting it in the process, and so possibly subverting any initial plan. Since even the most heightened awareness can never at any moment encompass the full significance of an action, there is always some meaning that is left out. More to the point, the very action may raise issues about the bodily medium through which it is expressed: to march in collective protest can be done in an infinite number of ways and styles which are not necessarily worked out beforehand. To return to my initial metaphor, even when the banners have captions and slogans written on them, they remain blank, and perhaps inchoate (see Fernandez, this volume), with regard to those areas of personal and bodily conceal-ment and exposure which cannot be talked about.

ISLAMIC FUNDAMENTALISM OR COUNTER-REVOLUTION

In Zanzibar in December 1992 and January 1993 I witnessed a particularly marked expression of a burgeoning Islamic fundamentalist movement. There were processions of young radical men, assemblies addressed by acknowledged sheikhs still only in their thirties, an attack on an Italian jeweller's shop, and demonstrations demanding two things: that the Zanzi-bar islands should be allowed to join the Organization of Islamic Confer-ences without impediment by the union government of Zanzibar and the non-Muslim mainland Tanganyika; and that tourism should not be allowed in Zanzibar. This prominence of youthful militancy, accompanied by excited debate in the older men's street-corner meetings or *baraza* and full coverage and comment by the media, all suggested that this was a turning point in Zanzibar's redefinition of itself. This is indeed what people in Stone Town and outside were saying themselves: Zanzibar's Islamic distinctiveness was about to be expressed in its political autonomy, its affiliation with the world's main Islamic states, including the most fundamentalist, and its repudiation of tourism and the sins and degra-dation associated with Western lifestyles. Islamic militant resurgence was also alive in the Kenyan coastal town of Mombasa, more than a hundred miles away, and, in fact, there had been earlier expressions of Islamic militancy in Zanzibar itself.

By summer 1993, the Islamic rallies, demonstrations and marches had died down, and the street *baraza* talked of other matters, mainly of the economy and the cost of living. The Muslim Zanzibar government had succeeded through a show of force and persuasion to quieten the move-ment. However, in Mombasa, Kenya, the militant struggle between Mus-lims and the non-Muslim government was continuing to intensify. Evidently, in the case of Zanzibar, the overt expression of Islamic funda-mentalism was a recurrent phenomenon, now resurgent, now quiet. Oral statements, press reports and my own impressions suggested this.

It may sometimes be characteristic of a small island community with dense intercommunity and cross-cutting kinship and affinal ties that government persuasion backed up by a minimal show of force can often curb popular movements which take to the streets. But this clearly is not always the case, as the example of Zanzibar itself shows. For, in 1964, there occurred one of the bloodiest island revolutions on Zanzibar, when many land and property owners, mainly of Arab descent, were killed or fled the islands, which were then ruled by a government of mainly African descent. One could certainly describe this as a struggle between proper-tied and non-propertied classes, which were, however, largely defined at the time on racial grounds, a distinction that was, however, never clear-cut, especially in the decades since the ending of slavery almost a hundred years ago, and which Zanzibaris today are often reluctant to endorse or even speak about.

Zanzibar in fact consists of two islands, Unguja with a population of 350,000 and Pemba with 250,000. Both are almost entirely Muslim. The main island of Unguja is commonly referred to in English as Zanzibar Island, but I refer to it by its indigenous name of Unguja and the two islands together as Zanzibar, which is in fact a semi-autonomous polity in the United Republic of Tanzania. Mji Mkongwe, or Stone Town as it is known in English, is the main town on Unguja island. Until the socialist revolution in 1964 it was the seat of the Sultan of Zanzibar, who was of Omani origin and whose links with Oman were strong. Zanzibar was in fact during the mid-nineteenth centry adopted as his residence by the then Sultan of Oman.

These few facts alone indicate some of the extraordinary complexity of this island state, which has for hundreds of years been a principal entrepôt in the Indian Ocean, not fully within any socio-geographical sphere, not African, Arabian or Indian, but partaking of each of these through a profession of boundary distinctions which are constantly shifting.

It is difficult not to try and relate this local expression of what I am calling Islamic fundamentalism to the global phenomenon of the same name. But I am aware also that, just as the Zanzibari Muslim marchers drew inspiration from Islamic movements elsewhere in the world, I was myself classifying it in much the same way. Had I observed such demon-strations thirty years ago at the time of the revolution, I doubt that I would have thought in terms of Islamic fundamentalism. 1964, the year of the Zanzibari revolution, was, after all, part of the ongoing period expressed in the language of satellite country and island revolutions, from Cuba to Vietnam, flanked by superpowers. Had Muslims risen up at that time, it might have been called a bourgeois counter-revolution and not Islamic fundamentalism.

If this was merely a question of a difference in the way we name a phenomenon, with the underlying conflict remaining the same, then we would be dealing with no more than a shift of semantic signifiers. But the totality of circumstances is never the same: what was named then and is named now are not repeated histories, and, anyway, our very naming of the events, counter-revolution as against Islamic fundamentalism, shapes our understanding and explanation of the phenomena. And of course I am aware that calling a demonstration either counter-revolution or religious fundamentalism is already to explain it, or at least to frame any explanation I wish to make of it.

Nevertheless, I think it is reasonable to argue that, in that prevailing 1960s world climate of socialist idealism, we can say that the overthrow of the Omani sultanate of Zanzibar was indeed a class-perceived revolution. Most of the land in Zanzibar was owned by a few families. Stone Town itself was made up of many luxuriously appointed mansions inhabited by the wealthy landed business class divided into different Muslim communities each historically linked to its own religious elite and mosque (Sheriff 1992). And, although by comparison with the mainland African population the majority of Zanzibar's population would not be judged poor, there was certainly a colossal difference between them and the landed and business families on the islands. More to the point, ideas justifying the division between a ruling and a servile class were being questioned at the time as a result of exposure to the global reports of revolutionary possibility. As far as I can judge, this explanation both fits the facts and the political rhetoric of the time. Moreover, the 1960s rhetoric provided us and the combatants we observed with clear-cut parameters within which explanation could occur.

I find it more difficult to explain the emergence of the current Islamic movement on Zanzibar in 1992–3. Compared with the 1960s, the 1990s provide no such easy classifications for the Western-trained social analyst, while, by contrast, the absolutism of the *jihad* apparently gives its adherents no problems of doubt.

Thus, there has been a kind of partial reversal. In the 1960s, observer and observed shared, or could share, a broadly marxist rhetoric, whether or not they formally subscribed to marxism. In the 1990s, and also during much of the 1980s, religious fundamentalist rhetoric clashed with current liberal social analysis. This is not simply a clash between theological absolutism and postmodernism. It is a broader intellectual conflict. Whereas it was conceivable in the 1960s for Western-trained intellectuals of marxist persuasion to join hands, sometimes literally, with Asian and African revolutionary movements, or at least to concur with their explanations of their struggle, few if any would nowadays subscribe to the tenets of fundamentalist religion, whether Islamic or Christian, for this would be seen as sacrificing intellectual scepticism for undebatable dogma.

However, we seem nowadays with regard to Islamic fundamentalism if not to confer critical charity at least to seek explanations, as we once used to, in terms of precipitating conditions. What else, we may ask, are we to expect of peoples whose distinctive sense of cultural identity appears to them to be under threat and who see themselves as economically and politically deprived in relation to media-imaged others. A positivistic return to explanation through social conditions and perceived relative deprivation seems an inevitable response to, if I may use the term, supposedly genuine global crises. In other words, with Islamic fundamentalism allegedly sweeping areas of the world including Europe, we are enjoined to address the reality of severe crisis and to put aside what others regard as anthropological 'trivia'. One can almost hear the ESRC saying: analyse your isolated rituals and small-people cosmologies in postmodernist language if you like, but, when it comes to the supposed growing global threat of militant Islam, now often characterized as communism's successor, tell us how it happens and how to combat it, and do so quickly.[1] And provided one remains at the level of highgrade media generalization, one can provide at least satisfactory answers to such questions. Thirty-odd years of Algerian independence do not appear to most people there to have brought them much except an erosion of cultural identity and living standards and political constraint as they see themselves and their relatives shuffled between North Africa and France and divided by different citizenries. Anthropology, of course, is a great irritant to this mode of thinking for, looking closely and intensively at a particular, local Islamic movement, such as is occurring in Zanzibar, we find so much at the level of explanation that simply does not fit the global rhetoric.

YOUTH AND RESTRAINT

The Zanzibari movement is driven by young men in their late teens and twenties, with even the few leading sheikhs only in their thirties. Such young men in Stone Town and in the surrounding urban area lack regular paid work, lack farming land and commonly must marry late, sometimes in their early thirties and even later, by which time they are expected somehow to have built a house and accumulated enough material property for the marriage settlement called *mahari* and for other payments to the bride's parents. Unlike their own parents in Zanzibar and young people of their own age in mainland Tanganyika, they were not taught either English or Arabic at school, but only Swahili which the revolutionary government insisted was the only acceptable truly African medium of instruction and communication, and so the teaching of English and Arabic was banned from 1964. The young men certainly have a deep pride in the richness of their Zanzibari brand of Swahili language and literature, but they express alarm that so-called progress in modern East Africa and the world necessitates a knowledge of English, while at the same time their status as Muslims is limited by no more than a recitational knowledge of Arabic. Finally, there is a strict Islamic code on pre-marital sexual relationships and, as far as I can gather from conversation with the young men, the sexual relations that do occur between them and young women are often perfunctory, restricted affairs desperately hedged around with fears of pregnancy and discovery, and carried out in the worst of clandestine conditions compared with mainland non-Muslims. When the girl does become pregnant, it is often necessary for her to live at the home of a parent or relative separately from her boyfriend until and unless he has earned enough to secure his own accommodation, which may take years or be precluded by the increasing distance separating the couple. Although separation and divorce rates are high, so possibly providing young men with at least some accessible women, I am struck, nevertheless, by the apparently genuine cases of long-term and total heterosexual abstinence that some men in their late twenties and early thirties are obliged to practise. Nor do I have evidence of significant homosexual practice, which is also thoroughly condemned by the clerics.

The issue of youthful restraint, both voluntary and imposed, is hedged around with ambiguity. Senior government-backed imams support tourism and so are here at odds with the radical youth. But the same radical young people, especially young men, may nevertheless heed the imams' Friday mosque sermons on other matters, most of which are aimed at youth. For example, one sermon acknowledged that young men could not find gainful employment and were likely to remain jobless until the economy improved. It urged them, however, not to sit talking on *baraza* wasting their time in idle thought and talk, but to pray in mosques, with more fervour and dedication than ever before. Another sermon also focused on the *baraza* congregation of youths and this time rebuked them for looking at and talking to young women passing by, urging them instead to cast their eyes down and to do no more than give the formal, Muslim greeting of *salaam alekum – alekum salaam*. Other mosque sermons and discussions have consistently reasserted the necessity of incorporating women more fully in mosque prayers as a means of safeguarding their virtuous character, while at the same time stressing the need for their separation from men on mosque premises and on entering and leaving them. This re-emphasis on women's concealment and seclusion reinforces the young men's concern to contrast Muslim and non-Muslim women.

Senior imams make authoritative moral pronouncements about the young, but it is young men themselves who take the initiative and lead the everyday, radical mosque-based activities that propagate fundamentalist morality. Outside the Ibadhi mosques in particular (those that are most associated with people of Omani descent), young adherents sell Islamic fundamentalist literature and try to reinvigorate belief in, and a strict textualist interpretation of, Islam among all Muslims and not just members of their own sect. At another part of Stone Town, a shop run by young men is entirely devoted to selling tape-recordings of sermons by radical sheikhs. This shop is well attended by other young men avidly buying the tapes with the enthusiasm of youth elsewhere buying popular music.

The Muslim sectarian differences of Sunni, Ibadhi and Shi'a are not strongly marked, nor seem to have been since at least the revolution. . Perhaps this is unsurprising. The Muslim population of the two Zanzibar islands is no more than 600,000, while Tanganyika, the mainland partner in the Union of Tanzania, is a country of some 30 million non-Muslims. Moreover, Zanzibar has only over the last few years been released by its revolutionary government from a range of constraints. Islam was never banned, but was not encouraged during the socialist regime: for instance, the former Muslim Academy was converted into an orphanage in 1964 by Zanzibar's revolutionary president, Karume, who also disallowed public Muslim gatherings of almost any kind, despite himself remaining at least a nominal Muslim. So-called free expression, like free enterprise, was only gradually allowed in Zanzibar from about the mid-1980s, and accelerated from about 1989, when one of Zanzibar's chief sources of aid, the Communist German Democratic Republic, ceased to exist. In this new political climate, the threat of the non-Muslims across the water in mainland Tanganyika has seemed to loom large and is now given as one reason for all Muslims of whatever persuasion to act together, although, as I soon show, another sectarian-type division has occurred.

There have also been attempts to revive links with the Arab Gulf States. Oman has a consulate in Zanzibar, though all other countries are represented in mainland Dar es Salaam. The Sultan of Sharjah, one of the Gulf Emirates, opened an historic conference in Zanzibar in December 1992 concerned with an international reassessment of the culture and history of Zanzibar, and publicly urged mutual forgiveness between Arab and African and pledged the rebirth of an old Arab Islamic relationship with Zanzibar. Middle Eastern money has made it possible once again to learn Arabic as a full and not merely recitational Koranic language, while the British Council is also trying to set up facilities in schools for the teaching of English again.

Islamic radicalism on Zanzibar is also set within a familiar and indeed global context, namely that of the division between Saudi-influenced Wahabi reformists, who call themselves Ahl-Sunna, and those, the majority, whom they call Wa-Bi'da, who are accused of having brought in Islamic innovative practices not present during the Prophet's lifetime nor sanctioned by the Koran and therefore disallowed. The reformists try to prohibit lavish *maulidi* celebrations of the Prophet's birthday, which usually means criticizing the use of tambourines and singing and dancing at these or other Muslim festivals. They also oppose saintly veneration, slaughtering animals for food at funerals, and insist on women wearing the *hijabu* and *buibui* in such a way that the whole body is covered, leaving only the eyes visible. Some might argue that it is the reformists' insistence on returning to the Koran, in particular, and to the Hadith and other holy texts, as guides to Islamic moral conduct, that really justifies their being called fundamentalists. However, I regard the recourse to the Koran and other literature as the textual plank in a developing discourse which is constantly attracting new causes as extra reasons for its existence.

I have already mentioned some of these other causes which go beyond the immediate, textually based demands of the Ahl-Sunna reformists, and which include demands for Zanzibar's religious and political autonomy of mainland Tanganyika and its right to affiliate with the Organisation of Islamic Conferences (OIC). In fact, having defended the move through marched protests, the reformists later dropped it, when they realized, in their own words, that the reason that the Zanzibar government wished to join the OIC was solely to receive aid directly from wealthier Islamic states and not, in the normal way, via the Tanzania Union government. Thus discredited as no more than a base economic move, the Zanzibar government's attempt to join the OIC ceased to have interest for the reformists.

We might conclude from this that the young reformists are indeed guided more by puritanical religious zeal than by hard economic motives, despite being jobless. Their own view is that you cannot create economic opportunities without also attending to the moral condition of society. They claim that through their religious zeal, they will in due course achieve their just economic deserts, and those of fellow Muslims who join them in their cause. Their message is: reform society according to the fundamentals of Islam, and prosperity will then follow according to God's will and ways, which only He can know.

This attitude converts what we might interpret as the young radicals' ambiguity concerning imamic dictates into a solution: thus, one should transcend the prospect of financial profit from tourism by turning from this-worldly issues and concentrate, as the imams urge, on the reaffirmation of Islamic values as enshrined in the sacred texts; one should substitute for the 'idleness' caused by joblessness the dedication of mosque-based activity and prayer; and out of prayer and devotion to the Koran, one can achieve God's will on earth. A story was once given in a mosque sermon to illustrate this concept of wealth and well-being. A young man and young woman wished to marry, but the man had no property or income. The Kadhi asked him if he could recite and understand the Koran, which the young man could. Then, said the Kadhi, you have all the wealth you need in marriage and life. This story narrated by a senior mosque sheikh is not as disingenuous as it might first sound, for it occurred in the context of calls publicly made at the mosque by senior clerics for the abolition or reduction of marriage payments and thereby a lowering of the age for men at which marriage might take place. It is in fact both a recognition and attempt to eliminate the problem of long sexual abstinence expected of young people. That said, the accompanying crucial problem of where the couple might then live and subsist after marriage is not however addressed.

SEXUALITY AND BODILY CONSUMERISM

The reliance on verbal rhetoric, story, homily and solution is unsurprising in all this. Mosque sermons are talked about afterwards, that of the main Friday mosque in Stone Town (Forodhani) is broadcast on Zanzibar radio, and sermons and other addresses in mosques and elsewhere given by radical sheikhs are complemented by literature and tapes handed out or sold at cost by young men. Speakers draw on the riches of the Swahili language, itself underlain by a centuries-old poetic and metaphorical tradition, and bring in Arabic expressions as deftly as they can for presentational effect. In this way, they sustain the interwoven tissue of concept and form, so that the circular pursuit of argument may serve the interests of stylistic as much if not more than logical competition.

The verbal rhetoric can, however, become verbal argument, and over one issue, that of tourism, the government and senior imams would not back down despite the views advanced by the radical youth and their five or so leaders that tourism led to Western-like moral decadence. The issue of tourism most clearly divided Ahl-Sunna radicals from the majority of more conservative Muslims supporting the government. The government and establishment countered that it was a fundamental principle of Islam that all peoples, Muslim or non-Muslim, should be encouraged to travel the world seeking God's knowledge, and that tourists could only gain by witnessing for themselves the splendours and virtue of Islam as practised in Zanzibar. They were to be welcomed, not shunned or attacked. This was the view of the government-supported Muslim imams and sheikhs. More pragmatically, and reflecting the government's encouragement of investment in tourism by outsiders as well as Zanzibaris, including Arabs and Indians returning to the islands for the first time since the revolution, tourism was presented by the government as the only realistic economic salvation for Zanzibar, given the depressed and unreliable world market demand for cloves and other crops. To this chorus was added, albeit almost mutely, the claim of certain Western-trained liberal economists, that, given the diversion of local people from subsistence and craft production to hotel wage employment, only the major players in the tourist industry ever really benefited.

What was distinctive about the issue of tourism, therefore, was that morality and the economy were clearly seen as separable categories and were each used to justify or deny the other.

While much was debated verbally, the issue of tourism also became expressed through pictures, images and bodily inferences as well as through words, for, in my view, it went beyond the complex of political and economic factors of contest and deprivation I have outlined. It touched on an amalgam of cultural and personal concerns to do with what at first sight we might call sexuality and consumption, not just of commodities but of the body. There is no ready-made language for these concerns, but they turn on notions of exposure, concealment, closure and loss. When the reformists are militant and marching, then tourism is indeed argued about openly between reformists and government in the politico-economic rhetoric of the day as well as in terms of moral decadence. But, during the periods of quiet, after the reformists have been quelled by government, the discourse of argument retains its complex, visual form and focuses on the problem of moral loss. But, I would suggest, it is this visual form and the concern with moral loss that is paradigmatic and is what I now explore. The economic deprivation is real and distressing but is, in the end, also a matter of concealment and exposure. In the young men's case, it concerns how they can retain dignity and a sense of the aesthetic in the face of joblessness and late marriage, while for young women the concern is more directly with how their bodies are presented.

It is significant that it is women's dress and bodies that are the main focus of concern. Crudely drawn posters were stuck by young Muslims to walls at various key points in Stone Town, for example near one of the few hotels allowed to sell alcoholic liquor, and which caters for visiting non-Muslims and is called 'The Bottoms Up Hotel', a title unsubtly combining drinking and sexual innuendos. The drawings had pictures of men drinking from a bottle and smoking hashish and cocaine (*bangi* and *unga* [flour]) and evidently suffering the effects, with written warnings against this deviant behaviour. Most striking was the contrast depicted between a very short-skirted European tourist with long hair and her upper as well as lower body scantily covered and a Zanzibari woman covered everywhere except the eyes by the *hijab*, including a face veil. The tourist was referred to as the Devil's whore, an unbeliever who walks naked ('huyu ni kahba shetani, mwenda uchi kafiri', cf. the Arabic-derived *kahba* instead of the more usual *malaya* for prostitute, and little used outside central Swahili-speaking places like Zanzibar, Mombasa and Lamu). By contrast, the Zanzibari woman was referred to as one of pious virtue, who covered her Muslim body ('kujisitiri mwili wake muislamu') and whose clothes indicated her self-respect (*kujiheshima*). Given its position, the visual messages could not have been lost on the European tourists. But the Swahili phrases would not have been understood by them and were clearly aimed at the Zanzibaris themselves, with the implication either that Zanzibari women could become whores or that, more generally, tourism begets prostitution practised and organized by outsiders, and indeed a few months previously an Italian-owned hotel had been raided and closed after disclosures that it had acted as a venue for mainland non-Muslim prostitutes and drug-dealing.

The Swahili expressions certainly presupposed closeness among Zanzibaris themselves and referred indirectly both to sermons and injunctions telling young men to avert their gazes from women and to those that warn young men of the seductive capacities of women. As is reported in numerous Middle Eastern and Mediterranean areas, women are regarded as having less control over their sexuality than men, whose responsibility it is ultimately to control women's lusts through their own self-restraint ranging from avoidance of women to communicating with them only formally in the language of Arabo-Islamic Swahili greetings.

During the time of the marches and demonstrations, sisters and wives of the radical young men, or in some cases young daughters of older men, wore the all-covering black *hijab* and face veil. During the quieter period, the young women reverted to the more colourful so-called *khanga*, two lengths of cotton wrapped around the lower and upper parts of the body, including the head but without a face veil. The black *hijabu* and face veil leave only a pair of eyes while the colourful *khanga* leave the face perfectly visible and have no strong connotation of youthful containment.

Women wearing the black *hijab* extending to a face-veil are a conspicuous minority and other men and women sometimes refer to them as adopting the guise of a *ninja*, the similarly black-covered hired assassins and bodyguards of Japanese film fables which are shown on video or in one of the two cinemas in Zanzibar. It has been suggested to me that, conscious of this effect, the *hijabu*-veiled and -covered women are able to accede to male demands for modest personal concealment yet at the same time enjoy connoting the assertiveness and modernity that is associated with the male *ninja* characters and exploits (Purpura, personal communication). It can also be suggested that, covered except for their eyes which they use to alluring effect, the women also enjoy a frisson from this licence to make sensual hints under the protective cover of religious clothing. It is the classic case of the woman who reveals both too little and too much.

I certainly have the impression that women constantly and consciously play on the ambivalences that their social position affords them. In addition to the example just given where they can turn an Islamic fundamentalist obligation into an expression of personal allure and even autonomy and defiance, there is a whole area of dress-play centring on the use of the *khanga* in which women communicate with each other and with men. Each *khanga* has a combined riddle–proverb or ascerbic saying written on it. Every month or so there is a proliferation of new sayings and new designs on the *khanga*. It is mainly women who compose and send in the sayings to the *khanga* textile designers and manufacturers, receiving a small payment. And it is mainly women who buy them, doing so as often as they can, which for those who can afford it, can be several times a month. The *khanga* are a big part of the clothing retailing and manufacturing business.

The key feature in all this is the fact that, as women themselves say and as I have observed, the written message on the *khanga* is more important than the cloth's colours and design. Even if the colour and design appeal immensely to a woman, she will not buy it if the saying is inappropriate. Nowadays, there may be some range in the colours of a particular design carrying a message, so that there is more opportunity than previously to make choices. But it is still the written comment or proverb that in the end qualifies the buyer or consumer's choices.

I have discussed these *khanga* riddle–proverbs at length elsewhere (Parkin, forthcoming), and here need only say that the themes of these silent messages have remained broadly the same over the last thirty years, increasingly focusing on men–women relations and sexuality, sometimes behind an apparently innocent and even pious declaration. A few proverbs and riddles are very old and precede their depiction on *khanga*, dealing more with exhortations to good moral behaviour than sexuality, but most are of recent origin. No sayings are ever repeated successively from one year to the next, and no woman would be seen wearing a *khanga* regarded as out of fashion.

Let me give an example: 'Tutakula nao wenye waume zao' (We shall eat with those having husbands). This is said to be the kind of oblique reference that a man's mistress might make to his wife. But, as with so many and perhaps all sayings, there are varying interpretations as to its meaning.

Thus, (a) it is said to be a way of belittling the wife, of indicating to her that she is obliged to share her husband with another woman: it thus is an assertion of competition between women for men. Or, (b) it is said to be a commentary on modern marriage, for infidelity is often alleged to be common, so that women find themselves sharing the same men. (This claim does not square with those of Muslim apologists who assert, for instance, that AIDS is rare in Zanzibar because Islam's strict pre-marital and marital codes preclude so-called promiscuity.) There are other interpretations but these give some idea of the chain-like possibilities. Thus, the first view privileges the idea of men as a scarce and valuable resource sought after by women and is offered as much by women as men. The second view connotes a sense of sisterly irony that, in a system of unstable marriages, women find themselves obliged to 'taste' the same 'food' (i.e. sexually and possibly financially share the same men). Here men are not privileged as in the first case but are reduced to the value of consumer objects to be handed on to each other by sisters. It echoes a view often expressed confidentially by women that it is they rather than men who really decide when a couple should separate and even divorce, having reached a point in the marriage when they, the women, have become, as they put it, 'tired'.

However, most current sayings reinforce the common view given by women even more than men, for women understandably see themselves as authorities on *khanga* strategies, that women buy and wear their *khanga* in order to spite other women whom they suspect either of trying to seduce their man, or of backbiting at her relationship with her man, by insinuating for instance that the couple are always quarrelling and are on the threshold of a break-up. It is said that 'Women riddle with each other' ('wanawake wanafubiana') through the use of the *khanga* and, indeed, their attacks on each other are made in the idiom of the riddle-proverb, a form that combines an element of apparent traditional wisdom with a puzzling verbal expression that invites a number of interpretations and is not easily settled as having a single meaning. There is always something incomplete about the *khanga* riddle-proverb, always more meaning that can be extracted from it, as women themselves insist, just as there is always to the onlookers a certain doubt as to which rival is being referred to when a woman chooses to buy and wear a *khanga*. Not even the rival will necessarily be aware. Unlike that kind of witchcraft accusation reported in other societies which settles on a particular and known individual, the identity of a woman's female rival is likely to remain publicly uncertain and known only to the wearer of the *khanga*, although there is the fear of public exposure.

A remarkably similar game of unvoiced and visibly connoted mutual recrimination among women over sexual relationships, including pre- and extra-marital affairs, occurs at *taarab* musical performances, which are heavily attended by women (see Topp 1994). Whenever the male or female singer at a *taarab* evening sings a line which especially expresses a woman's feeling of resentment against another woman, the woman will process to the front of the hall and place money in the hands of the singer, so communicating to her rival that she is aware of the threat and that she will deal with it, indicating this in response to another line of singing. At the *taarab* occasions the women dress in amazingly ornate clothes and finery and spend thousands of shillings. Their pronounced and assertive march to the singer, the handing over of the money, their equally swaggering walk back to their seats in their splendid dresses, their sometimes haughty glances at what some interpret as either the female rivals in the audience or the men in question, are, as with the use of *khanga*, all done in silence and through the use of body and bodily display, and yet, since no one can be sure who in the audience is being referred to, the results are inconclusive. As with the *khanga* riddling, we have a very powerful field of communication whose strength and efficacy, however, depend paradoxically on people not knowing precisely who is rival to who, and who desires who. The incompleteness of these communication games constitute their essence which is sustained provided the players do not insist on converting them into searches for unassailable truths. Quarrels and fights do occasionally erupt if a woman feels that she has been too obviously identified by an accusation and so turns on her accuser. But the game is kept effective through hinting rather than open assertion and, again, through the frisson that comes from veiled allusion which on the whole is protected by anonymity yet carries just an element of danger of discovery. Provided things do not get out of hand, the half-truths and innuendoes alert possible miscreants or objects of desire, while shielding them and their rivals and suitors from full public scrutiny and judgement.

This, then, entails an aim which is quite the opposite to that of the young men's fundamentalist Islamic march and demonstrations. The young men are marching for the revelation of absolute truth, even if its precise definition is subsumed under a claim that it is all in the Koran and Hadiths. Deviant Muslims should be exposed, as should the decadent practices of the non-Muslims. The unambiguous, anti-tourist drawings of the two kinds of women, one an amalgam of tourist-white-infidel-scantily clad-whore and the other a Zanzibari-Muslim-*hijabu*-covered-woman who could be a sister, wife or mother, are part of this truth-settling absolutism. The irony is that, by invoking such powerful visual images, the young men enter a field of communication in which, under Zanzibari women's own control of the dresses and finery they wear, the debate moves into the issues of sexuality that the young men had associated with the abominations of European tourism and lifestyle.

FROM BLANK BANNER TO CONCEALMENT AS ROOT METAPHOR

I do not see the above only as a covert struggle between young men wishing to control their womenfolk and these women seeking more personal freedom. Blank banners allude to indignities that cannot be talked about even during formal expressions of protest. But the root metaphor is that of concealment, or *setiri* (Arabic *setr*), which, like *hijabu* (Arabic *hijab*), is part of a whole domain of morality which urges people not only to cover their bodies and dress modestly but also to behave reservedly. The Swahili language has a remarkably wide range of Arabic-derived, as well as Bantu, terms denoting personal moral restraint and comportment. The ethics of modest concealment and reserve underlie also the reformists' attacks on bodily movement in chanting and singing in Muslim religious ceremonies and on exhibitions of what they regard as excess at funeral ceremonies and venerations of the saints.

It is not in fact that women are challenging men's attempts through the invocation of Islam to control the way women dress and behave.

Women may be exploiting brilliantly the ambiguities inherent in any ethic of concealment, but they are not thereby challenging either Islam or the ideal of marital fidelity or even chastity before marriage, although, like most other people, they are aware that these are not as common as clerics maintain. It can be argued that both men and women have an interest in subscribing to the ideas and proprieties of concealment, for it is only from this fixed position that improprieties and deviances can be criticized. For young men, it is a thin line between maintaining dignified Islamic status and being ridiculed as poor, jobless, unmarried and sexually unfulfilled. For young women, their own overall social powerlessness is buffeted by their clever and lavish manipulation of dress, dance, song, style, bodily movement and occasional displays of financial largesse.

The threat to concealment is disclosure. Stripping the body turns a virtuous woman into a whore according to the ethic. At first, you might say that this is underlain culturally by the great emphasis on the *setiri* complex, which is, after all, pervasive in other Islamic societies and especially those of the Middle East which have been most in contact with the Swahili East African coast.

However, the shift from bodily concealment to disclosure and from sister/wife to prostitute is also a paradigm for the conversion of woman into object, in the eyes of the Muslim men at least (which is why they protest against tourist influences) and, one may suppose, tourist men also.

In other words, this is a process of objectification and not just an affront to an intrinsic cultural complex, that of *setiri*. It is not, however, a simple case of women in Islam already being subject to the kind of treatment that, object-like, renders them mute and obliges them publicly to express themselves silently in dress rather than in public speech. There is here, I suggest, a new process of objectification, which sets up a distinction between modern-world consumers and consumed, and which is familiar to us elsewhere.

The threat is of the body, and women's bodies in particular, being taken and withheld from men in much the same way that in recent years a whole range of other consumer items have both entered the Zanzibar market and yet are tantalizingly beyond the reach of those who cannot afford them. The recent counter-revolutionary changes in Zanzibar and its sudden espousal of capitalism, foreign investment, tourism and petty entrepreneurship has given many economic opportunities for outsiders and has created a marked division between the few young Zanzibari men who have, through a small business or artisanship, managed to profit from the new changes, and the majority who are without work of any kind.

The focus appears to be on women's bodies and sexuality, but it is in fact the men more than the women who have been stripped and left naked. One way in which they can cover themselves with dignity is by appeal to the absolute principles of fundamentalist Islam which, being unambiguous, leaves no area of existential debate uncovered: it always has a totalizing answer based on textual references, so that what a European Enlightenment thinker might regard as undebatable dogmatism is for them full coverage. In this way Islam is seen as capable of revealing all and yet allowing nothing to slip past its inherent wisdom. It also achieves the feat of ceding to God the conditions of revelation as well of concealment: believers are enjoined to search for revelation or truth but only on His sufferance. Thus, while women may take it upon themselves to try and determine the conditions and terms on which they will use their bodies and body coverings to secure certain aims, the radical young men confer on God the terms of textual revelation. Even if it can reasonably be said that men control women, God does seem to rule men more directly than He rules women, and this, paradoxically, gives women a certain slippage in their own definitions of themselves. Part of this slippage is possible through the use by women and men of visual messages and idioms which allow departures from the textually based interpretations and pronouncements that are the hallmark of the religion.

Is there here a propensity for the visual or artistic to speak more laterally than scriptures? And is this why in Islam much has been made of the alleged ban, not in fact fully supported in the Koran nor indeed everywhere practised, on the pictorial and sculptural representation of living things, these being seen as created by God and as therefore only His to represent, reproduce and 'breathe life into', and as touching too closely on the worship of many idols and gods (*shirk*)? The ban on pictorial representation presumably originates in Judaism. But, once in place in Islam as a means of combating polytheism, it may have both informed and have been informed by the *setr* complex of bodily and other concealment, the two, *setr* and the ban on representation, thereafter going together. If this is so, then we do indeed have an Islamized ethic of sufficient strength to have found its way into the beliefs and practices of many peoples who have converted to Islam, and which, as in the case of Zanzibar and perhaps elsewhere, has provided a pre-articulated rationale for what we call economic deprivation and political marginalization.

While the historical and religious specificity of this ethic is clearly Arabo-Islamic and thence a feature of Swahili culture, it also provokes cognitive dissonance. On the one hand, it has to be observed (i.e. followed) as matter of personal, religious and cultural decorum. On the other hand, it is by its nature non-observable: hiding nakedness should not by itself be noticeable, for it should be subsumed within visibly acceptable behaviour, such as wearing the appropriate clothes and using gestures and the body in approved ways. The actual practice of concealing something should itself be subtly concealed. It is perhaps for this reason that persons' consciousness of concealment is constantly deferred and hence transferred on to other issues which have themselves been hidden from discussion or expression, such as young men's joblessness and poor marriage prospects in a society which insists nevertheless on the sanctity of a first marriage as an index of human dignity.

As if to raise to a level of more explicit visual debate the relative advantages of traditional ideas of modest concealment and purity as against the financial gains and losses of tourism, another representational complex has emerged in Zanzibar. It combines the three polarizations of tourism versus Islam, naked whore versus covered, pious Muslim woman, and consumer and non-consumer of new commodities introduced from outside. In the last three or four years canvas and batik artists have sold to both tourists and the new, rapidly emerging Zanzibari middle class who wish to decorate their refurbished homes. The artists often include in their paintings juxtapositions of what they, other Zanzibaris and the tourists have come to regard as the traditional and the modern: new buildings act as a background for old ones, and vice versa; audiovisual equipment lies within reach of ancient house interiors, whose elderly occupants can be seen clad in Islamic dress; a Swahili wooden fishing vessel lies off-shore next to a powered motor boat, with tourists and Swahili fishermen on the beach; and, most evocative of all, a scantily clad, blonde young tourist woman standing outside the door of an old Stone Town house faces a Muslim woman of the same age dressed in the *hijab*. In an example I have of this latter picture, it is difficult not to discern a hesistancy on the part of both women as they look at each other, one inside the house and the other a few paces outside it. Are they speaking or about to speak to each other? Will the tourist be invited into the house and will she enter? Or is it only the recognition of their difference that they have in common?

This chapter could have been a discussion of what would have been called a counter-revolutionary movement in the political language of 1964 or, as it has been, one of an Islamic fundamentalist demonstration in the rhetoric of the 1990s. But it could easily also become an enquiry into whether, in painting living creatures for a living, these Zanzibari artists transgress an allegedly major Islamic prohibition, or whether, as one group told me in response to my question: 'It is technically *haramu*, but, if it really is to earn money, then it is just about permissible.' As outside analysts, we simply cannot deny that alongside the apparent moral absolutism of the demonstrators, there is a flexible pragmatism that may strike anywhere, especially when it is said through pictures. I do not see the major epistemological problem as being the separation of the aesthetic from the moral. Rather, it is the aesthetic, defined as 'the body's long inarticulate rebellion against the tyranny of the theoretical' (Eagleton 1990: 13), that sets the terms of moral and political debate. The aesthetic provides the material precondition of conscious plans: we constantly rearrange and manipulate objects around us, including our bodies, which therefore not only pre-exist our thoughts about them, but are also inextricably involved in how we become conscious of our thought. However, the very consciousness of planning and strategy ends up by narrowing, stifling and so hiding its inarticulate visual and material origins. Small wonder that the metaphor of concealment flourishes. It is amenable to further metaphorical recasting but is always beyond total conscious capture.

NOTE

1 The ESRC (Economic and Social Research Council) is a government agency and is the principal funder of social science research in the UK.

REFERENCES

Ardener, E. (1971) 'Introduction', *Social Anthropology and Language*, London: Tavistock.
Durkheim, E. (1915) *The Elementary Forms of the Religious Life*, trans. J. W. Swain, London: Allen & Unwin.
Durkheim, E. (1964) *The Division of Labour in Society*, orig. trans. G. Simpson 1934, Glencoe: The Free Press.
Eagleton, T. (1990) *The Ideology of the Aesthetic*, Oxford: Blackwell.
Parkin, D. (1985) 'Reason, emotion and the embodiment of power', in J. Overing (ed.) *Reason and Morality*, London: Tavistock.
Parkin, D. (1993) 'Nemi in the modern world: return of the exotic?', *Man*, 28: 79–99.
Parkin, D. (forthcoming) 'The power of incompleteness: innuendo in Swahili women's dress', in B. Masquelier and J.-L. Siran (eds) *Rhétoriques du quotidien*.
Sheriff, Abdul (1992) 'Mosques, merchants and landowners in Zanzibar Stone Town', *Azania* 23: 1–20.
Sundkler, B. (1961) *Bantu Prophets in South Africa*, London: Oxford University Press for International African Institute. (Originally published in 1948.)
Topp, J. (1994) 'A history of *taarab* music in Zanzibar: a process of Africanisation', in D. Parkin (ed.) *Continuity and Autonomy in Swahili Communities*, Vienna: Afro-Pub. University of Vienna, and London: School of Oriental and African Studies.
Worsley, P. (1957) *The Trumpet Shall Sound: A Study of 'Cargo' Cults in Melanesia*, London: McGibbon & Kee.

Chapter 11

Usurpers or pioneers?

European Commission bureaucrats and the question of 'European consciousness'

Cris Shore

Europe's cultural dimension is there in the collective consciousness of its people: their values are a joint cultural asset, characterised by a pluralist humanism based on democracy, justice and liberty. The European Union which is being constructed cannot have economic and social objectives as its only aim. It also involves new kinds of solidarity based on belonging to European culture.

(CEC 1988b: 3)

The title for this chapter was suggested to me by comments from various informants, most of whom were European Commission (EC) bureaucrats: technically, these people are administrators and public servants, but this is neither how the public sees them, nor how they see themselves. The result is what Ardener (1982) called a 'critical lack of fit' between classificatory systems – which raises numerous issues about identity construction and stereotyping of importance to understanding European integration. As I argue below, systems of classification have a profound influence in shaping the way consciousness is constructed and articulated.

This chapter begins by exploring the image and self-image of EC bureaucrats and their relevance for debates about 'European consciousness'. More specifically, it examines what may broadly be termed the information and cultural policies of the European Community[1] and their role in creating a new Europe. The European Commission has frequently stated that a key objective of EC information policy is to 'promote consciousness of Europe' and to 'make Europeans more aware of their European identity' (see CEC 1988a; EP 1993a). For many EC officials the goal of full European union hinges on the creation of a truly 'European consciousness' that will transcend national divisions and mobilize Europe's 370 million citizens towards a new consciousness of themselves as 'Europeans' rather than as nationals. Like anthropologists, EC civil servants and policy-makers have a parallel interest in forms of collective consciousness (a term used frequently in EC discourse), and particularly with the measurement and promotion of European consciousness through such instruments as statistics and Eurobarometer opinion polls.

Drawing on ethnographic observations and case studies of EC initiatives for 'promoting the European idea',[2] this chapter explores some of the ways in which European consciousness is being created and disseminated, not only among the peoples of Europe, but also among EC officials.[3] The chapter asks not so much *who is conscious* of Europe or how that consciousness is manifest at local level, but rather, who do EC policy-makers identify as agents of European consciousness? What are the agencies that shape *their* consciousness and self-image? What does 'European consciousness' mean for them? And how does this notion *function* as a political technology and mobilizing metaphor?

I suggest that 'integration theory' might itself be classified as an agent of consciousness among EC officials. Following this, I examine attempts by EC bureaucrats to construct not only a 'consciousness of Europe', but more specifically, a 'European consciousness' among the peoples of Europe. Analysis of Community cultural initiatives leads to more theoretical reflections on the relationship between consciousness and power (Foucault 1991), the mobilization of bias (Lukes 1975), and the manufacture of consensus (Herman and Chomsky 1988). I conclude by suggesting some of the ways in which an analysis of EC policy initiatives might provide insights into broader questions concerning an anthropology of consciousness.

Studying the civil service of the European Community, particularly the permanent staff (or *fonctionnaires*) of the Commission and Parliament, also provides a context for exploring broader theoretical questions concerning European integration, state formation, bureaucracy, and the tensions between European and national identities. The EC civil service represents an extraordinary experiment in state formation: unlike other comparable international bureaucracies (such as the United Nations or NATO) it is composed of full-time, salaried, career professionals, who are independent of their member states and who must swear allegiance to the Community and its interests over and above their national governments. The European Commission is therefore an unusual social entity in the history of international organizations, perhaps even *sui generis*. As the Commission says of itself: 'We are in practice forging a new model of public administration to match the uniqueness of the Community' (CEC 1989: 51).

THEORY AS AN AGENT OF CONSCIOUSNESS: THE COMMISSION'S SELF-IMAGE

One of the canons of anthropological research is that we ground part of our understanding of social life in the folk-model: the 'actor's frame of reference' or 'the "native's" point of view'. Yet right away this introduces a complication, for the folk-model in question was, generally speaking, extremely theoretically informed – to the extent that EC officials frequently perceived and objectified themselves using models from the social sciences. The distinction between actors' models and observers' models was therefore blurred. This was not altogether surprising: these EC officials were highly educated civil service high-fliers, many of whom had come to their posts through the EC's increasingly institutionalized and formalized recruitment procedure (that is, an extremely lengthy and rigorous system of *concours*). Many also had some kind of academic training in European integration (including PhDs, MBAs and MAs from institutions such as the European College at Bruges and the Insead Business School in Paris).

If theorizing the EC is a problem for social scientists, it is equally a preoccupation of the EC itself. Since the 1950s there has been much debate about the Commission's role in the process of European integration, particularly among social scientists and EC supporters. As a result, two main theories of integration were developed during the 1950s, confusingly labelled 'functionalism' and 'neofunctionalism' respectively. These provide a key to understanding how the Commission sees itself.

Functionalist theory, as developed by Haas (1958) and others, argued that sovereignty depends on the loyalties of citizens, therefore policy should focus on creating the conditions for a transfer of popular allegiance from nation-states to a new European centre. As Taylor describes it, 'the process was one of building a socio-psychological community which transcended the nation state' (1983: 4).

This 'socio-psychological community' was understood in the sense implied by Tönnies and Deutsch: namely, a 'community' based on sentiment, affect, shared values – the kind of solidarity characteristic of Church, family or nation. The Treaty of Rome of 1957 saw cohesion and assimilation among people from different nations as a vital step towards creating such a community (Teague and Grahl 1992: 142; Barry 1993: 320).

By contrast, neofunctionalist theory saw integration arising incrementally out of the harnessing of pressures produced by competing interest groups in society. Gains from integration in one sphere would generate pressures for further integration in another. Increasing cooperation would therefore come about through convergence of mutual interests. The effect of harmonizing laws and economic regulations would have an unavoidable 'spill-over effect' in the political domain, culminating in an increasing functional dependency on a new pan-European political system.

Both neofunctionalism and functionalism are 'process theories'. The main difference between them is that whereas neofunctionalists stressed the 'psychology of elites' in the integration process, functionalism emphasized the importance of first establishing a 'popular psychological community' (Taylor 1983: 7). From an anthropological perspective, what is significant about these theories, particularly neofunctionalism, is that they seem to have become part of the folk-model of the European Commission. According to one optimistic scenario, EC personnel and institutions were to play the key role in forging the European Community. As George wrote (1985: 23),

> Encouraged by its success, the Commission appears to have come to believe the predictions of the neofunctionalist theory, that it was inevitable and that eventually unity would be achieved in its corner of Europe, and that it would emerge as the future government of this new supranational state.

Neofunctionalist theory therefore had considerable intellectual appeal to EC bureaucrats. My research supports George's observations. Not only has the neofunctionalist approach prevailed in the past, but this outlook continues to inform the Commission's consciousness of itself. Typically, the Commission describes itself as 'the engine of European integration', the 'unifying element in the Community process' (EP 1989: 1), or even the 'conscience of Europe' (Henig 1980: 39).

OTHER FEATURES OF THE COMMISSION'S 'FOLK-MODEL'

Four other observations can be made regarding the 'folk-model' of the Commission. First, most Commission officials generally held the view that the economic or customs union of the former EU was always a prelude to deeper political union (or 'Europe's federal destiny'). Indeed, the key protagonists in the development of the EC from Monnet, Schuman and Adenauer to Delors have all promoted a vision of a European state that would eventually transcend the nation-state.

Secondly, the Commission's view of itself clearly transcends the notion of 'public servant'. EC bureaucrats frequently define their task as one of 'informing' citizens about the Community. That is how they justify their campaigning work. Yet many go further, arguing that their mission is also to educate the general public and infuse a sense of 'Europeanness' among European citizens. As one young federalist put it (attributing his quote to Monnet): 'We are not forming coalitions between States, but union among peoples' (Löken 1992: 6). This idea that the Commission has a legitimate right to intervene in the 'cultural domain' was further endorsed by the Maastricht Treaty, which gave the EC new legal competencies in the field of culture and created as a legal category the concept of 'citizenship of the Union'.

The problem, as many EC officials see it, is that the peoples of Europe do not yet identify enough with EC institutions: that there is no tangible

'European public' to serve, and that despite the massive transfer of powers that they themselves acknowledge has taken place from the nation-states to the Community, the EC still lacks popular authority and legitimacy. In this respect, the view from Brussels echoes that of Massimo D'Azeglio, who allegedly commented after Italy had been politically unified in 1870: 'We have made Italy, now we have to make the Italians.' The new European Union has come into existence over the heads of the people, who have many disparate identities, but not one based on a common language, and still less a collective consciousness of themselves as 'fellow Europeans'.

Thirdly, most officials interviewed thought that the EC represented a higher, more advanced stage in the evolution of European society. They also believed that the new Europe they were building must become a 'community' rather than a common market. In many respects, these *fonctionnaires* are heirs of a Durkheimian tradition: their conception of society as object, as moral entity, and as a functionally integrated whole – and the social engineering implicit in their vision of their own role in bringing about this new European social order – seem to echo what Lukes (1973) and others have called 'Durkheim's Project'. This is reflected in the Commission's repeated emphasis on the need for 'social cohesion' in achieving European integration (see CEC 1990). As Pahl (1991) observes, there is an uncritical assumption here that the quest for social cohesion is self-evidently good, unproblematic and uncontentious – a view of 'cohesion' that recalls the structural-functionalist models of anthropology in the 1950s. Seen in these terms, the EC also represents a continuation of the Enlightenment ideals of progress, reason, civilization and rationality. Moreover, just as Durkheim tended to reify society and eventually deified it, similar tendencies can be detected in Commission discourse concerning visions of Europe. As former President Delors (1992: 1) declared:

> If in ten years ahead of us we do not succeed in giving Europe its soul, a spiritual dimension, true significance, then we will have been wasting our time. That is the lesson of my experience. Europe cannot live by legal argument and economic know-how alone.

This view was echoed in a recent European Parliament report on the EC's information policy which argued that 'popular confidence in the Community can be restored if the Community responds to the spiritual dimension and expresses it in policy objectives' (EP 1993b: 3). Fostering a public ethos and highlighting spiritual values, it suggests, is the key issue for the Community and should become the 'cornerstone of cultural policy' (EP 1993b: 4).

Finally, many voices within the Commission argue that the neofunctionalist approach to integration has reached its limits and that what is needed now to achieve full European union are more orchestrated interventionist measures to promote cultural and social cohesion – to transform the Community into an 'integrated field of communication' to use Karl Deutsch's term (1966). Critics within the Community argue that since 'Europe' came into being some forty years ago, it has been the enterprise of elites, technocrats and what Delors called 'benign despotism' (Gardner 1992b). Both the Parliament and Commission acknowledge that they have failed to establish their legitimacy with Europe's citizens. The problem, as they see it, is that Europeans are not sufficiently aware of their European identity or heritage, and this must be rectified through information and awareness campaigns. As the Commission's 1993 'Information and Communication Policy' document states: 'The information deficit is part of the democratic deficit. If the Community is to develop, the public must be convinced of the legitimacy of the values on which it is based and the benefits of what it has achieved' (Pinheiro 1993: 1).

Two questions follow from this. First, how is this 'consciousness of Europe' being created and diffused among the citizens of Europe? Secondly, is there evidence of a new 'European culture' and 'consciousness' emerging within the institutions of the Community themselves? To what extent might EC civil servants be agents or pioneers of a new kind of European consciousness? Before turning to address these questions it is useful to consider briefly how the public perceives the Community, and what European consciousness means for those outside EC institutions.

USURPERS OR PIONEERS? STEREOTYPES OF BRUSSELS BUREAUCRATS

The 'Eurocracy' has been repeatedly attacked by voices within the Community, who blame it for incompetence and waste, and sometimes outright corruption. As a result, several popular stereotypes of EC civil servants have developed, most of them derogatory. One construes them as overpaid, meddlesome *bon viveurs* or 'Fat Euro-cats' riding on the 'EC Gravy Train'.[4] As one official described it, 'the usual image of us is one of faceless, grey-suited bureaucrats, eating smoked salmon and enjoying big salaries and tax perks'. Alternatively, another stereotype presents the Brussels bureaucracy as a sinister, power-hungry, centralizing technocracy (Barber 1992: 2). According to this image EC civil servants are Euro-imperialists: zealots of a bureaucratic creed who wish to regulate and standardize all aspects of national life, from the cost of postage stamps and the permitted noise level for lawnmowers, to the shape of cucumbers and the correct definition of the European 'sausage'. These 'Euro-myths' seem to have powerful resonance at the level of popular consciousness. France's *Nouvel Observateur* caught perhaps the most powerful image of how many people visualize the workings of the EC when it published a photograph of a sharp-suited man against a backdrop of the twelve-starred Community flag and with a paper bag over his head.

The view among Commission officials is that they are made scapegoats by national politicians, and that whenever political capital can be made from attacking 'foreigners' and 'bureaucrats' the Commission provides a convenient target. Even Chancellor Helmut Kohl, traditionally a loyal supporter of the Community, has denounced the Brussels bureaucracy as 'too powerful, constantly expanding, and exterminating national identities' (Barber 1992: 2).

SOME FACTS ABOUT THE EC BUREAUCRACY

Stories of legions of Eurocrats hired on colossal salaries to perform useless or non-existent tasks are doubtless exaggerated. In reality, the EC bureaucratic apparatus is extremely small. When the EC grew from six to twelve members its total population more than doubled to 327 million. Yet there are only 10,000 *fonctionnaires* working for the Commission in Brussels, with a further 2,350 in Luxembourg, and 2,600 elsewhere. The other institutions of the Community – including the Court of Auditors, Court of Justice, Economic and Social Committee, European Investment Bank and the Council of Ministers – have a total workforce of less than 11,000.[5] The supposed 'army' of Commission bureaucrats therefore totals only 14,950, which, as Evans (1990: 42) notes, is about the same number employed by the city governments of Amsterdam and Lisbon, or in Britain's former Customs and Excise Department. Yet the Commission manages hundreds of Europe-wide programmes concerning technology, agriculture, industry, education, environment, transport, etc. The complaint from Commission staff is that the bureaucracy is too small to handle all the new powers and functions it has acquired. Indeed, the Commission's statutory role is very different from that of a secretariat, and unparalleled amongst international organizations. Its functions as the engine of integration are central to the Community. These include, *inter alia*, initiating policies, mediating national interests, administering common policies and ensuring that Community regulations are appropriately carried out.[6]

Within the Community institutions the environment is 'international' and cosmopolitan, but not necessarily multicultural. Evidence of an emergent 'European culture' is questionable. All those interviewed suggested that the experience of working for the Community had changed them; that officials did acquire a loyalty to the organization and that after a while they ceased to see themselves as primarily nationals, but rather as Europeans. Most also agreed that there was a tangible sense of 'Europeanness' developing within the institutions, and that this was expressed in their working relationships (all officials are obliged to work with other EC nationals and use a variety of EC languages), in patterns of consumption and lifestyle, in the way their children were educated (all EC staff are entitled to send their children to the European Schools), and in an intangible 'feeling' of difference. Many of these points were summed up by an official of the European Court in Luxembourg:

> We are the thirteenth tribe of Europe. All of us come from one of the twelve member states and bring with us our national identities, but you change. Bits of the other cultures rub off on you; your language changes, you end up speaking a kind of pigeon *franglais* where the sentences you use are full of technical French terms like *acquis communitaire* and *tour de table*. There is definitely some kind of European consciousness forming among the permanent EC staff: a sense of 'we' in the Community, 'we' in the Court, and 'we' in the English translation section, and 'we' Irish members in the House. But it's hard to put your finger on what it is exactly. I think it's to do with losing your rootedness; not so much loyalty to the organization as a question of psychological equilibrium. Everyone needs to belong to some sort of group: we belong to the Court.
>
> The civil service has a very distinctive French character in its language, structures and procedures. Newcomers find this changes the way they think. You find you slot in. Many Brits have great difficulty at first because even when they're talking English to their fellow nationals, the language is somehow French. It's as if there is an external French structure that overlays the whole organisation. This is often what people mean when they say someone 'goes native'.
>
> You definitely lose touch with the outside world. It's not just the high standard of living (though that does have an effect). It's a bit like a colonial situation: you don't really see much of the local people – except those who come in to run the services of the building. You lose all sense of the value of things outside here. Because we earn so much money, you lose any concept of what things cost in real terms at home.... Virtually everyone I know here is earning three times the salary they would get with an equivalent job elsewhere. Your expectations adapt in accordance with your earnings. So it becomes increasingly difficult to envisage going back home. You couldn't afford it. I remember when the Portuguese joined. They couldn't believe the size of the salaries. The Portuguese judge in the court was earning more than the Portuguese Prime Minister. I remember him joking that if he hadn't been appointed judge he would have been happy to settle for a *uissieur* [messenger].

Another indicator of whether a distinctive European culture is emerging within the institutions can perhaps be gauged by the reaction of Belgians to the presence of EC institutions and personnel in their midst. Here there are signs of growing polarization between EC employees and local residents, increasingly resentful of the soaring property prices and of what some describe as the 'transformation of our city into a builders' yard' (see FDF 1993).

EC BUREAUCRATS: PIONEERS OF THE 'EUROPEAN IDEA'?

In contrast to their negative public image, EC bureaucrats tended to see themselves as 'pioneers'. One common element of their self-identity was that of being the standard-bearers of 'Europeanism': agents of change engaged in a mission to build a new Europe and transcend the parochialism of the old nationalist order. This sense of being a vanguard bore striking similarities to the Leninist identity of the Italian communists among whom I carried out fieldwork in the early 1980s (Shore 1990; 1993b). In both cases that identity hinged upon a sense of being part of an intellectual elite, a vanguard, on the side of history and progress; the architects and visionaries of a new social order. This sense of mission, coupled with an often uncritical enthusiasm for any action that will promote 'European ideals and values', recurs throughout Community documents and reports. Even senior officials within the Commission admit that it is 'peopled by true believers' (see also Gardner 1992b: 14). But EC bureaucrats are performing their role as the 'engine of European integration' in ways more innovative and proactive than one might normally expect from public civil servants. They are actively engaged in building Europe – not only in the sense of creating a multinational environment or European culture within the institutions of the Community or among the bureaucratic elite, but also in their attempts to create a new Europe outside the EC institutions, at the level of public opinion and popular consciousness.

In pursuit of these ends the European Commission and Parliament have embarked upon various policies and initiatives in the field of audiovisual, information and media campaigns, to promote what they see as 'European' identity. I shall focus on just three ways in which Europe is being invented in what Commission discourse sometimes calls the cultural domain. First, in the EC's attempts to construct the imagined community of Europe through the invention of traditions and symbols for 'Europeanness' (Anderson 1983; Hobsbawm 1983); secondly, through its use of information and public relations; and, thirdly, through the creation of new 'European' statistics and measurements as instruments of bureaucratic surveillance and control (Foucault 1977; 1991).

INVENTING EUROPE THROUGH SYMBOLS

After the disastrous 1984 European Parliament elections when only 60 per cent of Europe's citizens bothered to vote, the European Council agreed to establish an *ad hoc* Committee for a People's Europe, whose task would be to suggest ways to 'strengthen and promote the Community's identity and its image both for its citizens and for the rest of the world' (Adonnino 1985: 5; CEC 1988b: 1). That committee produced two reports outlining a series of measures for improving the rights and freedoms of EC citizens, and for 'easing rules and practices which cause irritation to Community citizens' (Adonnino 1985: 9). These included simplifying border-crossing formalities, greater duty-free allowances, tax exemption for books and magazines, reciprocal recognition of equivalent diplomas and professional qualifications, and rights of residence for trans-frontier workers, plus longer term targets involving cultural policy, youth exchanges, and a series of special rights for Community citizens (such as voting in other EC countries).

The committee also argued that to transform the EC into a 'People's Europe' required new symbols and a new identity for the Community. It therefore recommended the adoption of a European flag and emblem which would be 'representative of the European idea'. That flag, adopted in June 1985, was taken from the logo of the Council of Europe: a circle of twelve yellow stars set against a blue background. The rationale for this emblem, as the Council of Europe described it, was because:

> Twelve was a symbol of perfection and plentitude, associated equally with the apostles, the sons of Jacob, the tables of the Roman legislator, the labours of Hercules, the hours of the day, the months of the year, or the signs of the Zodiac. Lastly, the circular layout denoted union.
> (Forum, Council of Europe, No. 3/89: 8 cited in Löken 1992)

The committee also recommended European postage stamps bearing portraits of leading EC statesmen such as Schuman and Monnet; a European passport, driving licence, and car number-plates, and a European anthem, taken from Beethoven's 'Ode to Joy' – which the Committee recommended be played at all suitable ceremonies and events since this music is particularly 'representative of the European idea' (Adonnino 1985: 29) – presumably because of its association with Enlightenment ideals of brotherhood, progress and Reason.

Other initiatives included an EC audiovisual policy based on the Commission's 'television without frontiers' directive, EC-sponsored sporting awards, educational exchanges, 'public awareness' campaigns, special Jean Monnet funds for new university courses or lectureships in European integration, and other forms of patronage, such as the 'Charlemagne Peace Prize' and the 'European Woman of the Year Award'. Perhaps more significant was the Commission's attempt to redefine the ritual calendar to include 'European Weeks', a 'European Year of the Environment' and 'European Year Against Cancer', and its proposal for new EC-wide public holidays commemorating decisive moments in the history of

European integration – such as the Schuman declaration and the birthday of Jean Monnet.

EURO-SYMBOLS AND POPULAR CONSCIOUSNESS

Flags, anthem, passport, Europe days are all attempts to touch familiar chords. Hobsbawm puts it this way: 'The National Flag, the National Anthem and the National Emblem are the three symbols through which an independent country proclaims its identity and sovereignty, and as such they command instantaneous respect and loyalty. In themselves they reflect the entire background, thought and culture of a nation' (1983: 11). In Hobsbawm's terms this is a clear example of a 'mass-produced invented tradition' created by intellectuals in order to hail the masses as 'citizens' of the new Union.

At first blush it would seem that the new Europe is being constructed on very similar symbolic terrain as that of the older nation-states of Europe; flags, anthems, passports, trophies, rituals, money, maps and citizenship – all become icons indelibly stamped with the presence of the state, which in turn reinforce the image of a bounded political community. In this sense, to paraphrase Anderson (1983), the EC – like the nation – is an 'imagined community' par excellence. Yet this is hardly surprising, for as Cohen (1985) and Anderson (1983) himself point out, all communities are imagined. Indeed, all political systems are constructed through symbols and realized as integrated fields of communication (see Cohen 1974; Kertzer 1988). That said, the extent to which nations and nationalism offer significant parallels for understanding European integration is debatable. If, as Anderson and others have suggested, 'the nation' was constructed largely through the printing press, the novel, the museum and the daily ritual of reading a national newspaper – all of which became instruments for diffusing national consciousness and the shared vernacular – then there is little to compare with these agencies at European level. While this situation will undoubtedly change in the future, the tendency towards deregulation and globalization is likely to undermine any attempt to create a 'European' audiovisual public. Thus the Commission's dream of 'television without frontiers' could become precisely that: a media landscape dominated not by European public service broadcasting, but by corporate, commercial global giants.

INFORMATION AS AN AGENT OF EUROPEAN CONSCIOUSNESS

The Commission may see symbols as vehicles for communicating 'the European idea' but whether the European citizen gets the message is unclear. The Danish and French referenda of 1992 on ratification of the

Maastricht Treaty suggested that the EC was failing to win popularity, despite spending almost 60 million ecu (or £48.06 million) on its information policy each year. Although France narrowly approved the Treaty, the French referendum was interpreted by the Commission as a public relations disaster. France had traditionally been the driving force behind integration and the rejection of the Treaty by some 49 per cent of the population shocked the Commission. Moreover, far from marking the eclipse of nationalism and the advance of 'Europeanism', the referendum debates were dominated by national issues, particularly the 'German question' and fears about Germany's domination of Europe – a theme exploited by both pro- and anti-Maastricht campaigns (Criddle 1993; Hoffman 1993).

Following the French referendum in October 1992 the Commission established a working group composed of communications professionals (mostly public relations experts) to examine the Community's information policy and to suggest ways of rebuilding its image. The subsequent report, drawn up by the Belgian Liberal MEP and former Commissioner, Willy De Clercq, was completed in March 1993, presented for approval to the Commission, then officially unveiled at a press conference in Brussels on 31 March. The presentation backfired, however, when journalists staged a walkout in protest. What angered them was the report's suggestion that the print and broadcast media should take a more positive line on European union, and that 'reporters must *themselves* be targeted, they must *themselves* be persuaded about European Union' (De Clercq 1993: 35). The Greek President of the Brussels International Press Association accused the Commission of behaving like a military junta. Other journalists were equally scathing. I mention this incident, which occurred shortly before I began my second period of fieldwork, because it provides important insights into EC constructions of, and strategies for promoting, 'European consciousness'.

The report noted a lack of 'feeling of belonging to Europe' and a lack of strategic direction, observing that 'European identity has not yet been engrained in peoples' minds' (De Clercq 1993: 2–4). The solution it proposed was that Europe should be treated as a 'brand product' to be sold with the slogan 'Together for Europe to the Benefit of Us All' (p. 25). It argued that EC governments should stop trying to explain the Maastricht Treaty – because 'treaty texts are far too technical and remote from daily life for people to understand' (p. 4) – and concentrate instead on presenting European Union to the public as a 'good product', with an emphasis on the beneficial effects 'for me' (p. 13). It also advised the institutions responsible for EC policy to be 'brought close to the people, implicitly evoking the maternal, nurturing care of "Europa" for all her children' (p. 9). At the heart of the advice given to President Delors was that the Commission should set up a central office of communications, similar to those of the United States and Japan, to ensure that Europe speaks with one voice and communicates 'the right message' to its target audience.

Among its other recommendations, the report advocated European Union birth certificates for all new-born children; a 'European dimension' to be included in school textbooks and syllabuses; an EC 'Medal for Merit' which would outrank all other national honours; a new banner for the Commission bearing the motto 'In Uno Plures'; and direct television appeals by Mr Delors to the women and youth of Europe (pp. 26–33).

Despite widespread condemnation of these proposals from most of the European press, the EC Commissioner for Culture, Mr Pinheiro, refused to distance himself from the report and said he would be using some of its suggestions (Johnson 1993). Most Commission staff that I spoke to admitted that De Clercq's approach was too commercial; none, however, questioned its basic premises about using 'information' as an agent for promoting European consciousness.

CREATING EUROPE BY NUMBERS: A FOUCAULDIAN PERSPECTIVE

The De Clercq report did not have the status of an official Commission policy document. However, the fact that communications professionals featured so prominently within the 'group of experts', and that the report had been commissioned and ratified by the Commission President himself, provide significant insights into the process of policy formation within the EC. It also suggests that the Commission's approach to communication and culture is highly instrumental and manipulative. In this sense, the Commission is perhaps as much an heir to the Jacobinist tradition as to Durkheim: its belief in the role of radical leadership; its assumption that *culture* can be created and disseminated from above, that citizenry can be penetrated using symbols, or that consciousness can be injected into the masses, these ideas are also embodied in the theory and practice of Leninism (Shore 1990: 157–63).

However, Foucault's work on knowledge/power and the 'art of government' highlights another, more subtle, area where European consciousness is being communicated and created: through the mobilization of discourse. The appropriation of the term 'Europe' by the European Community as a shorthand for itself is gradually giving a new meaning to the notion of 'being a European'. More importantly, 'European integration' itself has become a 'discourse of power'; one that precludes other discourses by couching unification in an ideology of neutrality within which it is presented as a 'technical process' governed not by political choice, but by principles of rationality, efficiency and sound management.[7] European-integration-as-discourse functions as a 'political technology', one that advances 'by taking what is essentially a political problem, removing it from the realm of political discourse, and recasting it in the neutral language of science' (Dreyfus and Rabinow 1982:196).

At another level, the invention of Europe is also occurring through the restructuring of certain key cognitive classifications. It is not the individual symbols in themselves that are likely to produce the conditions for a change in popular consciousness, but rather (and to paraphrase Strathern 1992: 163–80), the new systems of conceptual ordering through which new political relations are thought, since it is these classificatory systems (the *langue* rather than the *parole*) which enable new ways of thinking and talking about Europe to emerge. For example, the celebration of Jean Monnet's birthday or the nomination of Juliet Lodge as 'European Woman of the Year' are of secondary importance to the goal of fostering a European consciousness (indeed, few people are likely to have heard of these names); far more important is that these events open up the possibility for a new discourse on Europe. Monnet's birthday celebration thus becomes an instrument for creating (and reifying) a new category called 'European Community history' (presumably to challenge the hegemony of nationalist histories). Similarly, the 'European Woman of the Year' becomes a mechanism for hailing all women in the member states as 'women of Europe'.

On a wider canvas, these events can be seen as key elements in the re-ordering of people (as in 'citizens of the union'), places (as in the 'European Cities of Culture'), and the social organization of time. The 'technical' aspects of harmonization may therefore have implications for social cohesion that are closer to the goal of a 'People's Europe' than Community officials realize. Particularly important here are the new measurements and statistics – and the new agencies – for collating EC data that have been brought into being by the development of the Community. These include 'Eurostat' (the Commission's statistical office) and the six-monthly 'Eurobarometer' surveys of public opinion across the member states.

The Eurobarometer provides an example of the way new measurements create new subjects (and objects) for enhancing the 'reality' and power of the Community. Ten years ago the idea of 'EC public opinion' barely existed as a category; today it is cited increasingly to make political statements and influence policy. Thus, the Eurobarometer for June 1992 declares that 'people on average want to speed up the construction of Europe', that '76% of Europeans are for efforts being made to unify Western Europe', that 'EC citizens are very much in favour of the Single Market having a social dimension' and that 'the European public strongly supports the idea of a foreign policy and a common defence/security' (CEC 1992: i).

What is important here is not simply how one chooses to interpret these statistics or whether or not they 'speak for themselves', but the existence of such statistics in the first place. The creation of new instruments for measuring the attitudes and opinions of 'Community citizens' has deep ramifications for the way Europe is constructed and reflected in the mind's eye of the public. As Hacking notes (1991), statistics exert a powerful influence in the social construction of reality. They open up all sorts of possibilities for creating new conceptual domains: in this case, the construction, definition and mobilization of a new concept – the 'Community's public'.

The technical aspects of harmonization therefore invariably contain a (hidden) political and cultural programme. As Barry (1993) reminds us, standardizing the various systems of measurement (for time, space, quantity, volume and value) in order to unify political and economic space has long been a key feature of political rule, from the dynastic calendars and currencies of ancient Rome and China to the post-revolutionary French metric system and the 'imperial' weights and measures that served to unify the British empire. Such uniform systems of measurement are integral to what Foucault (1991) calls 'governmentality', or the rationality of government – for a population that can be counted and 'known' is also one that can be ruled and controlled more effectively; an idea summed up in what Rose (1991) calls 'governing by numbers'.

In short, the invention of 'European' statistical data creates new objects of knowledge/power over which the bureaucratic gaze of anonymous technicians and administrators can be cast. Yet, as Barry (1991: 25) argues, harmonization is not intended to centralize Europe under an all-powerful 'big-brother' Commission: rather, its goals are 'more liberal and federal... to create a Europe which is not just known by a central authority, but knowable also by a whole series of economic and political subjects' – not the least important of which are the interests of business and commerce. In this respect, the identity of Europeans within the new single market is perhaps more one of sovereign consumer than citizen.

CONCLUSION: QUESTIONS OF CONSCIOUSNESS

Returning to the questions posed at the outset, one conclusion seems to be that EC bureaucrats are both usurpers *and* pioneers. In order to create 'European consciousness' Commission officials have taken the lead in the integration process. They have pushed their statutory definition as 'public servants' to the limit – even tried to create their own public. Having identified themselves as the principle agents of European consciousness they have set out to create a 'People's Europe' in the domain of culture and communication. However, this emphasis on the socio-cultural aspects of European integration does not mark a shift from elitist neofunctionalism to a more populist functionalism. In many respects their activities are consistent with their role as outlined in neofunctionalist theory. What they have done, in effect, is pursue the technocratic and neofunctionalist goal using functionalist strategies. It is a case of what Herman and Chomsky (1988) might call the 'manufacture' of popular consent by a bureaucratic elite; the vision may be Durkheimian, the strategies for achieving it (and the rationality underlying it) are Foucauldian and Leninist.

This case-study of EC cultural politics raises several points of general significance for an 'anthropology of consciousness'. It suggests that an 'anthropology of consciousness' should not overlook the fact that 'consciousness' is a folk-category – of considerable importance in the case of policy professionals and politicians. An *ethnography of consciousness* might therefore best be pursued by focusing on particular *conceptions* of consciousness – and analysing them in their social and political context – rather than treating our definitions as unproblematic observers' models. The concept of 'agency' is equally problematic. Depending on how we define it, almost anyone or anything might constitute an 'agency' of consciousness; the only qualifying criterion is that these are persons or objects through which power is exerted. Again, the folk-model approach – analysing the ways in which our informants use such notions and what it means for them – provides useful insight into the problem. EC bureaucrats define themselves as 'agents' of European consciousness, but they see information policy, symbols, statistics, history books, 'communications experts' and the mass media as agencies through which European consciousness can be inculcated among European citizens. Yet their consciousness of themselves, their own sense of history and their sense of mission have been shaped by integration theory as well. European integration thus bears all the hallmarks of a modern political ideology.[8] The 'agents' of consciousness appear to be located in the realm of discourse, articulated at different times through Commission bureaucrats, policy initiatives, political theory, 'communications experts' and perhaps the technologies of communication themselves.

In this study of EC bureaucrats and state-formation I have avoided adopting an essentialist view of consciousness. Indeed, it is debatable whether consciousness has any fixed 'essence'. It should not, therefore, be treated as an explanatory tool but rather as a cultural notion that needs explaining through sociological methods. As I have tried to show, consciousness is inextricably bound up with institutions and webs of power and knowledge. As social anthropologists, I suggest we approach consciousness as a social fact rather than as an individual attribute. The interesting question for me is how 'European consciousness' functions as a discourse of power – a question one might equally ask of the use of the term consciousness in marxist and psychoanalytic discourse.

An anthropology of consciousness calls for a more catholic approach to the work of other disciplines of consciousness. However, turning to folklore, psychology or psychoanalysis is unlikely to provide satisfactory *anthropological* answers. How individuals construct their personal world-view may be a legitimate concern of the psychologist, the therapist and the literary critic, but the mind of particular individuals is a dubious concern for social anthropology. A more appropriate question for our discipline, perhaps, is how worldview constructs individuals. Even if social consciousness does *ultimately* depend on individual consciousness, it is important to remember that these are distinct and separate domains, the conflation of which does little to enhance our understanding of the social world. To say this is merely to reiterate arguments waged long ago by Durkheim, Marx, Engels and others in their attempt to establish the autonomy of social science from biological and psychological thinking.

The notion of bringing back 'the individual' into anthropological considerations (from whence, it is claimed, s/he has been banished since Durkheim) is equally problematic. In fact, anthropology has not ignored the individual. The critique of structural-functionalism in the 1960s led to a host of new 'action theory' approaches, from Leach's study of the political systems of Highland Burma, to the transactionalism of Barth, Bailey and Boissevain and the approaches of Bourdieu, Ortner and Dumont; all of these claimed to bring 'the individual' back into anthropological analysis. Like Leach (1967: 88–9), however, I suggest that the inner thoughts and feelings of individuals are not available to us as *social anthropologists*. What are available to us instead are social actions and cultural conceptions of constructions such as 'agency', 'individuals', 'subjectivity' and 'consciousness'; it is these collective representations – these 'social facts' – that I think offer the most fruitful area of enquiry for an anthropology of consciousness.

The final insight provided by this EC case study, particularly from a Foucauldian perspective, is simply a reminder that anthropologists concerned with consciousness should not ignore the fact that 'consciousness formation' is fundamentally a political process embedded in wider institutions of ideology, knowledge and power. If our questions of consciousness are reduced to the level of psychology or the individual, that wider political perspective is likely to disappear from sight.

NOTES

1 With the Maastricht Treaty, which came into force on 1 November 1993, the 'European Community' has been superseded by the 'European Union'. However, for the sake of clarity I shall continue to use the former term, except where the notion of 'European Union' is specifically referred to.
2 I would like to thank the Nuffield Foundation for supporting my fieldwork in Brussels between 1992 and 1993.

3 This chapter forms part of a larger research project on the bureaucracies of the European Community and EC activities in the 'cultural sector' (see Shore 1993a; Shore and Black 1994). This study situates itself theoretically within that body of anthropological literature concerned with the analysis of agencies and apparatuses of the modern state and international organizations, how these bureaucracies operate and the implications of their activities for policy (see Nader 1972; Britan and Cohen 1980; Donnan and MacFarlane 1989; Wright 1995).
4 This was also the title of a satirical novel and television series about corruption in the higher echelons of the EC by writer Malcolm Bradbury.
5 *Dossier de l'Europe*, Commission of the EC, 6 July 1991 (cited in FDF 1993: 17).
6 These tasks are listed in Article 155 of the Treaty of Rome.
7 To some extent these principles are enshrined in the Maastricht Treaty, particularly in the idea of an independent European central bank and in the Treaty's commitment to 'price stability' (see CEC 1992: 1).
8 Significantly, some textbooks have begun to describe it in exactly these terms (see Ludlow 1987: 86–8).

REFERENCES

Adonnino, P. (1985) 'A people's Europe: reports from the ad hoc committee', *Bulletin of the European Communities. Supplement 7/85*, Luxembourg: Office of Official Publications of the European Community.
Anderson, B. (1983) *Imagined Communities: Reflections on the Origins and Spread of Nationalism*, London: Verso.
Ardener, E. (1982) 'Social anthropology, language and reality', in D. Parkin (ed) *Semantic Anthropology*, London: Academic Press.
Barber, L. (1992) 'The ERM and Maastricht', *Financial Times*, 25 September: p. 2.
Barry, A. (1991) 'Europe to scale' *Marxism Today*, September.
Barry, A. (1993) 'The European Community and European government: harmonization, mobility and space', *Economy and Society*, 22(3): 314–26.
Britan, G. and Cohen, R. (eds) (1980) *Hierarchy and Society: Anthropological Perspectives on Bureaucracy*, Philadelphia: Institute for the Study of Human Issues.
CEC (Commission of the European Community) (1988a) 'A people's Europe: communication from the Commission to the European Parliament', COM (88). 331/final, Luxembourg, Bulletin of the EC, Supplement No. 2.
CEC (1988b) 'The European Community and culture', *European File*, 10, 88, Brussels: OOPEC.
CEC (1989) 'The European Commission and the administration of the Community', European Documentation Periodical 3/1989, Luxembourg: OOPEC.
CEC (1990) *Social Europe*, 1, Brussels: OOPEC.
CEC (1992) *Eurobarometer. Public Opinion in the European Community*, No. 37, Brussels: OOPEC.
Cohen, A. (1974) *Two Dimensional Man: An Essay on the Anthropology of Power and Symbolism in Complex Society*, London: Routledge & Kegan Paul.
Cohen, A. P. (1985) *The Symbolic Construction of Community*, London: Routledge.
Criddle, B. (1993) 'The French referendum on the Maastricht Treaty, September 1992', *Parliamentary Affairs*, 6: 228–38.

De Clercq, W. (1993) 'Reflection on information and communication policy of the European Community', R.P./1051/93, Brussels.

Delors, J. (1992) Summary of Addresses by President Delors to the Churches, CEC Forward Studies Unit, Doc. No.704E/92, Brussels: OOPEC.

Deutsch, K. (1966) *Nationalism and Social Communication: An Enquiry into the Foundations of Nationality*, 2nd edn, Cambridge, Mass.: MIT Press.

Donnan, H. and McFarlane, G. (eds) (1989) *Social Anthropology and Public Policy in Northern Ireland*, Aldershot: Avebury.

Dreyfus, H. L. and Rabinow, P. (1982) *Michel Foucault: Beyond Structuralism and Hermeneutics*, Brighton: Harvester.

EP (European Parliament) (1993a) 'Draft report on the information and communication policy of the European Community', Part A: DOC EN/PR/227/227207.

EP (1993b) 'Explanatory statement on the information and communication policy of the European Community', DOC EN/PR/221/22140.

EP (1989) *Fact Sheets on the European Parliament and the Activities of the European Community*, Luxembourg: OOPEC.

Evans, R. (1990) 'Eurocrats – public servants or usurpers?', *Geographical Magazine*, XII(3): 40–4.

FDF (Front Democratique des Francophones) (1993) *L'Europe à Bruxelles*, Brussels: FDF/ERE.

Foucault, M. (1977) *Discipline and Punish: The Birth of the Prison*, Harmondsworth, Penguin.

Foucault, M. (1991) 'Governmentality', in G. Burchell *et al.* (eds) *The Foucault Effect: Studies in Governmentality*, Hemel Hampstead: Harvester Wheatsheaf.

Gardner, D. (1992a) 'Pandora's box or panacea', *Financial Times*, 14 October: p. 14.

Gardner, D. (1992b) 'Maastricht – after the French vote', *Financial Times*, 22 September: 2.

George, S. (1985) *Politics and Policy in the European Community*, Oxford: Clarendon.

Hacking, I. (1991) 'How should we do the history of statistics?', in G. Burchell *et al.* (eds) *The Foucault Effect*, Hemel Hempstead: Harvester Wheatsheaf.

Haas, E. (1958) *The Uniting of Europe*, Oxford: Oxford University Press.

Henig, S. (1980) *Power and Decision Making in Europe*, London: Europotentials Press.

Herman, E. and Chomsky, N. (eds) (1988) *Manufacturing Consent: The Political Economy of the Mass Media*, New York: Pantheon Books.

Hobsbawm, E. (1983) 'Introduction: inventing traditions', in E. Hobsbawm and T. Ranger (eds) *The Invention of Tradition*, Cambridge: Cambridge University Press.

Hoffman, S. (1993) 'Goodbye to a united Europe?' *New York Review of Books*, 27 May: 27–31.

Johnson, B. (1993) 'Image-builders hit by walkout', *Daily Telegraph*, 1 April.

Kertzer, D. (1988) *Ritual, Politics and Power*, New York: Yale University Press.

Leach, E. (1967) *Genesis as Myth and Other Essays*, London: Jonathan Cape.

Löken, K. (1992) 'European identity. What about us?', *The New Federalist*, 5–6: 6–7.

Ludlow, P. (1987) 'European integration', in M. Riff (ed.) *Dictionary of Modern Political Ideologies*, Manchester: Manchester University Press.

Lukes, S. (1973) *Emile Durkheim. His Life and Work*, Harmondsworth: Penguin.

Lukes, S. (1975) 'Political ritual and social integration', *Sociology*, 9: 289–308.

Nader, L. (1972) 'Up the anthropologist', in D. Hymes (ed.) *Reinventing Anthropology*, New York: Random House.

Pahl, R. (1991) 'The search for social cohesion: from Durkheim to the European Commission', *Archives européennes de sociologie*, XXXII: 345–60.

Pinheiro, J. (1993) 'The Commission's information and communication policy', 30 June, Brussels: OOPEC.

Rose, N. (1991) 'Governing by numbers: figuring out society', *Accounting, Organisation and Society*, 15(7): 673–92.

Shore, C. (1990) *Italian Communism: The Escape from Leninism*, London: Pluto.

Shore, C. (1993a) 'Inventing the "people's Europe": critical perspectives on European Community cultural policy', *Man*, 28(4): 779–800.

Shore, C. (1993b) 'Ethnicity as revolutionary strategy', in S. MacDonald (ed.) *Inside European Identities*, Oxford: Berg.

Shore, C. and Black, A. (1994) ' "Citizens' Europe" and the construction of European identity', pp. 275–98 in V. Goddard, J. Llobera and C. Shore (eds) *The Anthropology of Europe: Identities and Boundaries in Conflict*, Oxford: Berg.

Strathern, M. (1992) *Reproducing the Future*, Manchester: Manchester University Press.

Taylor, P. (1983) *The Limits of European Integration*, London: Croom Helm.

Teague, P. and Grahl, J. (1992) *Industrial Relations and European Integration*, London: Lawrence & Wishart.

Wright, S. (1995) 'Anthropology: still the awkward discipline', in A. Ahmed and C. Shore (eds) *The Future of Anthropology: Its Relevance in the Modern World*, London: Athlone Press.

Index